Nightmares of Anarchy

Nightmares of Anarchy

Language and Cultural Change, 1870–1914

Wm. M. Phillips

Lewisburg
Bucknell University Press
London: Associated University Presses

Associated University Presses
2010 Eastpark Boulevard
Cranbury, NJ 08512

Associated University Presses
Unit 304, The Chandlery
50 Westminster Bridge Road
London SE1 7QY, England

Associated University Presses
P.O. Box 338, Port Credit
Mississauga, Ontario
Canada L5G 4L8

The paper used in this publication meets the requirements of the American National Standard for Permanence of Paper for Printed Library Materials Z39.48-1984.

Library of Congress Cataloging-in-Publication Data

Phillips, Wm. M.
    Nightmares of anarchy : language and cultural change, 1870–1914 / by Wm. M. Phillips
        p.   cm.
Includes bibliographical references and index.
    ISBN 0-8387-5525-9 (alk. paper)
    1. English literature—19th century—History and criticism.   2. Anarchism in literature.   3. English literature—20th century—History and criticism.   4. American literature—History and criticism.   5. Language and culture—Great Britain.   6. Language and culture—United States.   7. Anarchism—United States.   8. Anarchism—Great Britain.   I. Title.

PR468.A5P48   2003
820.9'358—dc21   2002154926

PRINTED IN THE UNITED STATES OF AMERICA

For Ann, whose love, support, patience, and prodding
were absolutely necessary.

Contents

Acknowledgments

My DEEPEST THANKS GO TO MY WIFE ANN, WHO MANAGED A PERFECT BAL-
ance of encouragement and firmness through four moves, two children, and a book of her own. She has been indispensable as a
sounding board and an editor as well. Special thanks go to the members of my dissertation committee at the University of North Carolina for their feedback and perceptive criticism: John McGowan,
Beverly Taylor, Townsend Ludington, Linda Wagner-Martin, and
James Thompson. Also deserving of thanks are the library staffs of
the University of North Carolina, Beloit College, the University of
Northern Illinois, the University of North Alabama, and Maryville
College for their patience and help. Thanks also go to Evelyn Hinz,
editor of *Mosaic*, who published a much altered version of chapter
four, "Industrialism and Utopia," under the title "Tropes and Parodies of Capitalist Biography: Andrew Carnegie and *The Memoirs
of an American Citizen*," published in *Mosaic* 32:1 (March 1999),
p. 17–34.

$\sim$

Permission to reproduce Peter Kropotkin's *Mutual Aid* is courtesy
of Black Rose Books.

Nightmares of Anarchy

Introduction

OVER 150 YEARS AFTER IT WAS FIRST USED TO DENOTE A POLITICAL MOVEment, the word "anarchism" is still charged with controversy and contradiction. The word conjures associations of both private utopias and Hobbesian societies based on force, the bloodthirsty nihilist as well as the genteel individualist. The Internet is said to be "anarchistic," even as Albania is said to be an "anarchy." These contradictory associations have always been a part of the history of the word, a history that was nearly forgotten after the birth pangs of industrial society ended in the early twentieth century. Nevertheless, the rhetoric of both the United States and Great Britain carries a latent anarchism, and, in times when social institutions seem out of date and incapable of ordering the world, anarchism once again becomes an active part of the cultural dialogue. Anarchism as a term has always denoted both the hopes and the fears of cultural disorder. By examining the first period of anarchist activism in Great Britain and the United States, we can begin to understand the complex history that the word embodies. Such an exercise also suggests that modern society and its history likewise carry forward the same conflicts between authority and liberty, and order and freedom that the anarchists voiced during the last century.

The late nineteenth- and early twentieth-century literary associations of anarchism and anarchists suggest ways to trace reactions to the social change that occurred during the period. It was a time of much social unrest, when the social consensus had weakened in the wake of industrialization and immigration. The increasing power of the working classes and the diminishing power of the landed aristocracy led many to fear for the breakdown of the old order. At the same time, the example of the French revolution and the dizzying pace of technological change that the period witnessed convinced many observers that sudden, catastrophic change was possible. Many anarchists, arising out of populist traditions in Europe, worked to hasten the fall of an old order they considered unjust. Although never numerous or powerful enough to actually effect

13

the revolution they hoped for, anarchists were a symbol for the hopes and fears of the new era and became associated with the negative effects of the new economic and political orders which were established during the transition from the nineteenth to the twentieth century. As anarchism waned as a mass movement (or became institutionalized as syndicalism), the concept of anarchism remained vibrant as a cultural symbol, and concepts of anarchist ideology became part of the discourse of the larger culture.

The 1880s and 1890s witnessed a flurry of thought and publishing on the question of how best to harness the new industrial technologies of the period and how to incorporate the modern factory into the existing social fabric. The new economy, more reliant than ever on trade and specialization of tasks, diminished individual control as it created unprecedented material wealth. The needs of industry created vast urban populations that suffered from cyclical unemployment resulting from the boom-and-bust cycle of unregulated financial markets. People were confronted with vast populations, separated by profound differences in culture or ethnicity, placed in close proximity and under great stress. Just as people felt more overwhelmed by the currents of industrial society, so did their institutions struggle to adapt their missions and understandings to the new social order. The cultures of Great Britain and the United States lurched from one crisis to another in the late nineteenth century as individuals in each culture struggled to create new, more effective understandings of the social forces which had been birthed in the early part of the century.

Anarchism was one social theory among many during the last decades of the nineteenth century, but the attacks it received from all sides in contemporary political debates, despite the decidedly nonradical nature of many of its main ideas, reveal the symbolic role that the anarchist movement and individual anarchists played in the cultural dialogue. Anarchism was perceived as a threat far out of proportion to its power and characterized as a far more alien doctrine than it actually was.

The roots of anarchism were often traced to insanity or simple greed in the popular press, which was sympathetic to the established professional and propertied classes or to the emerging industrial plutocracy. However, anarchist ideas and anarchist rhetoric were deeply rooted in several cultural discourses of the late eighteenth and nineteenth centuries. William Godwin, the founder of anarchist thought, postulated that, as the Enlightenment project of progressive reason brought individuals closer to perfection, government as a coercive power would become a barrier to further progress and be abolished. The idea that government causes rather than cures social ills and that individual freedom is the highest ideal found expression in Romanticism as well. The tradition of peasant revolt and the idea of revolution that was inspired by the partial success of the French Revolution also inspired anarchists to believe that radical social change was not only possible, but inevitable. Individual anarchists constructed their own philosophies out of the disparate traditions upon which anarchism was based; these individual constructions led to a diverse number of opinions being grouped together as "anarchist"—communal anarchists, anti-authoritarian socialists, radical individualists, proponents of free love and violent nihilists all were associated with, or claimed to be, anarchist.

This lack of conformity within the movement, although perfectly in keeping with anarchist ideals, produced much confusion for outside observers. Anarchists could not be contained in tidy labels, and this lack of definition and unified voice created a perceptual vacuum, so to speak, which outsiders filled by making anarchism stand for many cultural developments that were perceived as threatening or disorderly. Anarchism was primarily associated with the rise of the working classes and the threat of a revolution by the "masses." Anarchists encouraged this association, which coincided with many anarchists' opposition to institutions that robbed workers of the product of their labor, as well as a widely held faith in an inevitable social revolution. From Matthew Arnold's equation of anarchy with the populace in *Culture and Anarchy* to Henry James's fears of "the Democracy" in *The Princess Casamassima*, writers used the figure of the anarchist to stand in for the perceived threats of mass culture and the eroding power of older elites. A number of cheap thrillers that used anarchists as villains testify to the cultural fears associated with anarchism, including Griffiths's *The Angel of the Revolution* and Savage's histrionic *Anarchism: A Story of Today*.

Anarchists came to stand for the general cultural fears of degeneration and revolution that gripped the propertied classes in the closing years of the nineteenth century. The discourses of science, literature, economics, and politics all elaborated the narrative of the anarchist threat by using the word "anarchist" to describe disturbing trends within their own disciplines. Cesare Lombroso designated anarchism as a pathology after describing the physiognomy of anarchists, transforming a set of ideas into the symptoms of a medical disorder.[1] Trends in literature that offended established taste, from the decadents and symbolists to the naturalists, were declared to be "anarchical," as was any attempt to question social mores by people in favor of free love or women's rights. Particularly, any legislation which removed impediments to labor's right to organize, or sought to control the behavior of capitalists in any way, was often described as "anarchical," and attempts to rein in police abuses in Chicago were seen as the equivalent of giving anarchists the keys to the city. Even Henry Adams describes the new forces of electrical power and radiation as "anarchical" in their incomprehensibility within established modes of understanding.[2]

Despite the fears and numerous narratives in which anarchists figured in both Great Britain and the United States, their political power in English-speaking countries was never very great: the propaganda campaign mounted against them (and the outright repression which often followed the propaganda) dwarfed the resources of the anarchist movement. Anarchism declined in the early years of the twentieth century, but the language of propaganda that had been employed against anarchism served to keep the ideas current in the language. The horrific power of the wild-haired anarchist was supplemented by other narratives which either contained the fear associated with the anarchist, or transformed the context of anarchist ideas and language.

As writers began to reflect on the events of the last years of the nineteenth century, narratives were more distant from the fear of social collapse that had lent so much virulence to the anti-anarchist campaign. Anarchism could be characterized as a relatively harmless phase of adolescence (as is done by Ford Madox Ford or Helen and Olivia Rosetti), and the anarchist rhetoric of freedom from convention could be recontextualized (as in Charlotte Teller's *The Cage*), losing its associations with the lower classes or contemporary political issues. As individual anarchists ceased to play an active role in the cultural dialogue, the ideas of anarchism could be more safely expressed.

Such safety was never complete, however. The state and the corporation had implemented the centralized, hierarchical model of social organization through force, economic strength, and persuasion, and even the Marxist opposition embraced the ideal of centralized authority. Anarchism's vision of local and individual control and a society based on consensus rather than authority was seen as an impossible utopia when unconnected to political action, but whenever an anarchist attempted a political act (such as Emma Goldman's crusades in support of workers' rights or birth control), the image of the threatening anarchist would be invoked, justifying state repression.

Although anarchism slowly waned as a political movement, it blossomed as a language of opposition in literature and the arts.

Anarchism became a metaphor for society itself. Convention was seen as authoritarian and opposed to individual expression; the social order which had been idealized in the Victorian period and laboriously pasted together by the Edwardians was seen, through the lens of anarchist language, to embody potential chaos and to create the very social ills it claimed to avert. Writers such as Joseph Conrad and G. K. Chesterton divorced anarchism from its explicit political context and expanded it into a comprehensive vision of social reality, embodying both the nihilism and the comic absurdity of modern culture. Although anarchism as a political movement had failed to achieve its goals, anarchism as a trope had passed into the general social language.

Despite their lack of numbers, anarchists obtained notoriety in the late nineteenth and early twentieth century because anarchist narratives exposed the hidden conflicts of other ideological discourses; each group feared and opposed the anarchists for reasons that reveal the assumptions and internal narratives of that group. In addition to capitalist language, anarchists were vilified in a wide range of discourses: the established professional class, invested in the republican institutions of Britain and America, were repulsed by the foreigners and other members of the working class which did not respect either the professional classes' self identity as a cultural elite or their faith in parliamentary government and saw in the threatened loss of prestige a disorder which was anarchical; liberals, in sympathy with the anarchist focus on the individual, were nevertheless repulsed by extreme anarchist rhetoric and terrorism in the service of the ideal of revolution; socialists and communists found the anarchists dangerous for their opposition to centralized planning and even more dangerous because of the enmity which anarchists generated among conservatives. The battle against anarchism waged in the cultural dialogue of America and Britain became a shadow, obscuring the consolidation of social power in the hands of centralized institutions.

It was not the real anarchist movement—a small, motley collection of idealists, eccentrics, and malcontents—but the cultural fears associated with the anarchist movement, that gave anarchism its power. At the same time, the propaganda against anarchists allowed anarchist ideas and narratives to become part of the general discourse, perpetuating those ideas long after the movement which first voiced them had subsided. Interpreting the cultural depictions of anarchism allows us to see the cultural forces which created the first "red scares" and justified the growing corporate and governing institutions which have dominated society in the twentieth century.

1

The Haymarket Affair

CHICAGO WAS A CITY OF STARK CONTRASTS IN THE SPRING OF 1886. THE CITY had been transformed after the Great Fire into a monument to the new American economy, with high-rise buildings and luxury hotels testifying to the newly created affluence of the leaders of industry. At the same time, the slums and tenements around Chicago were also growing, as a large population of workers—many of them foreign immigrants brought to America as cheap labor—eked out their living away from Chicago's Gold Coast. The palaces which the new industrial rich were building were supported not only by brick and mortar, but also by the press, the police, and the Pinkerton agents who warned of the threat to social order represented by labor's calls for fairer wealth distribution, better working conditions, and shorter hours. In 1877, a series of wildcat strikes had shut down commerce from Pittsburgh through Chicago, and the immigrant newspapers of the laboring classes—most written in a foreign language and several openly proclaiming themselves as socialist and anarchist—were talking of another strike to reduce the working day to eight hours. Although the first of May had come and gone without the feared general strike in favor of the eight-hour day, there were still several strikes throughout the city that kept many Chicagoans on edge. One of the larger strikes was at the McCormick Reaper Plant on Chicago's south side.

The actual events of May 1886 occurred in the context of years of labor unrest and police corruption and brutality. On 3 May 1886, police opened fire and killed several strikers as they shouted at the replacement workers whom McCormick had hired. Without waiting for the details, August Spies, a German immigrant who was active in Chicago's anarchist movement, printed a circular calling for an open-air meeting to discuss this latest use of force by the industrialists of Chicago. Expecting a large turnout, the group planned to meet in Haymarket Square, a large area that could accommodate a crowd; the actual meeting was rather small (under a thousand people, according to observers), so the meeting was moved to a nearby alley on Desplaines Street, out of the traffic flow through Haymarket Square. After some delays and several mild speeches, the meeting began to break up under threat of rain.

The mayor of Chicago (who had been present at the meeting) went by the nearest police station to inform the captain, Jack Bonfield, that the event was unlikely to develop into a riot. Bonfield was known as "Black Jack" because of his predilection for violence against workers, and he once promised that, should he get the socialists without their women and children present, he would "make short work of them." Despite the mayor's assurances, Bonfield hurried to the square with 300 men and commanded the meeting to disperse. A bomb was thrown from a nearby alley into the first rank of policemen, and the panic-stricken police then opened fire on the crowd. One policeman (named Degan) was killed instantly, and six others died from wounds; an uncounted number of spectators were wounded. As far as can be determined, all casualties except Degan's were caused by the police during the chaos; however, this fact and other evidence of the one-sidedness of the "riot" were suppressed by the police, with press cooperation.[1]

Everyone assumed that a radical had thrown the bomb. The events near Haymarket Square confirmed the worst stories associated with the anarchist movement, and the police fed the conservative newspapers with talk of secret conspiracies and bomb caches. Carl Sandburg, then eight years old and living in Galena, Illinois, remembers that:

> We learned the word for the men on trial, anarchists, and they hated the rich and called policemen "bloodhounds." They were not regular people and they didn't belong to the human race, for they seemed more like slimy animals who prowl, sneak and kill in the dark. This I believed along with millions of other people reading and talking about the trial. I didn't hear of anyone in our town who didn't so believe then, at that time.[2]

Conservative stereotypes about anarchists were incorporated into an authoritative-sounding narrative, and many in the press ignored evidence which did not support a portrayal of radicals as a secret conspiracy of bloodthirsty, working-class foreigners bent on destruction.[3] The anarchists were associated with too many controversial issues—immigration, labor, social change—for their usefulness as scapegoats for capitalist excesses to be ignored. Anyone who had publicly sympathized with radicalism was arrested and questioned by the police, who, led by the publicity-seeking chief of investigation, Captain Schaack, suspended proper procedures in order to prove the conspiracy which he had assumed must exist; eight men were eventually imprisoned for the murder of the police officer killed by the bomb, although no evidence linked those men to the bomb or the unknown bomb thrower.

Henry David describes the actual trial as grossly unfair. Judge Gary's courtroom conduct was in complete sympathy with the anti-anarchist hostility of the press. The bondsman, employed by the chief prosecutor, Grinell, stacked the jury pool with those who would be prejudiced against the defendants, and Judge Gary often cajoled jurymen into saying that they might be swayed by evidence (despite the prospective jurors' own protestations that only "preponderant" evidence could make their change their opinions) so that he could approve them and exhaust the defense's jury strikes. During the trial, Judge Gary consistently sided with the prosecution on every issue and allowed the prosecution wide latitude in evidence. After Judge Gary gave the jury instructions that essentially reiterated the prosecution's case, the men—August Spies, Oscar Neebe, Michael Schwab, Adolph Fischer, Louis Lingg, George Engel, Samuel Fielden, and Albert Parsons—were found guilty of the murder of Officer Degan. All but Neebe were sentenced to death. The prosecution never bothered to connect the defendants to the bomber or prove who the bomber was; instead, the prosecution used a broad interpretation of conspiracy law to connect the bomb to the violent rhetoric of the anarchists, and then used a wide body of anarchist literature (even statements of anarchists who had never been to the United States) to depict the defendants as threats to American civilization.[4] In his closing arguments, Grinell declared that "Anarchy is on trial."[5] Adolph Fischer, in his speech to the judge after the trial, summarized the prosecution's case: "I was tried . . . for murder, and I was convicted of Anarchy."[6] The defense had ably shown that there was no secret conspiracy, and that all activities by the anarchists had been open to the public; nevertheless, the inflammatory arguments and wide latitude allowed the prosecution enabled Grinell, the prosecutor, to cast the jury in the role of defending American civilization from an anarchist conspiracy that he and Captain Schaack of the Chicago police asserted, but never definitively proved to exist. The jury, pressured by prosecutor, judge, their own employers, and the screaming voices of journalists, did not take long to return their decision. Seven of the anarchists were to be executed. One man, Oscar Neebe, whom Grinell had considered dropping from the case for lack of evidence but did not because he feared it would undermine his conspiracy case against the others, was sentenced to fifteen years.

Commercial industrialist culture had won a victory over the anarchists. The "American civilization" which the judge and prosecutor defended was explicitly a mercantile, not a moral, culture; Judge Gary himself commented after the trial that "The people of this country love their institutions. They love their homes. They love their property. They will never consent that by violence and murder their institutions shall be broken down, their homes despoiled, their property destroyed."[7] Despite the fact that no homes were destroyed by the bomb, the judge in the trial explicitly understood the trial to be one of anarchism versus property. In Gary's understanding, the protection of commercial property was more important than the protection of the rights of workers, and the violence and judicial murder conducted in the name of American institutions mattered little against the threat of anarchy presented by a histrionic press.

The anarchists had few defenders amid the screams for immediate execution. Nevertheless, some liberals felt that public prejudice, not the evidence, had doomed the men. Many defended the anarchists out of an older American ideal of civic responsibility and were careful to distance themselves from the violent rhetoric of the anarchist movement; instead, they cast the debate as one between aggressive capitalism and individual rights, including the right to free speech—the key component of citizenship, according to the intellectual classes. William Dean Howells led a public campaign to enlist support for amnesty, including a public letter to the *New York Times* which brought him much criticism: some newspapers "abused me heartily as if I had proclaimed myself a dynamiter."[8] Others who had called for their execution later had second thoughts. "A notable example was Melville E. Stone, editor of the *Chicago Daily News*. Few men had done more to whip up feeling against the anarchists, yet he was now the most active in the effort to save their lives."[9] William Morris and Peter Kropotkin in England joined thousands of labor union members in signing petitions for the pardon of the anarchists, and Morris concluded that the promise of American democracy was revealed to be a "pernicious fallacy" by the trial.[10]

Under Illinois law, prisoners were required to make a formal appeal for clemency to the governor. Fielden, Schwab, and Spies had made the required formal request at the urging of the defense committee, but Engel, Fischer, Lingg, and Parsons all refused to appeal for clemency, demanding either exoneration or death. The prisoners who refused clemency were acutely aware of the role they would play as martyrs. While awaiting execution, the prisoners had been writing autobiographies and articles for inclusion in anarchist newspapers in which they outlined their devotion to the anarchist cause. William Dean Howells and others had compared the men to John Brown (echoing the equation of slavery with the treatment of the working classes), and many who disagreed with radical politics urged clemency on the grounds that to execute the men would make them martyrs.

However, those who urged clemency for whatever reason were outshouted by those who saw this trial as a chance to defend American civilization against a pernicious foreign doctrine. Despite a few defections, most capitalist newspapers still cried out for blood. The *Interior*, a Presbyterian newspaper, claimed that "the pardon of the anarchists would be a tacit surrender of the city"; in particular, Marshall Field, the prominent Chicago businessman, influenced Governor Oglesby to deny clemency for fear that it would destroy the rule of law.[11] That a handful of radicals in the poorer sections of Chicago could be believed to represent such a dire threat to the entire city reflects not so much the power of the anarchist movement as the paranoia of the propertied classes. The capitalist press insisted that any show of mercy would be fatal; any dissent would doom the fragile discourse on which the police and capitalists had built their authority.

On the anarchist side, "the plea for mercy by Spies, Schwab and Fielden was bitterly attacked by many Chicago revolutionaries, to whom it was a sign of weakness and loss of revolutionary courage."[12] The narrative of martyrdom was exerting an influence on its victims as well. Although Schwab and Fielden had both been involved in the anarchist movement, they had been quiet and temperamentally unsuited to the role of martyr. Nevertheless, the narrative expectations of the anarchist community called for the solidarity of the defendants, and an eagerness to use their executions to further the cause. The Amnesty Association within the anarchist community still worked tirelessly for the release of all the defendants, however.

Lingg, denying the police the right to execute him, committed suicide by exploding a blasting cap in his mouth. As the day of execution approached, Governor Oglesby commuted the sentences of Fielden and Schwab to life imprisonment. Parsons, Spies, Engel, and Fischer were hanged on 11 November 1887. As they were on the scaffold, Spies cried out "the time will come when our silence will be more powerful than the voices you strangle today!"[13] The script of martyrdom had been fulfilled.

As the executed men passed into martyrdom, the social unrest feared by the propertied classes failed to occur. The executions were widely criticized by liberals around the world, who proclaimed that free speech had been dealt a death blow by the trial, and that America had lost any claims to moral leadership. The gallows became, among anarchists, a symbol equivalent to the crucifix: many anarchists would wear a small gold gallows as a brooch in the years after Haymarket.[14] Even after the executions passed quietly, the red scare continued, and the police would occasionally break up some meeting in order to convince the businessmen who paid the police to crack down on anarchists that their money was still needed. The fiction of the secret conspiracy continued to prove useful as a rationale for an actual conspiracy to expand police power for several years. In July 1888, Bonfield claimed to have uncovered a "dynamite plot" against Judge Gary, although the evidence was far from conclusive. As late as 1892, meetings to commemorate the Haymarket martyrs were broken up by police.

As time passed, however, more and more people began to question the justice of the decision and bristle at the "police terrorism" which used the anarchist scare as an excuse to suspend free speech and free assembly. The 1889 indictments of police Captains Bonfield and Schaack (principal investigators in the Haymarket trial) for corruption and the subsequent attempt by Bonfield to shut down the *Chicago Times* for printing the allegations bolstered the perception that the trial was unjust and the police out of control. The remaining anarchists, together with many liberal supporters, persuaded John Peter Altgeld, who had been elected in 1893, that the trial was flawed and the three anarchist defendants still living should be pardoned.

In an effort to persuade Altgeld not to pardon the men, Judge Gary wrote an article in the *Century Magazine* defending the verdict by claiming that they were found guilty of murder, not their opinions.[15] This article earned him much criticism; as M. M. Trumbull responded in the *Arena*: "If this was a trial for murder, why does he take so much pains to show the sanguinary character of anarchy? . . . Why does he devote nine-tenths of his article to abstract anarchy, and only about one-tenth of it to that promised evidence for murder? The truth is that he tried Spies and the rest of them for anarchy in 1886, and he is trying them for anarchy now."[16] On 26 June 1893, Altgeld pardoned the remaining defendants, aware that he would suffer politically for doing so, but convinced

that the trial had been unjust. Altgeld "was burned in effigy, de-
nounced from the pulpit . . . cartoonists portrayed him as a depraved terrorist, an instigator of bloodshed and evil . . . to Theodore
Roosevelt he was 'a friend of the lawless classes.'"[17] Despite this
outcry and his subsequent defeat at the polls, Altgeld remained a
respected figure on the left and was active in the Democratic party
on a national level for many years.

The events of 1886 and 1887 made a permanent mark on American culture. Despite the fact that none of the defendants were unkempt lunatics, the image of the wild-eyed anarchist bomber dates
back to the political cartoons of this period. The anti-labor and anti-
immigrant sentiments aroused in Chicago would be employed many
more times in a succession of "red scares" over the next seventy
years. Perhaps most importantly, the advocates of corporate capitalism successfully propagated a narrative in which capitalism, far
from being the engine of social change, was synonymous with order,
and that the violence of the times was part of a massive, secret conspiracy on the part of workers and radicals to overthrow American
civilization. This narrative valued the institution over the individual
and expanded the cultural bias toward centralization to encompass
even its enemies. After the First World War, radicalism in the
United States would increasingly follow this state-centered pattern
and call for an increase in the power of government in the name of
social justice, rather than government's abolition.

THE CHICAGO ANARCHISTS AND ANARCHIST CULTURE

The events surrounding the Haymarket trial exemplify several
themes as they play out in society, journalism, and literature. The
first theme involves the interaction between a dominant culture and
the radical immigrant community with which it was in contact, and
between the authoritarian discourse of propertied, English-speaking, native Chicagoans and the subversive narratives of a predominantly working-class, multiglot immigrant culture. The social
distance between these two groups allowed ideology to displace real
interaction, and the extremes to which all participants in the events
of 1886 and after would go show how the choices made by many
involved were misunderstood in the context of other narrative understandings. This ideological distance and lack of communication
between social groups finds its logical expression in the notion of a
conspiracy writ large, in which anyone even remotely associated

with the main enemy (the anarchists) can be found guilty and punishable for beliefs outside of the dominant ideology.

The Chicago anarchists had created a "movement culture" within several immigrant communities that strengthened the weak anarchist social institutions. Unlike their individualist counterparts such as Benjamin Tucker, Chicago's anarchists were mostly European immigrants, and their culture was derived from the European communist-anarchist tradition. Most of Chicago's anarchists were active in the labor movement and the immigrant communities, and most rallies had speakers in English and German. The anarchists used the existing social-support infrastructure of the immigrant and labor communities as forums in which their ideas could be heard and spread, and they presented an alternative narrative language by which the group could understand American history and society. This group culture was centered around several concepts: the mutual aid and defense necessary to any minority group which experiences persecution; an explanation of the persecution which many workers, both native and immigrant, experienced; and the promise of eventual victory through the social revolution. The reaction centered in Chicago in 1886 undermined the myth of revolution, but raised interest in the other narratives within anarchist culture.

The anarchists defined themselves, created goals for the group, and enforced a shared sense of history through stories and rituals. Bruce Nelson describes the immigrant anarchists, a minority within a minority, as raising their peers' class consciousness by several means: the group held picnics and dances, performed amateur plays, published a German-language newspaper, and organized public lectures as ways to publicize their narrative understandings and spread the use of their own language. These narratives fostered a self-understanding of the workers as victims of capitalism, kept in place by a church which defended an unjust social order ideologically and a government which functioned as a hired gun for the rich. Against this machinery of oppression was the worker's movement, which had a history of noble struggle, a few promising victories, and the promise of a coming change—the "social revolution" which would create a just division of property and labor. Until that time, the radicals' job was to educate the workers, practice mutual aid, and prepare for the armed repression of the upper classes.[18]

The anarchists and other radicals affirmed their group solidarity and defined themselves against the dominant capitalist order through speakers, art, and holiday celebrations. Anarchist holidays included the anniversaries of the French and American Revolutions, the rebellions of 1848, the Paris Commune of 1871, and the strikes of 1877. All events were understood as important moments in the struggle for individual liberty that the anarchists were carrying forward. Of these, the anniversary of the Paris Commune was the largest, and the one that aroused the fears of the propertied classes of Chicago most effectively. Chicago's workers celebrated the Commune from 1872 until 1909, and the 1879 celebration attracted between 20,000 and 40,000.[19] For many middle- and upper-class residents of Chicago, the Commune was understood as a time of violence, destruction, radical excess, and a warning against revolutions in general and radical-left politics in particular. For the anarchists, the discourse surrounding the Commune identified the workers as the beneficiaries of the coming revolution and reassured them that revolution was indeed possible. The fact that the Commune was such a source of fear in the minds of conservatives, far from hindering its use by the radical community, transformed the story into a source of power for the relatively powerless radicals; ignored when they attempted to debate conservatives and corporate advocates in lecture halls, they could at least get an audience from conservative journalists with violent propaganda (according to Avrich, many reporters were instructed to only note the violent parts of speeches, and ignore the rest). Unfortunately, the cost of this attention was high: police brutality on a wide scale, and the danger of playing the part of the violent revolutionary in a conservative narrative rather than the part of the seeker of justice in one's own story.

Seeing themselves as the victims of capitalist and police aggression, anarchists, socialists, and other immigrant groups organized private militias whose role was to defend workers against the police, Pinkertons, and state militias that forwarded the employers' interests in strikes around Chicago throughout the 1870s and 1880s. The brutal police crackdowns on labor during the strikes of 1877 were used to justify the creation of private militias, which would defend workers against the police during future strikes. These private militias were a constant source of fear for the police, government, and monied interests of Chicago. Although their equipment and numbers were no match for the Chicago police force, the sight of armed revolutionaries marching down the streets of Chicago was seen as an intolerable threat which awakened visions of labor violence and the Paris Commune. Although the state of Illinois outlawed such assemblies, the armed groups continued to meet and drill secretly in parks outside of town. The secrecy which became necessary as their group activities were declared illegal, together with the social segregation which existed throughout Chicago,

helped to create the caricature of the anarchist as secret and subversive, when in fact most of Chicago's anarchist leaders were
happy for the publicity they could get and rarely operated secretly.

Most radicals of the time argued that force would be necessary
for social change because those who benefited from the current social order would use force to protect their own positions. This acceptance of force separated radicals from more reform-minded
groups who embraced the ballot and incremental labor reform as
the proper strategies for social change. Anarchists saw the way that
Socialist candidates could be "counted out" (votes for leftist candidates were routinely undercounted by electoral judges) or co-opted
by the political system, and became hardened in their stand against
political action. "After 1883 it is almost impossible to find anything
but the most mordant criticism of political action. Those who still
adhered to that method suffered from 'politico-phobia.'"[20] Far from
being a system of institutionalized revolution, the American democracy (according to anarchists) was a system whose corruption and
conservatism fought true social change. The anarchist distrust of
permanent institutions was extended to the institutions of representative democracy, which helped an entrenched propertied class
to hold on to power by creating the illusion of self-government while
actively providing troops to protect the property of the wealthy
against the claims of the working class.

The Chicago anarchists, whose own narratives proclaimed a war
between the forces of capital and the working classes, were quite
willing to discuss preparations for battle. Instruction in street
fighting and terrorism was conducted in several parts of the city,
and recipes for explosives were published in various newspapers:

> Thus the *Alarm* and the *Arbieter-Zetung* . . . published articles on the
> manufacture of dynamite, gun-cotton, nitro-glycerine, mercury and sil-
> ver fulminates and bombs. They also offered instruction in the use of
> dangerous explosives. One article in the *Alarm* bore the heading "A
> Practical Lesson in Popular Chemistry—The Manufacture of Dynamite
> Made Easy." Another on the manufacture of bombs was subtitled "The
> Weapon of the Social-Revolutionist Placed Within the Reach of All."[21]

Dynamite in particular was described as a miracle of modern science, the revolutionary's weapon of choice, and a metaphor for the
entire anarchist project. One particularly extreme passage from the
anarchist newspaper the *Alarm* (not written by one of the Haymarket defendants) exults: "Dynamite! of all the good stuff, this is the
stuff. Stuff several pounds of this sublime stuff into an inch pipe,

gas, or water pipe, plug up both ends, insert a cap with fuse attached, place this in the immediate neighborhood of a lot of rich loafers, who live by the sweat of other people's brows, and light the fuse. A most gratifying result will follow."[22] Although Johann Most (a prominent anarchist writer who lived in New York at the time) and others often wrote of dynamite, there is no evidence that any of the writers actually planned to use bombs themselves. Nevertheless, this passage was eagerly used as "evidence" of conspiracy by Grinell during the Haymarket trial.

Dynamite had been used in labor strife before in the United States, and, in Zola's novel *Germinal* (published the year before the Haymarket bomb) the anarchist Souvarine uses dynamite against his employers. This extreme rhetoric was matched by many of the proponents of capitalism, however: the president of the Pennsylvania Central Railroad, Thomas A. Scott, had called upon the militia to give the hungry strikers a "rifle diet for a few days and see how they like that kind of bread" during the 1877 strike. Captain Bonfield of the police is reported to have "said that the greatest trouble the police had in dealing with the Socialists was that they had their women and children with them at the meetings so that the police could not get at them. He said he wished he could get a crowd of about three thousand together, without their women and children, and he would make short work of them."[23] In the face of the brute force of capitalism, as represented by an abusive police force and small armies of Pinkerton detectives who did not hesitate to provoke strikers, anarchists considered their own drills and experiments with explosives to be in self-defense.

Although members of Chicago's working-class communities often experienced violence from the hands of the police and Pinkerton agents, most stopped short of advocating specific acts of terrorism. Anarchist leaders could please the victimized crowd by using violent rhetoric, but most believed that individual acts of terrorism would only strengthen the police power of the current regime rather than hasten social change. However, a small minority within the movement embraced violence as a means of hastening the collapse of capitalism. This faction was often called the "autonomist" faction because they embraced strategies of autonomous revolutionary action described by Bakunin and Nechaev in the "Catechism of a Revolutionary" (which, along with Johann Most's writings on insurrectionary strategy, were often excerpted to appear in anarchist newspapers). This "hard line" minority engaged in bomb manufacture and bloody rhetoric, and were the focus of capitalist paranoia.

Despite the occasional "dynamite scares" which various cities experienced in the 1880s, most anarchists discussed violence only in terms of the coming revolution, and not in the present situation. Like Peter Kropotkin in Europe, Chicago's anarchists talked of the social revolution as an historical inevitability that no individual could bring about or hope to control; one could only be prepared for it through education in "correct" economic principles. According to David, Chicago's radicals never bothered to define the coming revolution beyond a few vague phrases—the abolition of private property, economic justice, and the right of the producer to a fair share of what was produced. The nature of society (whether controlled through a central government, local collectives, or private individuals) and the means of achieving that society (whether reform and education would produce a bloodless revolution, as imagined by Morris and Bellamy, or whether force would be necessary) were never clearly defined, because different individuals within the radical community had different answers to those questions.

David describes Chicago's anarchists as ideologically unclear. The leaders of the movement used "communist," "socialist," and "anarchist" practically interchangeably and often adopted the terminology used against them by the popular press. In the 1870s, while memories of the Paris Commune were fresh, the groups sympathetic to that cause were labeled "communists"; when the Socialist Labor Party came into being in 1878, the main term used was "socialist," and, as the red scare mounted in the 1880s, the term "anarchist" came into more frequent use. Albert Parsons wrote that the label "anarchist" was initially applied by the conservative press as a pejorative term, but was adopted by the Chicago radical community in a gesture of defiance: "the capitalistic press began to stigmatize us as anarchists, and to denounce us as enemies to all law and government . . . we began to allude to ourselves as anarchists, and that name which was first imputed to us as a dishonor, we came to cherish and defend with pride."[24] Despite their own community's preference for the term "socialist" (as evidenced by the name of their political party, the Socialist Labor Party), the radical community in Chicago came to embrace a name loaded with negative associations.

The adoption of the label "anarchist," despite the negative baggage that the word carried, shows the curious interplay between the socially distant groups and their associated narratives. The labor movement itself was split along various lines, some ethnic and some ideological. The anarchists of Chicago sought for understandings which would transcend the particular differences: in the face of a movement which did not even share a common language, the language of the International movement promised that these differences were less important than the struggle against authority. However, within the framework of the International there were several opposing factions: Marxists (who espoused a strong state controlled by workers as a balance against the strength of corporate institutions) were opposed by anti-authoritarian followers of Proudhon and Bakunin (who found any authoritarian institution to be objectionable); reform socialists (who felt that political action could remove the objectionable elements of capitalism) were opposed to revolutionaries (who found government to be so hopelessly tied to corporate interests that only violent revolution could alter the situation). With their experiences of police brutality and civic corruption, Chicago's anarchists could not put much faith in either central authority or reform; as the group split from more reform-minded labor organizations, the label "anarchist" was more and more appropriate within the late nineteenth century's radical discourse.

Another perverse appeal of the label "anarchist" was the terror that the term held for proponents of the social order. One important narrative rationale for government power was the idea that human beings were savages with a thin veneer of social control, and that the current social order was all that stood between the blessings of civilization and a world of Swiftian Yahoos. By adopting a label which implied the sweeping away of every social control, the anarchists were able to attract the mainstream attention which had eluded their reasoned criticisms of the status quo. The easiest way to be heard by a group is to play a role within a narrative of that group. The anarchist label and the rhetoric of revolution gained Parsons, Spies, and other radicals a hearing in the capitalist press and a publicity which their own resources could not provide, but at the cost of conforming their public identities to fit the nightmare-image of social disorder which the savage justifications of social discipline and police repression had created. In order to gain a hearing in the capitalist media, anarchists were forced to adopt a language that cast them as the enemy.

Despite the fact that all major newspapers, publishing houses, and government institutions followed the same general ideology, the discourse of capitalism shared the fragility of most authoritarian forms of speech. The capitalist discourse confirmed its dominant position within the larger culture but was hampered in its ability to address language outside its discourse. Because their ideology was framed by a restricted language, capitalists did not directly address radical ideas but would instead reframe those ideas within a different discourse, portraying anarchism as either tyrannous (political revolutionaries are a foreign force bent on taking over America) or criminal (radicals are no better than armed thugs who manipulate working men). These frames transformed anarchism into a shadow image of capitalism itself and concealed the gaps in capitalist ideology; although there was never a credible anarchist conspiracy to take over America, there were many instances of collusion and political corruption, as well as violent provocation, within the ranks of capitalists. By screaming at a created enemy, capitalists directed attention away from their own activities. In the wake of the Haymarket Affair, most prominent businessmen were quite willing to donate money to the police effort designed to root out conspiracy, as well as efforts to station federal troops nearby to be used to "defend private property" against the evil anarchist conspiracy, while at the same time they would collude to fix prices, blacklist agitators and radicals, and employ Pinkertons to fabricate evidence and incite riots which would further undermine the sympathy of the larger community for striking workers.

The extremes to which business interests went in defending their ideas of order betray the events of Haymarket as occurring completely within the conservative nightmare of social disorder. The anarchists had not provided the social revolution that would justify the government's police power, so the police had to stir up the disorder which their own narratives predicted. "Police and Pinkertons were used to penetrate [anarchist] organizations, filing wild, fantastic reports of dynamite conspiracies, if only to show how vigilant they were in carrying out their assignments."[25] The police and business interests who were the most fervent partisans at the Haymarket trail committed many of the atrocities of which they were finding their scapegoats, the anarchists, guilty. In one speech at the end of the trial, Neebe reversed the charge of anarchism, as it had been defined by the prosecution and in the newspapers:

[The police] searched hundreds of houses, and money was stolen and watches were stolen, and nobody knew whether they were stolen by the police or not. Nobody but Captain Schaack; he knows it. His gang was one of the worst in the city. You need not laugh about it, Captain Schaack. You are one of them. You are an Anarchist, as you understand it. You are all Anarchists, in the sense of the word, I must say.[26]

If anarchy means lawlessness, the rule of force, and the overthrow of accepted codes of conduct, then the actions of the Chicago police force and the vengeful mob of journalists and business leaders were

the anarchists of the story. Predictably, this argument fell on deaf
ears during the trial.

Despite the excesses of the police, most newspapers demanded
that the anarchists be executed. This unanimity demonstrates the
powerful effect that the conspiracy narrative had on people's perceptions. The ideological threat which a decentralized economic
and social order posed for the advocates of corporate organization
had always been framed as an attack on the foundations of civilization itself, and an actual act of violence was talked about in terms
of the opening act of a revolution. Many refused to believe that such
a disruptive act could be the work of an individual, and that the anarchist leaders, even if they had nothing to do with the actual bombing, were guilty in some way.

The universal condemnation of anarchism led many less radical
social groups to distance themselves from anarchism in order to
avoid the guilt of association. Many labor organizations, who had
viewed anarchist sections as affronts to the ideal of centralized, hierarchical discipline, used the event as a pretext for ousting various
German and Bohemian locals from their organizations. The Democratic mayor of Chicago was attacked for tolerating these organizations for as long as he had; as was the case in Britain (and in the
present day), the specter of social disorder was used as a pretext
to deprive targeted groups of free speech rights.

MICHAEL SCHAACK'S *ANARCHY AND ANARCHISTS*

Michael Schaack's book, *Anarchy and Anarchists*,[27] grew out of
his role as the chief investigating officer for the police in the wake
of the Haymarket affair. By all accounts, he was zealous to a fault;
even his own police commissioner rebuked him on several occa-
sions for manufacturing evidence and using his role as investigator
to increase his own notoriety. The conspiracy for which the Haymarket defendants were condemned was largely a fiction he created,
packaged to appeal to the narrative understandings of a panicked
public.

Schaack's own corruption in matters outside the Haymarket Affair was a matter of public record. In January of 1889, the *Chicago
Times* printed allegations that Schaack and Bonfield had, for some
time, been trafficking in stolen goods and receiving payments from
saloon-keepers. When Bonfield tried to shut the paper down in response, the public rallied against the continuing abuses of police
power which Chicago had witnessed since Haymarket, and Bonfield

and Schaack were discharged in disgrace. This revelation of the corruption of the anarchists' accusers gave new life to the Amnesty Committee, and the officer's discharge was bemoaned by the conservative *Chicago Tribune* as a victory for wild-haired, beer-swilling anarchists everywhere.[28]

Schaack's book was an attempt to strengthen the weakening anti-anarchist coalition by reinforcing the conspiracy narrative around which that coalition was built. By 1888, when Schaack was compiling his own account of the investigation, the public panic had ebbed, and serious questions about the justice of the trial and police conduct surrounding the events had been raised publicly. A fund set up by prominent businessmen which paid police to root out the anarchist "menace" was losing contributors, and Schaack, along with others including Captain Bonfield, felt the need to maintain the fear of anarchists, both to continue to receive money and to justify their past actions. The book, which portrays the anarchists as part of a secret worldwide conspiracy with the aim of destroying American civilization, was a way to reinforce the conspiracy narrative which had been spun during the trial. To this end, Schaack claims that he includes much evidence which was never used in court, but which was uncovered by his "investigation," and that this evidence will "vindicate the law" (v). Throughout his narrative, Schaack uses many of the tropes found in sensationalist and detective stories in order to make his own story seem more plausible to the general reader; the monstrous conspiracy he describes would be out of place in a more sedate narrative frame.

The book, almost 700 pages long with illustrations, includes nearly all the evidence for conspiracy which Schaack was able to find or manufacture and also contains a history of anarchism that, although claiming to be fair-minded, categorically ignores or rejects the possibility that anarchists, communists, or socialists have anything but nihilistic destruction in mind. Like the detective novels which it echoes in tone, *Anarchy and Anarchists* tells stories of the danger which he and his men faced throughout this investigation, along with a healthy dose of sinister femme fatales and evidence given in secret meetings with shadowy, cloaked figures. The stories which make up Shaack's book are built from a wide variety of established narrative patterns: good versus evil, fortitude versus corruption within the police force, the Byzantine world of secret conspiracies, and even the machinations of mysterious women. Schaack's work includes a broad sampling of narratives of the struggle between order and disorder; the choice of narratives itself skews the interpretation of the actual events and betrays the ways in which an ideology of hierarchy and order permeated the journalistic language of the time. The lines between fact and fiction are intentionally blurred, and Schaack's book becomes simply one narrative among many which seek to convince the majority of the existence of a pernicious anarchist involvement in women's rights, intemperance, free love, and other conspiracies to destroy America's conservative civilization. Because he relies so heavily on established narrative patterns to make his case against the anarchists, his book is a useful way to summarize popular stereotypes about anarchists.

Schaack's narrative begins with a history of the anarchist movement, in which he rehearses many of the strategies by which conservatives reject radical ideas in the United States. Most of these rejections hinge on anarchism's foreign heritage. Anarchism, argues Schaack, arises out of the oppression of the peasants. "It caught the unthinking, impressionable throng as the proper protest against too much government and wrong government. It was ably argued by men capable of better things,—men who turned their great talents toward the destruction of society, instead of its upbuilding,—and the fruit of their teachings we have with us in Chicago today" (17). In this argument, Schaack is alluding to a form of American patriotism which can be seen in Emerson and many others: Europe is despotic, jaded, and corrupt. Anarchism, as Schaack understands it, is an atavistic disorder of Europe's fevered brain; it only makes sense in the context of Europe's dispossessed masses.

Of course, what is a suitable distaste of government in the context of a corrupt and unfree Europe is completely out of place in the land of liberty:

> The Anarchists of Chicago are exotics. Discontent here is a German plant transferred from Berlin and Leipsic and thriving to flourish in the west. In our garden it is a weed to be plucked out by the roots and destroyed, for our conditions neither warrant its growth nor excuse its existence. . . . As long as the American citizen can buy his own land and raise his own crops, as long as average industry and economy will lead a man to competence, Socialism can be only like Typhus fever—a growth of the city slums. (25–26)

Within this argument lie several narratives that have their roots in capitalist language. The underlying assertion of the passage is that the market system obeys the narrative of social Darwinism, a struggle in which the fit prosper and the unfit do not. The corollary to that narrative is that all who fail are, by definition, unfit. Socialists and anarchists, who champion the cause of the unemployed and the destitute, are therefore working for a system which would benefit the unworthy at the expense of all those who are productive: "they would substitute . . . for the will of the people the will of a contemptible rabble of discontents, un-American in birth, training, education, and idea, few in numbers and ridiculous in power" (26–27). The criticism of the radicals is reversed through this argument. It is not the rich who live idly off the work of labor, but the socialists who want to live idly off the fruits of despotism. Anarchism, not capitalism, is anti-egalitarian, and its foreign nature allows Schaack to characterize it as a foreign invader, eager to plunder America.

Schaack expands the notion of anarchism as a foreign transplant by tracing the unrest in Chicago to the asylum of radicals by England:

> England is really responsible for the present strength of the conspiracy against all governments, for it was in the secure asylum of London that speculative Anarchy was thought out by German exiles for German use, and from London that the "red Internationale" was and probably is directed. This was the result of political scheming, for the fomenting of discontent on the continent has always been one of the weapons in the British armory. (19)

The toleration of anarchism is a matter of British strategy, according to Schaack, because Britain wants to see other governments weakened by the anarchists. In the context of the debates in the press on whether Britain and America can be allies, this can be seen as another expression of the xenophobic and nationalistic sentiment which is aroused by the attacks on anarchism. Furthermore, the claim that the sinister strings of conspiracy cross the ocean from London to Chicago places the investigation of Haymarket on an epic scale—a struggle between good and evil through which the fate of the world will be determined. At the same time, this accusation contains anarchism within a larger order—the scheming of foreign agents using radicals for more statist goals. This idea that anarchism is simply a secret arm of government will be taken up later in novels by D. W. Griffiths, Joseph Conrad, and G. K. Chesterton.

In order for the police to be absolute good, the anarchists must be portrayed as absolute evil. To that end, Schaack divorces the anarchists from their idealistic roots and their economic reform agenda and portrays them as followers of Nechaev's *Catechism of a Revolutionary*,[29] desiring destruction for its own sake. This caricature of anarchists as beings more akin to rabid dogs than human beings justifies the extreme police crackdown which Schaack was a part of and helps to split the radicals from their natural allies in the labor movement. Schaack goes so far as to include illustrations of nameless "specimen rioters" with messed hair and wild eyes, in order to evoke the caricature of the anarchist which had been established by Thomas Nast of *Harper's Weekly* and others (122, 123). Likewise, when Schaack describes Michael Schwab, he emphasizes the features which associate him with the anarchist stereotype: "[Schwab] looked like an exclamation point, and had his long, bushy hairs been porcupine quills, each would have stood straight on end. He was bewildered, dumbfounded, and there was a distant, far-off expression in his eye" (164). Despite the fact that none of the anarchist defendants even remotely resembled this caricature, the stereotype, designed to play off fears of immigrants, the unemployed, and the insane, was a visual shorthand which Schaack employed to reinforce his attack on anarchists.

Against this force of evil, Schaack portrays members of the police department as the sole defenders of public order, surrounded by shortsighted city officials (who were Democrats at the time) and passive bureaucrats. Given the controversy surrounding the police at that time, Schaack feels compelled to elicit sympathy for the police against what he argues is a dire threat:

> Thus, while the police entertain no animosity against these men, we feel—I feel and every officer under my command feels—that we are bound by our oaths to the State and to society to meet force with force, cunning with cunning. . . . We have a government worth fighting for, and even worth dying for, and the police feel that truth as keenly as any class in the community. (27)

Just as Grinell argued during the trial, Schaack sees the anarchists as a threat to the State and conservative ideals (which are equated, in his view), a threat which justifies the full force of the police in any attempt to destroy it. Against the wild, foreign faces in the crowd which symbolize anarchism, Schaack individualizes the police through this interrupted sentence and attributes his own understanding and motives to society as a whole. In this attribution he is following the authoritarian discourse of the group he serves: the capitalists who saw themselves as central in America to the point of terming their own segregated community "society."

The power of the rich in Chicago was well understood, so, in order to be a credible threat, the power of the anarchists must be magnified accordingly. To justify his claims of conspiracy, Schaack retraces the history of the anarchist movement in Chicago, casting public meetings as midnight conspiracies, and public processions as direct threats to property holders. The caption to a picture of members of the armed group Lehr und Wehr Verein reads "A group of anarchists" (87), and claims that the group was nothing more than an anarchist army, wisely driven underground by the state legislature.

Every labor disturbance in Chicago, Schaack claims, can be blamed on the anarchists: "take each formidable strike in the city, and invariably they have instigated the rabble to deeds of disorder and violence" (110). Schaack singles out the demonstration against the Chicago Board of Trade as an example of the threat which anarchists posed to the city as a whole and the farsightedness of the police, who prevented the demonstration from getting within several city blocks of the building itself:

> A tougher-looking lot of men than those who composed the procession would be difficult to find, and once started in the direction of violence against the building, there is no telling the extent of damage they might have inflicted. The toleration of such a parade by the municipal authorities was severely criticised by the community, for, had it not been for the action of the late Col. Welter, then Inspector of Police, in intercepting the procession, a serious riot would have occurred.
>
> Parsons, when asked subsequently why they had not blown up the Board of Trade Building, replied that they had not looked for police interference and were not prepared. "The next time," he said, "we will be prepared to meet them with bombs and dynamite." (81)

According to Schaack, the violence around the McCormick Works was, like all other disturbances, the result of anarchist agitation. Aggressive police methods (including storming into saloons and arresting crowds for no reason) were preemptive strikes against anarchists plotting violence and therefore justified methods for defending American democracy.

The killing of two members of the crowd at McCormick's by the police was Spies's inspiration for the infamous "Revenge" circular which was printed in the offices of the *Arbieter-Zietung*, then recalled when the editors of the paper thought it too inflammatory. Schaack includes both the English version and the German version in translation. The circular, composed in the heat of the moment, calls upon workers to defend themselves against police brutality:

> Your masters sent out their bloodhounds—the police—; they killed six of your brothers at McCormick's this afternoon. They killed the poor

wretches because they, like you, had the courage to disobey the supreme will of your bosses . . . they killed them to show you, FREE AMERI-
CAN CITIZENS, must be satisfied and contended [sic] with whatever your
bosses condescend to allow you, or you will get killed! (130)

The *Chicago Times* had reported six casualties, although Spies had
witnessed only two (those two were the only deaths from the police
attack). Schaack describes Spies's speech in this fashion: "Mark
well the language,—seeking to inflame the minds of the Socialists
by maliciously stating that four men had been killed, when in fact
not one was fatally injured,—its bitter invective, its cunning phraseology, its rude eloquence and its passionate appeal" (131). Spies is
transformed into the glib-tongued villain of a melodrama; the basic
contradiction between the American ideal of political freedom and
the reality of economic servitude is hidden behind Schaack's make-
believe.

For his version of the events near Haymarket Square, Schaack
relies on the testimony of Harry Gilmer, a man whom he had paid
for testimony, and whose credibility was so undermined by defense
and prosecution witnesses during the trial that Grinell dropped any
mention of his story from the closing arguments. Within his book,
however, Schaack is not subject to cross-examination. He delivers
the police version of events: after the mayor left, the meeting took a
suddenly violent turn, which necessitated the rush of troops, led by
Captain Bonfield, to the meeting. Fielden's declaration, "we are
peaceable," according to Schaack "must have been a secret signal"
(146), for the bomb was thrown and members of the crowd brought
out revolvers and fired on policemen. The police regrouped quickly
in the face of a crowd which attacked as if with one mind—"even
on the instant the crowd began firing" according to Schaack—and
quickly routed the anarchists. [30]

Like everyone else, Schaack does not question the anarchists'
culpability for the bombing, and assumes the motives and background of the bombing before the investigation has even begun:

> It is not difficult to locate the moral responsibility for the bold and
> bloody attack on law and authority. The seditious utterances of such
> men as Spies . . . clearly pointed to the sources from which came the
> inspiration for the crowning crime of Anarchy. It was likewise a strongly
> settled conviction that the thrower of the bomb was not simply a Gui-
> teau-like crank, but that there must have been a deliberate, organized
> conspiracy, of which he was a duly constituted agent. (156)

Having begun his conspiracy narrative as part of his history of Chicago's anarchists, Schaack does not have to prove the conspiracy

so much as narrate the drama of its "discovery." As the investigation is the part of the story in which he becomes directly involved, Schaack's book begins to adopt the manner of a detective story, with Schaack as the intrepid hero.

Of course, Schaack must first overcome the inertia of the police bureaucracy. This thread of Schaack's narrative is a direct attack on his many critics, who saw Schaack as overly paranoid and over-zealous. In fact, Ebersold, Schaack's superior on the force, castigated Schaack for using the investigation to increase his own personal notoriety and accused Schaack of planting bombs and paying informants so that he could have the glory of "uncovering" other conspiracies.[31] In Schaack's narrative, the opposition to his investigation comes from incompetence and internal rivalries within the police department:

> It cannot be denied that, had the case been left in the hands of the Central Office, the prosecution would have come to naught, and these red-handed murderers would have gone unwhipped of justice. . . . From the very first I was satisfied that the men at headquarters neither appreciated the gravity of the occasion, nor were they able to cope with the conspirators—a set of wily, secret, and able men, who had made a special study of the art and mystery of baffling law and avoiding the police. There was neither order, discipline, nor brains at headquarters. Every officer did as he liked, and the department was rent and paralyzed with the feuds and jealousies between the chiefs and the subordinates . . . Knowing what I did of the manner in which the detective work was apt to be done, it will not be wondered that I at once made up my mind to do what lay in my power to hunt these murderers down. (184–85)

According to Schaack, his superiors discouraged any work which might make others look better than the chiefs themselves, but he steadfastly pursued every lead in his investigation of the conspiracy. However, the lackadaisical attitude of some police officers allowed Rudolph Schnaubelt, whom Schaack asserts was the bomb thrower, to go free: "it is any wonder the officials did not offer him a cigar in acknowledgment of their kindly feelings" (171), he writes with disgust.

In particular, Schaack praises Bonfield and accuses Chief Ebersold of being jealous of the praise Bonfield received "in connection with the labor troubles. . . . The Chief accordingly concluded to attend to all the business himself, assisted by his pet gang of ignorant detectives, and they made a fine mess of it" (185). When Schaack later meets with success, he attributes Ebersold's orders to stop talking to the press and manufacturing conspiracies to jealousy:

"he declared that he wanted me to stop the newspapers writing anything more about me and to let the credit be given to the head of the
department" (197). Schaack almost despairs; despite the good work
of "Black Jack" Bonfield, the investigation is failing to uncover the
anarchist conspiracy he knows is responsible.

Fortunately for Schaack, citizens come to the aid of his investigation. The first anonymous source—fearing that the anarchists will
kill him—inspires Schaack to begin his own investigation, without
the supervision of the Central Office. As help, Schaack recruits
trusted associates, and he tells them that "they must expect a forty-
eight hours' stretch of work frequently before we got to the end; that
they must keep in mind that their lives would often be in danger,
but they should only kill in dire necessity. Insults and abuses they
must not take from anyone" (189). The group of policemen begin
their investigation, and quickly find a "bomb factory."

Throughout his investigation, Schaack is aided by mysterious
strangers who come during the night and leave cryptic, but ultimately productive, leads: "we received a great deal of good information from persons who would not have told us anything without
positive assurances of secrecy" (192). Several people with information crucial to the case only talk to Schaack at night, in masks.
These leads (delivered through the familiar and unverifiable plot
device of the secret informant) allowed Schaack to tie together the
threads of the anarchist plot and help the prosecution's case.
Schaack has the chief prosecutor Grinell say, "You have found the
missing link, and you have it right . . . Schaack, I want to say that
you are one of the greatest detectives in America" (192). Despite
the difficulties inherent in discovering a conspiracy by anarchists
skilled at hiding evidence and daily threats to them and their wives,
Schaack's detectives work tirelessly.

Some hint of the twists which a conspiracy investigation can be
prey to are contained in a comic interlude in which two officers,
both secret agents infiltrating the anarchist conspiracy, end up spy-
ing on each other. Schaack laughs when he discovers this, and he
resolves the matter by telling each man "that the other was working
for Billy Pinkerton" (205). Anticipating Chesterton's *The Man Who
Was Thursday*, Schaack's efforts to uncover anarchists turn up as
many police agents as they do genuine revolutionaries; even in this
account, the conspiracy can be seen as a dark double of the allied
forces of government and capitalism. In fact, Schaack claims that
he relied heavily on these outside (Pinkerton) agents, who filed
many useful reports on anarchist activity, with "funds for this purpose supplied to by public-spirited citizens" (206). That Pinkerton

agents were often accused of making up stories that would justify themselves to their employers Schaack does not mention. [32]

Schaack describes the women associated with the anarchist movement as more dangerous than the men; they hide bombs up their skirts, and shriek most loudly for revenge. However, their most detestable feature, according to Schaack, is an ugliness which is decidedly non-Anglo-Saxon:

> A lot of crazy women were usually present, and whenever a proposition arose to kill some one or blow up the city with dynamite, these "squaws" proved the most bloodthirsty. . . . They were always invited to these "war dances". . . . At one meeting, held on North Halsted Street, there were thirteen of these creatures in petticoats present, the most hideous-looking females that could possibly be found. If a reward of money had been offered for an uglier set, no one could have profited upon the collection. Some of them were pock-marked, others freckle-faced and red-haired, and others again held their snuff-boxes in their hands while the congress was in session. One female appeared at these meetings with her husband's boots on, and there was another about six feet tall. She was a beauty! She was raw-boned, had a turn-up [sic] nose, and looked as though she might have carried the red flag in Paris during the reign of the Commune. (207–8)

Not all anarchists were ugly, however. One of Schaack's officers drowned in a boat during a day off, but Schaack's keen skills as a detective convince him that "a deliberate crime was committed" (214). Under a picture captioned "betrayed by beauty," Schaack tells a story of this young officer, who bragged of his work on the investigation to a young girl despite Schaack's warnings against such behavior. "From the moment that girl ascertained his secret occupation he was a doomed man. She let other Anarchists into the secret, and they at once set about devising means for ending his life" (214). Schaack has no doubts about this story, but he was unable to find any evidence to establish guilt. In Schaack's narrative of paranoia, conspirators lurk everywhere, despite the detective's unceasing vigilance and surveillance.

Having established the conspiracy within his narrative, Schaack's description of the trial consists mainly of showing that the defense witnesses "were simply perjurers" (224), while the prosecution's witnesses were telling the truth. The number of "anarchists" arrested who became witnesses for the prosecution (after coercion and bribery) Schaack attributes to their base and cowardly nature.[33] Schaack, in his zeal, continues his attempt to ferret out every anarchist in Chicago, and many pages contain short narratives in which Schaack arrests one anarchist, who, being a craven coward, gives up the name of other anarchists during the investigation. The fact that much of his strongest "evidence" of conspiracy was never used in the trial is explained away: "of course much of the information given in the preceding pages was not used either in the grand jury room or at the trial. It was not necessary. State's Attorney Grinell, with his usual wisdom and tact, selected only the best, strongest, and most reliable witnesses" (376). Just as Judge Gary would write in his own defense years later, Schaack claims that most of the evidence of the conspiracy was never brought up during the trial; Schaack's book is, in part, an effort to fire the imaginations of readers with a narrative of this threat so dark and so secret that it could only be hinted at in the courtroom.

Venturing further into fiction, Schaack creates narratives of what might have happened had the anarchists not lost their nerve on the night of 4 May 1886. He does not doubt that the anarchists planned to begin their social revolution on 4 May 1886 and institute the Commune in Chicago. Nonetheless, he assures his reader that the police would have been up to the task: "The loss of life no doubt would have been appalling on both sides, but the outcome, as far as the triumph of law and order is concerned, would have been the same. The bomb would have done its deadly work at the start, but the Gatling gun would have come to the rescue had the police been seriously crippled" (369). According to Schaack, many anarchists were lurking around the police stations that night, ready to cause widespread destruction. The only thing which prevented the anarchists from blowing up every police station in the city was the fact that they "could not do without beer while awake" (370), an allusion to the stereotype of the drunken (usually German) anarchist.

Even after the trial, Schaack must be vigilant against the desperate plots by anarchists to free their doomed comrades. Luckily, the anarchists "had discovered that many of their secrets were in my possession" (639). Sometimes, the anarchists would attempt vicious deeds in order to discourage surveillance; once, when they discovered that a police officer had bored a peephole into a meeting-room, they planned to blind the officer by shooting a syringe of vitriol into the hole. Fortunately, Schaack discovered the plan and warned the officer in time (640). As the day of the executions approached, Schaack claims that he learned of numerous plots, not simply to free the prisoners, but to cause wanton destruction throughout Chicago. One plot against the city's water supply was discovered, but the extra guards which the police placed around the waterworks prevented the attempt.

Schaack laments that there are many "who probably never will be hanged, who are morally as guilty" as the executed anarchists (655); this thought only inspires further vigilance, however. He concludes his book with the warning that anarchists are still active in Chicago and have become even more secretive and insidious after their defeat. He lists the names of organizations he knows to be anarchist "fronts" (mostly labor unions) and closes with a description of the real threat which faces not only Chicago, but the world:

> The organizations named are only what appears on the surface. Underlying and controlling all these is a secret organization, which in Chicago consists of an "invisible committee." It must be understood that the movement toward the object to which the Internationale looks forward—the social revolution—is local, national, and international, and it is probable that the committee for Chicago was appointed from the headquarters of the Internationale in New York, at the suggestion of that arch-conspirator and mischief-maker, Johann Most. (662)

Schaack repeats the trope of the ironclad anarchist hierarchy. The local troubles are the work of a corporation of troublemakers that makes no community safe from anarchist influence; like Standard Oil, the anarchists are everywhere. Newspapers and anarchist Sunday schools complete the conspiracy's secret arsenal, and Schaack moves to expose the true nature of these seemingly innocuous organizations as subsidiaries of the international anarchist conspiracy. Schaack's description of the secret conspiracy is uncannily similar to the organization of the contemporary corporation—with local offices controlled through a hierarchy by outsiders, often from New York. The anarchist conspiracy is transformed into the evil twin of corporate society, responsible for all the ills of industrialization, and associated with materialism, atheism, immigration, the breakdown of families, and urban violence. Schaack takes the growing alienation and the lack of local control in society which corporate social organization brings, and lays them at the feet of a small group of people categorically opposed to authoritarian institutions. If the Internationale had not existed, men like Schaack would have invented it.

Schaack ends his book with a warning, which would open the way for other writers to build on his idea of conspiracy:

> All over the world the apostles of disorder, rapine and Anarchy are to-day pressing forward their word of ruin, and preaching their gospel of disaster to all the nations with a more fiery energy and a better organized propaganda than was ever known before. People who imagine

that the energy of the revolutionists has slackened, or that their determination to wreck all existing systems has grown less bitter, are deceiv-
ing themselves. The conspiracy against society is as determined as it
ever was, and among every nation the spirit of revolt is being galvanized
into a newer and more dangerous life. (687)

All over the world, writes Schaack, the Reds are planning the overthrow of governments. The only defenses against this monstrous
conspiracy are constant vigilance and the strengthening of the
forces of law and order. Any weakness or unrest—strikes, dissen-
sion, or laziness—may lead to the destruction of civilization at the
hands of these implacable and not-quite-human anarchists.

Schaack's *Anarchy and Anarchists* reads, in 100 years of hindsight, as a wildly paranoid delusion, made more sinister by his custom of naming the persons he believes are involved in anarchist
conspiracies within the pages of his book and occasionally providing addresses. Schaack's willingness to see conspirators in every
occurrence, and to ascribe the most malevolent of goals to anyone
who questions the social order, provides a way to frame and distance the dislocations which modernity and corporate capitalism
cause. Complementing the individualistic discourse of Darwinian
capitalism with the narrative of a centralized conspiracy bent on
destruction for greed or reasons no sane person can comprehend,
the anarchist conspiracy provides an ideological counterweight to
the increasing powers of the large-scale corporation and the central
government.

Although technically a work of nonfiction, Schaack's *Anarchy
and Anarchists* reads like a detective story. The almost clichéd
narratives—the beautiful but deadly woman who seduces the investigator, the anonymous tip, the necessity for the investigator to fight
both his quarry and his superiors—underscore the essentially ficti-
tious nature of the anarchist conspiracy narrative itself. That
Schaack himself must have believed his stories on some level is un-
fortunate; that his stories led to the deaths of four men and the suffering of many others as part of an intentionally generated public
panic is tragic.

Schaack's narrative, and other fiction and nonfiction works like
it, were built on a larger cultural discourse which shaped public
perception of anarchism and skewed public debate to favor the
forces of capitalism and centralization. The stereotypes, assumptions, and stories that were used to support the increasing dominance of corporate institutions in society continue to exert an
influence on our understanding of the world. Anarchy was never the

dire threat to civilization that Schaack and others claimed it to be, but the ideas of anarchism—rooted in the same Enlightenment philosophy which was the foundation of the contemporary social order—represented another possible path of social development, and the dream of other social arrangements is always the direst threat to any dominant ideology. By tracing the uses and abuses of the concept of anarchism during a crucial period in the development of corporations, we can recover a cultural debate which has been obscured, but never quite forgotten, over the purposes and powers of the institutions which dominate our lives.

2

The Anarchist Background

IN ORDER TO UNDERSTAND THE ROLE OF ANARCHISTS IN THE LATE NINE-
teenth century, we must first understand the history of the anarchist movement itself. Although some early Christian communes repudiated the authority of civil government, the modern anarchist
movement found its basis in Enlightenment rationalism with the English philosopher William Godwin. Max Stirner, a disciple of Hegel,
took Romantic individualism to an anarchist extreme in *The Ego
and His Own*,[1] which argued that the liberated individual must
obey no received ideas, but rather create his own morality. This individualism was the basis of the individualist tradition within anarchist discourse. The word "anarchism," which always carried
associations of disorder and mob action, was adopted as a political
label by Pierre-Joseph Proudhon in the 1840s. Proudhon favored action through nonauthoritarian collectives and directly inspired Michael Bakunin, who unified the individualist, collectivist, and
Romantic strains of anarchist thought in the figure of the committed
revolutionary and inspired a generation of anarchist terrorists.

The philosophical tradition of anarchism was advanced by another Russian, Peter Kropotkin, whose writings on cooperation in
animal and human communities gave anarchism a rhetorical foot-
hold in scientific discourse and inspired the modern environmental-
ist movement. While communal anarchism, which encouraged the
growth of locally based production cooperatives, dominated the European anarchist tradition, American anarchists tended toward the
individualist model as a logical extension of American democratic
ideas. In both America and Europe, anarchism was savagely repressed even as anarchist ideas were finding a larger audience; by
the beginning of the twentieth century the word "anarchism" had
gained a positive meaning which stood against several centuries of
negative associations.

The word "anarchy" had been in use since the mid-fifteenth century and had already acquired a pejorative meaning and an associa-

tion with the fear of mob violence. The *Oxford English Dictionary* first records the use of the word "anarchy" in 1539 as a protest against "this unleful lyberty or lycence of the multitude . . . called an anarchie." Over the next 300 years, the word carried connotations of excessive liberty and disorder, whether practiced by the mob, unjust rulers, or priests with foreign doctrines.

"Anarchy" and its derivations were frequently used during the French Revolution. George Woodcock writes that "they were terms of negative criticism, and sometimes of abuse, employed by various parties to damn their opponents, and usually those to the Left." Woodcock quotes the Directory's description: "by 'anarchists' the Directory means these men covered with crimes, stained with blood, and fattened by rapine, enemies of laws they do not make and of all governments in which they do not govern, who preach liberty and practice despotism . . ."[2] In both the English and French traditions, "anarchy" was laden with negative associations of unjust power and self-serving destructiveness. Just as the word "atheist" was used to label all who did not believe in God or those who simply acted without regard to God's dictates, so "anarchist" was associated with those who denied social authority or acted with disregard to the forces of authority. The tyrant, the mob agitator, the common criminal, and all who opposed the ideal order of the speaker could and were often labeled "anarchists."

Nonetheless, the ideal vision of society ordered without earthly authoritarian hierarchies is an old one. Throughout history, groups have attempted to rectify society by denying the authority of hierarchical power structures. Although Peter Kropotkin and other anarchist writers sought out these early anti-authoritarians as a way to create a history for their movement, most of these early communes were religious in nature, rejecting earthly authority in favor of a spiritual one. The Albigensian heretics of France advocated an equality of goods, and the Taborites thought that they should live according to the coming Kingdom of Christ, which meant there would be no class distinctions or private property.[3] The many peasant revolts of the 1500s all proclaimed a denial of civic and religious authority, but any promise of a new order was framed within the Christian narrative of the Kingdom of God.

Anarchism achieves its modern form through the discourse of Enlightenment philosophy. In some ways, the ideals of anarchism are a natural progression from the enlightenment assumptions of a orderly universe and the innate perfectibility of rational human beings. William Godwin was the first to write a systematic treatise on the ideal of a stateless society. Inspired by the writings of Rousseau, Godwin wrote his lengthy treatise on the logical foundations of a just society, *An Enquiry Concerning Political Justice and Its Influence on General Virtue and Happiness.*[4] Writing in the midst of English debates over the French Revolution, Godwin created a justification for anarchism based not in Christian millenarianism but in the discourse of science and rationalism. In doing so, he established several narratives which are central to anarchist ideology.

For his systematic description of a stateless society, Godwin is often placed at the beginning of the modern anarchist tradition. His grounding of anarchism in rationalism was a rhetorical strategy repeated by many later anarchist writers, including Pierre Proudhon and Peter Kropotkin. Godwin saw the tyranny of his day as stemming from an irrational and unjust notion of property. As the individual advances in reason, bad governments—those governments which do not proceed from reason, but rather seek favors from the rich and powerful—become an impediment to the happiness of the individual. For Godwin, virtue is rational understanding, and all forms of vice are simple ignorance. As education and rationalism become more widespread, the need for governments that try to suppress vice and encourage virtue by edict and force will diminish.

Godwin argues that governments pervert human understanding by replacing individual reason with the force of convention. Godwin finds the notion of the social contract to be a myth, just as irrational as the notion of the divine right of kings; in fact, no one is given the option of agreeing to a particular form of government. People are instead coerced into obeying and bribed into supporting the institutions of the state. This coercion results in the perversion of humanity:

> Man, while he consults his own understanding, is the ornament of the universe. Man, when he surrenders his reason, and becomes the partisan of implicit faith and passive obedience, is the most mischievous of all animals. Ceasing to examine every proposition that comes before him for the direction of his conduct, he is no longer capable of moral instruction.[5]

By requiring people to submit, government encourages people to remain in ignorance. If one could remove the bondage of institutions, people would naturally learn the truth, and error would disappear. Godwin's utopian faith in human nature becomes a central strain in the anarchist thought of subsequent generations. Although Godwin himself rejects violence as a method unsuitable for spreading the true light of reason, later anarchists adopt his characterization of governmental institutions as obstacles to liberty and call for their immediate destruction.

Godwin did not describe himself as an anarchist, but his contention that governing institutions are the leading causes of vice and disorder forms a central narrative of anarchist discourse. Governments teach selfishness rather than altruism, hypocrisy rather than virtue; therefore, the abolition of authoritarian government would be a progressive act. Any kind of force which does not allow people to act according to their own reason is tyranny, and the accumulation of property beyond personal needs (which allows one to control others) is the most benighted selfishness. Godwin's emphasis on individual rationality makes him an inspiration for individualist anarchism. Although Godwin opposed violent revolution as irrational, his critique of government also becomes a primary justification of revolutionary anarchists.

Godwin described an anarchist utopia, but was content to observe the slow progression of human understanding. Pierre Proudhon, a self-taught scholar who took pleasure in controversy, was the first to proclaim himself an anarchist and seek to change people's minds through activism. Like Godwin before him, Proudhon traced the ills of the current society to the mistaken and pernicious notion of unlimited private property, which the powers of the state supported against the best interests of the majority. Unlike Godwin, Proudhon was a proletarian by background and temperament and sought to advance the cause of the working classes by all the means at his disposal. His work—sprawling and often contradictory—is a natural by-product of his Hegelian penchant for thesis and antithesis; nevertheless, he was able to transform Godwin's intellectual utopian statements into a rhetoric capable of influencing others.

Proudhon worked in a printing shop, where his ability to edit manuscripts caught the attention of several learned men. Through their encouragement, he won a scholarship to the Academy of Besancon. While at the academy, he published his first book, *What Is Property?*[6] (1840). He answered the question of the title with the now famous phrase, "property is theft." This and other radical publications lost him his scholarship and, in 1849, caused his prosecution and imprisonment.

Proudhon was not the first to identify the role of the state in protecting the property of the rich against the poor. Adam Smith wrote that "civil government, so far as it is instituted for the security of property, is in reality instituted for the defence of the rich against the poor."[7] Proudhon, who claimed Adam Smith as one of his intellectual masters, defined property as "the right to enjoy and dispose at will of another's goods,—the fruit of another's industry and labor."[8] Workers are ignorant of the true worth of their labor, and so the capitalist appropriates all of that worth beyond the worker's sustenance; because the worker is ignorant of the true value, the relationship between employer and employee cannot be said to be a contract between equals.[9] Nevertheless, Proudhon did not desire a society in which all things were owned in common; although property (in the sense of capital) is theft, private property is liberty in the sense that everyone is free to dispose of his or her own production. It is not property in itself, but the imbalanced ownership of property which Proudhon attacks.[10] His solution was a form of credit union, in which the middleman of the for-profit bank would be replaced by a system of mutual aid, of people pooling their money together for the purpose of providing the money each needed. In 1849 he attempted to make this Peoples' Bank work; but even in watered down form, it did not succeed.[11]

Although his political career ran from radical to reactionary, Proudhon remained committed to free, collective action throughout his life. His final work, *The Political Capacity of the Working Classes*,[12] which lays the foundation for syndicalism, had a profound effect on the French labor movement in the early twentieth century. Here, he stresses the importance of raising workers' political consciousness as a prelude to unified political action. "To possess political capacity is to have the *consciousness* of oneself as a member of the collective, to affirm the *idea* that results from this consciousness, and to pursue its *realization*."[13] Although no activist himself, Proudhon laid the groundwork for the revolutionary activism of Michael Bakunin and others and presented a model which the wider anarchist movement would follow.

Proudhon's work expresses the essence of communal anarchism: not simply the destruction of the current order (as the caricature which the critics of anarchism maintain), but also "the replacement of the authoritarian state with non-governmental cooperation between free individuals."[14] Like Kropotkin after him, Proudhon does not envision anarchism as an individualist ethic, but a social one. Both Proudhon and Kropotkin assume that people will form social groups, and both seek to ensure that those groups do not themselves become machines of tyranny.

As Proudhon was writing in Paris, Max Stirner was pushing Hegelian logic to its individualist extreme in Germany. In *The Ego and His Own* (1845), Stirner creates a radical individualist manifesto that anticipates the writings of Nietzsche. Whereas Proudhon had focused on the social institutions that exploit the poor economically, Stirner argues that received ideas themselves are a form of force, which the individualist will discard. For Stirner, modern society has replaced the idea of a God who demands obedience with an ideal of a conventional morality that must be followed. Both are fixed ideas that demand that the individual privilege the idea over personal desires. Stirner argues that internal disciplines are more dangerous to the freedom of the creative individual than physical restraint, and the abstract love of "mankind" is as pernicious as the love of God it has displaced:

> Better an unmannerly child than an old head on young shoulders, better a mulish man than a man compliant in everything; the unmannerly and mulish fellow is still on the way to form himself according to his own will; the prematurely knowing and compliant one is determined by his "species," the general demands—the species is law to him.[15]

Stirner describes the same phenomenon that later captivates Michel Foucault—the internalization of the law, of "conscience." Stirner's association of the subtle demands of conventionality with the more overt forms of social force transformed modern anarchism from a purely political movement into a broader social movement that would tie revolutionaries, utopists, radical artists, and advocates of "free love" together through a set of shared narratives and understandings.

This servitude to an external idea has many terrible consequences and demonstrates the true powerlessness and hypocrisy which "morality" engenders. Internalized morality allows people to tolerate tyrants; "good" people are ashamed of the immorality of the tyrant, but paralyzed by the immoral means necessary to depose the tyrant. Only when an individual sheds morality and acts from the pure desire to do so is the tyrant deposed, and this immoral act is welcomed by the supposedly "moral" people.

> Where then in the "good" was the courage for *revolution*, that courage which they now praised, after another had mustered it up? The good could not have this courage, for a revolution, and an insurrection in the bargain, is always something "immoral," which one can resolve upon only when one ceases to be "good" and becomes either "bad" or— neither of the two.[16]

Stirner's critique of convention echoes Godwin's from fifty years earlier: authority, claiming to be a protection against vice, actually encourages vice and is an impediment to individual progress. There are some important differences, however; Godwin, writing before the French Revolution had run its course, grounds his narrative in an Enlightenment rationalism which Stirner, incorporating the narrative of the Reaction and Romantic notions of the individual, would reject as yet another fixed idea. The anarchist movement would incorporate both of these incompatible understandings: on the one hand, the anarchist revolution was inevitable as human beings progressed; on the other hand, the subtle effects of conventionality were so strong that only the free individual who had discarded morality could bring about social change through violence. Michael Bakunin will later embrace this Romantic individualism in his characterization of the committed revolutionist.

Stirner also creates the criticism of liberals (who might be natural allies of anarchists against conservatives) as closet reactionaries. In keeping with his understanding of the evils of conventional morality, Stirner attacks liberalism as worse than older forms of authoritarianism. At the same time that liberals proclaim a love of freedom, they demand a total subservience to abstract concepts that leaves no room for individual thought or action. "The bourgeoisie is nothing else than the thought that the State is all in all, the true man, and that the individual's human value consists in being a citizen of the State."[17] Marx's communism, which expands the State to encompass all of society, is even worse from Stirner's point of view. Any system of thought which demands that the individual follow that thought rather than her or his own desires is pernicious; Stirner celebrates only personal creativity without regard for others.

Godwin, Proudhon, and Stirner create the central narratives of anarchism in the late nineteenth and early twentieth centuries. Each writer adapts a dominant discourse of his time to the cause of individual freedom. For Godwin, Enlightenment rationalism leads inexorably to the diminution of the state; Proudhon learns from the course of the French Revolution that state mechanisms are more easily turned to reaction than revolution and that the proletariat can and must help themselves; Stirner's rejects Hegel by rejecting the claims of all thought systems on human behavior and championing a Romantic individualism. All three writers accept the French Revolution as proof that societies can transform themselves quickly and that the people are capable of governing themselves despite the effects of authority, convention, and force. However, none of the three attempted to build a mass movement out of their theories; Godwin and Stirner were both too individualistic, and Proudhon argued that a working-class movement must originate in the working class rather than the intellectual class. The task of building a movement out of the scattered followers of anarchist ideas belonged to the leading anarchist of the next generation, Michael Bakunin. Although Bakunin added little to the intellectual heritage of anarchism, he gave anarchists a sense of purpose and, through his romantic love of violent revolution and secret societies, associated anarchists with terrorist methods in the public dialogue.

Michael Bakunin is a controversial, contradictory figure. Although raised in the Russian aristocracy, he was the first anarchist activist, spending his time crafting conspiracies, building revolutionary cells, and leading insurgent movements against Marx within the International. Bakunin was never a theorist; he was less interested in the shape of society after the revolution than he was in sowing the seeds of the revolution itself. Bakunin in the 1830s and 1840s had no coherent social vision beyond the promise of the revolution itself. In his essay, *Reaction in Germany*, Bakunin ends with his most familiar celebration of revolution for revolution's sake: "Let us put our trust in the eternal spirit which destroys and annihilates only because it is the unsearchable and eternally creative source of all life. The urge to destroy is also a creative urge."[18] Bakunin's own presence also inspired comparison with elemental forces, and both Wagner and Turgenev based characters on the bearded, hulking Russian aristocrat.

Bakunin's life is a history of failed revolutionary movements, jail sentences, and dire economic circumstances. As a youth, he had been a follower of William Weitling, a social revolutionary with a love for creating secret societies. Weitling, who preached of a merciless revolution which would lead to an idyllic utopia, betrayed anarchist leanings in what vague social vision he espoused: "the perfect society had no government, but only an administration, no laws, but only obligations, no punishments, but means of correction."[19] From Weitling, Bakunin gained a love of revolution, training in the organization of secret societies and, after Weitling's arrest produced records of Bakunin's involvement, a trial in absentia in Russia.

From Switzerland, Bakunin went to Paris, where he befriended Proudhon and learned from him. Bakunin was never a profound thinker, and he preferred action to theory. Under Proudhon's influence, Bakunin began to call for a social revolution in addition to a political revolution. This call for a total change in the organization of the economy and society grew from the developing rationalization of the failings of the French Revolution—the middle and upper classes, which still controlled property, could use their social power to thwart the revolution. Although he called for an end to elites, he did not reconcile that call with his vision of a revolutionary elite which would guard against reaction; he later admitted this inconsistency in his thinking. After the Revolutions of 1848, Bakunin was arrested and, after two years during which he was sent from country to country, deported to Russia, where he rotted in Peter and Paul Fortress for six years of solitary confinement. After four further years of exile in Siberia, Bakunin escaped through North America and returned to Europe, ready to further the revolution.

Bakunin settled in Italy and, among the Italian revolutionaries, commenced to forming secret societies. The extent of these societies is not clear; Bakunin loved to fool others about his plans and most likely fooled himself as well. However, the formation of the International Working Men's Association in 1867 gave Bakunin a stage from which he could exercise some influence. The conference was not originally revolutionary in character—John Bright and John Stuart Mill were among the sponsors—but Bakunin used his oratory and his reputation to dominate several key committees. For the next several years, Bakunin and Marx sparred for control of the International; Marx stressed the need for political action by skilled workers and centralized planning, and Bakunin stressed the revolution of what Marx labeled the *lumpenproletariat* and collectivist anarchism.

During his battle with Marx, Bakunin became involved with Sergei Nechaev, a Russian nihilist who was even more bloodthirsty than Bakunin. Nechaev, who collaborated with Bakunin on several publications in 1869 and 1870, is probably the writer of the infamous *Principles of Revolution* which set forth the formula and principles of revolutionary terrorism. An even more extreme (but unpublished) document, the "Catechism of a Revolutionary" was found in Nechaev's possession when he was arrested in Switzerland in 1870. The "catechism" created the character of the committed revolutionary, unknown to all save the fellow members of a subversive cell, who knows no morality and employs all means, including murder and theft, in pursuit of revolution. The "catechism" is not specific to any political position and in fact outlines the organization of many contemporary terrorist groups. Bakunin later disavowed the document, which most historians agree was probably mainly the product of the more extreme Nechaev; nevertheless, the document had a decisive effect on Bakunin's career and helped create the association between anarchists and terrorism within the larger cultural discourse.

Marxists eagerly used the discovery of these papers to embarrass Bakunin, while anarchists tried to fix the blame on Nechaev; Bakunin and his followers were ousted from the International, which soon collapsed. Nechaev and Bakunin's collaboration had more far-reaching effects, despite the uncertainty of authorship. Whatever Bakunin's actual motive, these documents "openly linked the doctrine of anarchism with the practice of individual terrorism . . . from 1870 on there was always to be a section of the anarchist movement ready to commit acts of terrorism, if not for their own sake at least to symbolize a total revolt against society."[20] Before 1870, anarchism was one of several radical social theories; after 1870, as common criminals claimed that they were pursuing "anarchist" goals by robbing others, the political aims of anarchism were lost in a flood of criminal associations.

Throughout his life, Bakunin believed that every uprising might be the first shot of the Revolution; the complicated and often contradictory causes of most popular uprisings in the late nineteenth century, and their swift suppression, led him from one fiasco to another as he would help organize revolutionaries, witness their defeat, and sneak away in disguise in order to avoid capture. The use of violence as a means of bringing about revolution was never fully accepted in anarchist circles, but Bakunin's example led others to emulate or parody his actions. Although by no means the only perpetrators of violence, anarchists would become scapegoats in America and Britain, blamed for inciting violence in the native working classes. Just as Bakunin's own deeds did not bring about the Revolution, so would the era of "propaganda by the deed" succeed only in provoking a violent reaction.

At the same time that the capitalist press was characterizing anarchists as possessed demons of pure destruction, another Russian nobleman was attempting to depict anarchism in a different light. Peter Kropotkin, who had already established a reputation as a geographer, left the pursuit of pure science for the task of anarchist propaganda. Kropotkin sought to provide anarchism with a foundation in the natural sciences and answer the social Darwinism used to bolster the claims of capitalists. By grounding anarchism in a discourse with widespread authority, Kropotkin helped anarchist ideas make the transition from the earlier Romantic and rationalist mindsets to an age dominated by ideas of progress, science, and efficiency. By being an ascetic and peaceful man himself (often described as "saintly"), Kropotkin provided a counterpoint to the caricature of anarchists as sinister madmen hurling bombs at every opportunity.

The "Anarchist Prince," Kropotkin was a brilliant student who abandoned a promising career in the tsar's court for a post in Siberia, where he learned to prefer ascetic simplicity to the lavish intrigues of St. Petersburg. His growing radical views led him first to attempt to reform the treatment of serfs, then to renounce his commission in the army. When offered the secretaryship of the Russian Geographical Society, he realized he must decide between the pursuit of science and the pursuit of social justice; he rejected the secretaryship and, learning that conditions in Russia in the 1860s precluded any serious effort toward reform, moved to Switzerland. While living among some anarchistic communities in the Jura, he was converted to anarchism, and he returned to Russia as an active propagandist.

In 1874, Kropotkin was arrested and sentenced to the Peter and Paul Fortress. After two years his health broke down, and, during his hospital stay, he escaped to Switzerland, where he edited and published several anarchist newspapers, the most prominent of which, *Le Révolté*, stimulated a revival of anarchism among the workers of Lyons. In 1881, pressure from the Russian ambassador caused Kropotkin to be exiled from Switzerland; he settled in France. His articles during this decade would outline a coherent anarchist system of thought, as much an ethics as a revolutionary program. In 1882, he was arrested as part of a crackdown on anarchists following a series of riots and dynamite explosions; he was imprisoned until 1886, when he moved to London. He would remain in London for more than thirty years. At the end of his life, he returned to Russia, but the increasing tyranny of the Bolsheviks disillusioned him. To the best of his ability, he fought Lenin's increasing power and crackdown on the anarchists, who had been Bolshevik allies during the revolution. His funeral in 1921 marked the last time the anarchist flag would fly openly in the Soviet Union; a five-mile-long funeral procession bore testimony to Kropotkin's dedication and power to inspire.

Like Proudhon, Kropotkin was a communistic anarchist; that is, he assumed that the natural tendency of human beings was to form social groups, and the goal of the anarchist was to make sure these social groups did not unduly infringe on personal liberty. He envisioned human society as organized into small, local communes that would enter into agreements with other communes for items needed through trade. Everyone in the community could take what she or he needed from the community stores; Kropotkin believed that human sociability and peer pressure would ensure that everyone worked to the best of his or her ability. Like Godwin, Kropotkin was profoundly optimistic about human nature. Unlike Stirner and Godwin, however, Kropotkin assumed that people must work cooperatively in the modern economy. Trained in the natural sciences, Kropotkin argued that communistic anarchism would be the natural result of human progress, and he pointed out examples of "mutual aid"—individuals freely cooperating with one another without the benefit of an authoritative institution—in both the animal kingdom and throughout human history. He shared the anarchist reluctance to write utopias which attempted to dictate what society would be like after the Revolution, but he did write several books describing possible methods of ordering society without resorting to hierarchy or monopolies of force. His scientific methods and scholarly background earned him respect within both the radical movement and the larger culture.

However, Kropotkin was committed to the anarchist cause, and this commitment earned him much criticism. He acknowledged the appeal of violence against the repression of the propertied classes and voiced sympathy for those who were driven to desperate acts by the current unjust system. He once wrote "we who, in our houses, seclude ourselves from the cry and sight of human sufferings, *we are no judges* of those who live in the midst of all this hell of suffering. . . . Personally, I hate these explosions, but I cannot stand as a judge to condemn those who are driven to despair."[21] Kropotkin was part of the London conference which adopted "propaganda by the deed" as one strategy for anarchist agitation; however, he later repudiated that endorsement and never encouraged any individual act of violence.

Kropotkin and Bakunin, both anarchists, yet with diametrically opposed characters, would be the pattern for a narrative which anarchists and their critics would adopt when describing the small anarchist movement in the late nineteenth and early twentieth centuries. On the one hand were anarchist terrorists inspired by Bakunin's bloody romanticism. These terrorists, sometimes criminals or emotionally unbalanced individuals whose anarchism was adopted after the fact, were "seized upon and exaggerated all out of proportion by the press. Anarchists were presented as the perpetrators of a massive attack against civilization itself."[22] This exaggeration was contradicted by the number of highly visible, peaceful exponents of anarchism such as Kropotkin[23]. As Hong describes:

> The solution to this contradiction was both simple and opportune. The writers on anarchism proclaimed the existence of two very different types of anarchists. *The Nation* [p. 336 in E. L. Godkin's article "The execution of the Chicago anarchists," 10 Nov. 1887] announced that there were the "militant or homicidal anarchists" and the "dreamy per-

suasive anarchists." This theory of two antithetical groups of anarchists was then repeated again and again by subsequent writers.[24]

Anarchists found themselves caught on both sides. If they acted, they were classified as dangerously insane; if they did not, they were harmlessly insane. In either situation, anarchism as a political philosophy was not given a hearing, although many of the ideas espoused by anarchists were, in fact, similar to those voiced by more "acceptable" groups.

In the face of a determined propaganda campaign against it, anarchism survived. The appeal of anarchism lies in its appropriation of the same narratives and discourses that have currency in the broader culture. The proponents of anarchism adapt the liberal discourse on liberty and human progress into an argument against the abuses of power by state, church, and moneyed individuals. The history of the French Revolution provides the promise of radical social change and the possibility of collective action by the lower classes. Variations on Hegel's ideas provide a narrative of historical inevitability in which the excesses of the current systems of capitalism and the nation-state will produce a decentralized antithesis—anarchism. Although Stirner was briefly popular in Germany, the dominant form of anarchism in Europe during the late nineteenth century was communist-anarchism, and most anarchist writers concerned themselves with possible models for social organization which could control the forces of industrialization without becoming oppressive centralized bureaucracies. Coming from traditions that did not recognize the rights of every individual, most European anarchists of the late nineteenth century were more concerned with the liberation of the local community from economic and political forces beyond its control than they were concerned with the total freedom of the individual.

The United States, with a rhetorical tradition of radical individualism enshrined in the Declaration of Independence and other documents, was a more congenial environment for individualist anarchism. Anarchists in the immigrant communities carried on their traditions of communist anarchism, but many native American anarchists, such as Benjamin Tucker and Emma Goldman, popularized an individualist anarchism based on American rhetorical sources. Tucker in particular tried to ground anarchism in the political traditions of the United States, proclaiming that "Anarchists are simply unterrified Jeffersonian Democrats. They believe that 'the best government is that which governs least,' and that which governs least is no government at all."[25] The dominant anarchism of the United States is an individualistic anarchism, and suspicion of state power is a constant theme in American political discourse from the writing of the Constitution to the present day. Anarchistic ideas are found in the writing of Emerson and Thoreau, who in *On the Duty of Civil Disobedience* subscribed to the motto that "that government is best which governs not at all" and proclaimed that the individual conscience was the highest authority.[26] In addition to a tradition of suspicion of government and respect for individual liberty, the United States has a strong tradition of freethinkers and utopian activists.

The most inspirational anarchist activist in the United States in the mid-nineteenth century was Josiah Warren. Warren grew up in the golden age of American utopias, when the opening frontier encouraged a diverse group of people to attempt to build their own ideal communities. Of these, Robert Owen's colony at New Harmony was one of the largest; however, it did not escape the factionalism and eventual disintegration shared by most of these utopian communities. Warren, who had been involved in the New Harmony project, felt that its weakness was in the rigidity of organization, which failed to take individual desires into account. Instead of rigid, centralized socialistic utopias, Warren argued that "society must be converted so as to preserve the SOVEREIGNTY OF EVERY INDIVIDUAL inviolate."[27] To that end, he founded in Cincinnati what he called a Time Store, which sold goods at cost in exchange for "labor notes" that stood for an amount of work time. Warren hoped that this procedure would educate people in the idea of exchange based on labor rather than money. Warren decided the idea was workable, but spent the next few years editing a newspaper, the *Peaceful Revolutionist*, and founding a series of utopian communities structured along anarchist lines. The villages, called Utopia and Modern Times, were founded on individualist, mutual associations; both lasted in that character for about twenty years, after which they were slowly transformed into conventional villages and absorbed into the surrounding communities.[28]

For his ability to put anarchist ideas into practice, Warren inspired Stephen Pearl Andrews and Lysander Spooner, and the two writers elaborated on Warren's ideas. When Proudhon's ideas were introduced in the United States, many anarchists noted the similarities between Proudhon's ideas and Warren's; the followers of the two thinkers contributed much to the American Populist movement of the time.

American anarchism became associated with various radical social movements of the late nineteenth century. Because of their strong advocacy of individual freedom against state power, anarchists were supporters of free love and birth control, opponents of state censorship, and advocates of women's rights (although the suspicion most anarchists felt toward the ballot box made them lukewarm on the subject of female suffrage) and the rights of labor. Anarchist participation in movements that directly attacked many of the central tenets of conventional morality helped conservative partisans to characterize their position as under siege on numerous fronts. This characterization created a sense of alarm (and an increased loyalty) in many that blunted interest in anarchist ideas and narratives and replaced them with tales of secret conspiracies and atrocities. The violence associated with the labor movement (often the product of agents hired by industry), when combined with anarchist calls for political, social, and economic revolution, made the middle and upper classes in America especially nervous about challenges to their authority.

Anarchists gained most of their visibility in the United States in association with the labor movement. Most anarchists were members of labor organizations, and there were occasionally anarchist sections of various labor organizations. The anarchist presence within organized labor was regarded ambivalently by the leaders of the movement. The anarchist critique of power, whether economic, institutional, or ideological, was useful to the labor movement; the anarchist suspicion of democratic institutions undermined the goals of most labor leaders, and anarchist independence made discipline among the rank and file much more difficult. As the anti-anarchist propaganda intensified, labor leaders were quick to disavow any connection with anarchism, and, like in Germany and Britain earlier, Terence Powderly and other union officials worked to expel vocal anarchists from their labor organizations. Working against Powderly's wishes was the fact that the anarchists were important agitators, and their ties with immigrant workers were strong, so anarchism remained an important discourse within the labor movement in America.

The anarchist advocacy of the rights of labor created common ground between the anarchists of the native individualist tradition and those immigrants who ascribed to a more European form of communal anarchism. Although individualist anarchism was practiced by a few (most notably Benjamin Tucker), most anarchists in the United States were immigrants from central Europe, and communist-anarchism fit in neatly with the other institutions which were created to help recent immigrants survive in this new country.

The most prominent immigrant anarchist was Johann Most, who

for many in America and Britain was the stereotype of the dangerous anarchist. Most was a German immigrant trained as a bookbinder. His rhetoric was violent and excessive, and he printed directions for the manufacture of dynamite and nitroglycerin in his newspaper, *Die Freiheit*. "All these matters Most discussed with the sinister enthusiasm of a malevolent and utterly irresponsible child. He never used and probably never intended to use such methods himself; he recommended them to others instead."[29] Most was the inspiration of many vile caricatures of the anarchist hypocrite, who preaches dynamite but allows others to take the risks.

Most first published an anarchist newspaper in London before he was arrested; he later moved to the United States where he continued his vitriolic attacks on the powerful and calls for violence. Like Bakunin, Most was known more for his passion than his philosophy. In 1878, he left Germany for London after articles critical of the Kaiser and the clergy had earned him a brief imprisonment; in 1881, an article defending the assassination of Tsar Alexander earned him another six months' imprisonment. He left for America, where his revolutionary agitation met with much success in the context of the heightened labor and immigrant tensions in the United States. His advocacy of violence, combined with anarchist involvement in the labor movement, helped to create a climate of panic—and subsequent justification of violence—on the part of the more prominent capitalists. Woodcock goes so far as to blame him for almost single-handedly inspiring the Haymarket tragedy, causing the first repression of anarchists in America in the aftermath of a bomb in Chicago that killed one policeman in 1886.[30]

Aside from these prominent, published anarchists, there were thousands of others, scattered about Europe and America in small, informal groups. Each group (or schism within a group) had its own agenda—whether unionism, socialism, or free love—and may or may not have been violent. These groups were connected only by sympathy of ideas, and it was only in the minds of police investigators that they could be termed a "conspiracy." Spain, Italy, and Russia all had groups of anarchists that would rise to prominence in the years after World War I. In America and Britain, most anarchists were to be found in the immigrant communities of the large cities. Rudolph Rocker chronicles the activities of Jewish anarchists in London's east end in the last years of the nineteenth century, and anarchist immigrants in Chicago had founded numerous mutual aid and social societies and even presented a play based on the plot to assassinate Tsar Nicholas. These anarchists were never very numerous, but had an influence larger than their numbers because of the appeal of anarchism to those who were victimized economically and through established discourses of ethnicity and class.

The history of anarchism establishes several important narratives which define anarchists as a group. The primary narrative concerns the primacy of the individual over society. This idea was informed with language from several discourses. The innate worth of the individual is derived from the Christian tradition, and the Protestant Reformation creates the precedent of each person having authority over her or his own spiritual development; for some, including Leo Tolstoy, this was a sufficient basis for a kind of anarchist ideal. The Enlightenment elevated human reason to the position of supreme power, and Godwin explicitly associated the promise of human perfectibility with anarchist individualism. The Romantic narrative of the individual reaching the limits of human potential despite confining social norms, which builds on the two previous traditions, allows Stirner, Bakunin, and others to describe themselves as heroes and to understand the misunderstanding and persecution that often followed their careers. The shadow of the French Revolution promised the real possibility of social revolution and inspired two generations to attempt to create their own revolution on more individualist lines.

Individualism alone does not differentiate anarchists from more conservative writers such as Herbert Spencer and William Graham Sumner, however. Following the example of Proudhon in Europe and Josiah Warren in America, anarchists defined economic justice as one of their primary concerns, and this concern, combined with the exaltation of common people derived from the Christian tradition, encouraged anarchists to identify with the poor and the working class. The Romantic vision of the individual hero led to an anti-institutionalism that differentiated anarchists not only from the liberals and Christian Socialists of the middle and professional classes, but also from other revolutionaries (such as Karl Marx) who advocated centralized power in the name of revolution.[31] The nihilist use of atheism, as well as violent rhetoric and violent action, further alienated those groups within the middle classes that would otherwise have had sympathy with various anarchist narratives. The ideals of social justice and individual empowerment that could have served as bonds of alliance between anarchists and other groups in society were weakened by competing discourses within anarchism.

These competing discourses within anarchist rhetoric were fully exploited by those whose visions of social change were diametrically opposed to anarchist decentralization. Advocates of corporate organization of the economy and a strong governmental ability to maintain order created narratives that made the anarchist a sinister caricature designed to frighten the general population. The figure of the anarchist became a symbol for any destabilizing force of the time, be it atheism, atavism, the loosening of moral codes, or economic change. Nathaniel Hong has grouped the attacks on anarchism into several broad categories: the capitalist equation of the attack on the centralized state and the economic hierarchy as an attack on society; the religious characterization of liberty as dangerous, and obedience divine; the scientific characterization of anarchists as atavistic deviants; and the nativist attacks on anarchists as foreigners, or members of the faceless "masses."[32] Each anarchist "outrage"—and many more violent outbreaks during this period were attributed to anarchists than were actually committed by them—brought a new round of attacks in the mainstream media that were designed to shore up the loyalty of individuals to various authoritative discourses by painting the enemy to those discourses (anarchists) in diabolical terms. The fact that there was a threat at all was used to shore up loyalty to established institutions as the only defense against the evils that those very institutions claimed would follow an anarchist victory, as was demonstrated in Chicago in 1886.

In the United States and Great Britain of the late nineteenth and early twentieth centuries, the dialogue between anarchists and the larger culture is punctuated by events that were associated exclusively with anarchists (whether accurately or not). These "outrages" served as focal points, as evidence for particular ideologically charged discourses, and as turning points in the perception of anarchist ideas. Many of these "outrages" took place in foreign countries, but were zealously reported because of the danger associated with anarchism. Anarchist attempts to garner publicity through peaceful means—mainly congresses and public speeches—were given only mocking attention if they were reported at all outside the radical press. This treatment was not due to some organized conspiracy, but rather to the narratives associated with anarchists—most people, informed by the negative stereotype of the anarchist, were unprepared to accept any other type. In some cases (as in Chicago), anarchists themselves bowed to the pressure and played upon the negative stereotype, often with disastrous results.

The United States witnessed more anarchist activity within its borders than Great Britain. Amid much anarchist agitation within the labor movement and the free love movement, the events surrounding the Haymarket Affair were followed in 1892 by Alexander Berkman's attempt to assassinate Carnegie Steel Works' manager Robert Frick, and in 1901, by Leon Czoglosz's (whose anarchist credentials were dubious at best) assassination of President McKinley. The anarchist movement in America, that had been strong and growing through the 1870s, weakened as each of these events was used to alienate those who might have had sympathy with anarchist ideals. Only a few individuals, notably Emma Goldman (whose *Mother Earth* was published from 1906 until 1917) kept the American anarchist tradition alive. By the end of the First World War, laws against anti-war activity and the deportation of important anarchists under the 1919 Palmer Act suppressed what remained of the American anarchist movement. Radicalism in America after that point generally supported the gradual dominance of American society by corporate or governmental institutions.

Although anarchists often found asylum in Great Britain, their influence was generally confined to the immigrant communities in which they lived. Aside from a few radicals and artists, anarchism never overcame its foreign taint with the British worker. Reported "outrages" on the continent, however, would provide sufficient material for British newspapers and provide rationales for government crackdowns on free speech by radicals of all stripes. The assassination of Tsar Alexander II in 1881 led to the imprisonment of Johann Most, who rashly praised the act in print and crossed an unwritten line of decency; the dynamite explosions of the Frenchman Ravachol in 1892 led to an anarchist scare and trial in Walsall, England; in 1894, an explosion outside the Greenwich Observatory killed one Frenchman, likely the person who attempted to plant the bomb. Although the London *Times* often reported on anarchist activities in France with much alarm, anarchism in England was mainly associated with various aesthetic movements and artists such as William Morris, Oscar Wilde, and members and acquaintances of the Rossetti family.

For most in the United States and Great Britain, anarchism was a mediated phenomenon: most people knew of anarchists only what they heard or read. For that reason, the coverage of anarchists in newspapers, popular magazines, and books written to capitalize on that journalistic coverage is important as the forum through which anarchist discourses were heard, subverted, or drowned out.

3
Revolution, Anarchism, and the Mob

ONE OF THE CENTRAL NARRATIVES OF THE ANARCHIST MOVEMENT IN
Europe and the United States was the idea of "social revolution"—
the complete overturning of outmoded institutions and customs
which would create a clean slate on which a more just and natural
society could be designed. This yearning for an ideal society, akin
to a religious yearning for a paradise outside of history, was to be
achieved (so anarchists thought) through anarchistic means: individual acts which would lead to a spontaneous revolt. The anarchistic practice of "propaganda by the deed" was envisioned as a means
of educating people about the revolution and as the steps that could
hasten it; most anarchists, however, thought that the revolution
would come of its own accord, and all that was required of the anarchist movement was education.

The faith in an imminent revolution coincided with a larger social
malaise that manifested itself in the cultural dialogue as a fear of
social degeneracy or collapse. The details varied widely. For some,
such as Henry James, the advent of democracy and commercialism
spelled the end of the older aristocracy and its support of high culture, which he understood as the end of European "civilization."
Others saw society degenerating into disorder, either through advancing democratic principles, racial impurity, genetic atavism, or
loosening moral standards. This narrative of decay, which was independent of the anarchist movement, reflected an eroding faith in
cultural institutions in the wake of widespread cultural change.[1]
Nevertheless, conservatives attacked anarchists as the symbol of
this cultural fear, turning anarchists into a malevolent force outside
of the cultural order, the face of the feared mob. This symbolic association replaced the voice of anarchists with the stereotype of the
anarchist as a mad bomber, bent only on destruction. Although anarchists gained a measure of attention they could not have achieved
otherwise, the fear of revolution ultimately marginalized anarchism
and justified extreme repressive measures.

The ideal of revolution was a central narrative of the anarchist culture, taking the place of institutional bonds for the nonauthoritarian anarchists. The anarchist faith in a coming new order was bolstered through the remembrance of attempted revolutions in the past. In Chicago, the local anarchists celebrated the French and American Revolutions, the rebellions of 1848, the Paris Commune of 1871, and the strikes of 1877 as precursors of the coming social change. Several anarchists, notably Peter Kropotkin, sought to strengthen this faith by writing histories of the French Revolution which reaffirmed the possibility of wrenching social change and suggested ways to avoid the counterrevolutionary reaction which the French Revolution had witnessed.

Like many eschatological narratives, the story of the social revolution was a source of inspiration and consolation for radicals who in their daily lives saw mainly disappointment, injustice, and oppression. By framing their own experiences within the historical scope of the revolution, anarchists, communists and socialists could minimize their defeats and find tremendous promise in their small victories. The eschatological narrative, embedded in the Christian tradition, also proved attractive to many people whom the anarchists wished to recruit to their cause: displaced workers, peasants, and others whom Marx derided as *lumpenproletariat*. By divorcing the eschatological promise from the doctrines of Christianity, anarchists could use an established discourse to communicate their own ideas. When combined with the language of exploitation and class struggle which anarchism shared with other radical economic doctrines, this faith in revolution created a narrative framework for people's lives that could inspire iron perseverance and courage.[2]

The violent simplicity of the social revolution that made the narrative an effective bridge between popular traditions and radical discourses could also justify extreme acts of terror. In 1877 and 1878 a wave of assassinations occurred in Europe, led by the terrorist faction of the Russian Populist movement. The notoriety that these terrorist acts brought to their respective movements attracted many anarchists who were not otherwise disposed to advocate violence. In 1879 and in 1880, anarchist congresses issued proclamations in favor of terrorism as a method of propaganda for the cause, and the normally peaceable Kropotkin himself advocated the formation of secret groups separate from the labor-oriented International to plan and carry out acts of terror.[3] "Propaganda by the deed," as it came to be known, was a concrete act of revolt and a symbol of revolution; the act was seen as an ideal way to educate the semiliterate workers whom anarchists considered crucial actors in the narrative of revolution: "As the French Federation said, the back-ward masses read little, while Benvenuto and the Italians had tried to demonstrate their programme through a living fact."[4] With vio-lence, anarchists thought they could gain the attention which had eluded them when they had simply tried to educate workers in the language of the class struggle.

The bomb was seen as an ideal symbol of the anarchist revolu-tion: it started as an individual object, but spread out; the dynamite bomb was thought to equalize the power of the individual with that of the police; and bombings did not require a large organization to be effective and thus could be carried out through the decentralized, nonauthoritarian groupings preferred by anarchists; the bombing also satisfied the urge to "do something" concrete, to exact some revenge against capitalists. The effectiveness of the bomb as a sym-bol for the revolution within anarchist discourse explains its promi-nent place in the rhetoric of various anarchist activists, notably Johann Most, who was on trial during the London Congress of 1881 for printing a defense of the tsar's assassins. Many anarchists who would never have actually thrown a bomb were not hesitant to talk about it; several of the anarchists of Chicago were said to keep bombs in their newspaper offices to show off to curious reporters.

The tragedy of the era of "propaganda by the deed" is that the true significance of the acts of terror committed could be under-stood only by those who were already familiar with anarchist dis-course. For the anarchist, the bomb was a symbolic act imbedded in the narrative of social revolution, a symbolic revenge for the insti-tutional violence committed by those who had gained wealth through exploitative capitalism. Within the anarchist movement, many opposed individual acts of violence but could understand the emotions which lay at the center of the narrative—frustration, re-venge, and hope of the revolution. In fact, many acts of terror were as much acts of revenge (against brutal policemen or judges who condemned friends to prison) as they were acts of political protest.[5]

The effectiveness of "propaganda by the deed" and the language of revolution outside anarchist discourse had less to do with anar-chist persuasion than it did the general anxieties of the propertied classes. Far from being an effective tool of anarchist propaganda, terrorism bolstered the claims of the state for more power in com-bating "disorder"—which was defined as any activity not sanc-tioned by the laws and conventions which were shared by the propertied classes. The bomb as an image was used to displace the entire anarchist discourse, allowing others to define anarchism as a simple creed of bloodlust and destruction and effectively silence anarchists in the ongoing cultural conversation.

Many anarchists realized the ineffectiveness of violence after the bombing near Haymarket in Chicago in 1886, which led to an extended period of police terrorism and the suspension of individual rights in the name of "preserving order." By the 1890s, most anarchist leaders, notably Peter Kropotkin, had begun to denounce individual acts of terrorism or theft as counterproductive. However, the power to strike fear into the hearts of many in the name of the cause led to one series of anarchist outrages in France, beginning with the bombings of Ravachol in 1892.

It is in some measure ironic that the most significant string of anarchist bombings would occur nearly ten years after the London Congress called for it, at a time when most anarchist writers had lost faith in the individual terrorist act and were discouraging others from sacrificing their lives for the cause. The bombs and assassinations which occurred from Ravachol's bombing of a judge to the assassination of President Carnot in 1894 were also not the result of a conspiracy, but rather a chain reaction in which the punishment of one terrorist inspired the next terrorist to revenge.[6] Ravachol, the first terrorist, blew up the home of a judge who had given what Ravachol considered to be harsh sentences to several people involved in an uprising in 1891; after his arrest, Emile Henry blew up the café where Ravachol had been arrested because of a tip from the owner (no one was killed in either attack, although Ravachol did murder another person). The bombs were given an interpretive framework in the anarchist press which other journals repeated, so that most people understood that the bombs were not targeted at individuals but at representatives of authority. This interpretation, and the fear it generated among the propertied classes, inspired other individual anarchists in the Parisian community to avenge their arrested comrades. The cycle ended in 1894 with the pardon of several activists who had been rounded up in the police crackdown that followed the bombings.

Although any explosion or assassination can be a cause for concern, the fear of anarchists was far out of proportion to the threat they presented or the actual plots they carried out. Fenians in London, as well as numerous labor organizations, carried out acts of violence in pursuit of their own agendas, but neither group was as reviled, feared, or tied as closely to the concept of terrorism as the anarchists. The excessive fear of anarchism when compared to other groups that employed terrorist strategies during the time is related to the anarchist's basic questioning of social assumptions.

Fenians and labor groups pursued specific goals that could be met without undue strain on the social order. Anarchists sought the very overthrow of that order, and their call for the ending of civilization associated them with fears (already present, as Patrick Brantlinger has described in *Bread and Circuses*[7]) of cultural decline and the ascendancy of working class power.

The main inspiration for the fear of revolution came not from the anarchists, but from the terrible conditions in which poor people lived in the 1880s and 1890s. Charles Booth's statistics painted a dire picture of abject poverty throughout London, and the apparent inability of any social institution to alleviate that poverty created a sense of impending doom throughout society. Ford Madox Ford described the feelings of the time in a rather tongue-in-cheek fashion: "it was a day of nightmares universal and showing no signs of coming to an end. Nothing could happen but what did—a worldwide flood of disorder ending in Anarchism."[8] Society was perceived to be in disorder, and the anarchists were found to be a convenient symbol of that disorder. What happened in the late nineteenth century was a tremendous expansion of the powers of social authority to deal with a breakdown in order that was mainly imaginary.

Just as the social Darwinist narrative placed the causes of poverty within the moral character of the impoverished, so did many commentators on the impending decline of civilization identify the causes of the decline in moral trends present in society. Gibbon[9] traced the fall of Rome to its citizens' abandonment of civic ideals for personal pleasure, which had allowed the barbarians to subvert the government. The press in Great Britain and America characterized their respective countries as imperial republics and were quick to use the example of the fallen Roman Empire to warn against the threats of relaxed custom or the fecundity and materialism of the lower classes.

In the late nineteenth century, many writers tried to frame narratives around this fear of the numerous poor and the associated sense of social decline. In addition to the various utopias that promised vast social changes within the reader's lifetime, there were numerous novels which described the horrors of an impending violent revolution. Donnelly's *Caesar's Column*[10] described the leader of a mob, ironically named Caesar, who inspires the lower classes to rise violently against their masters. He glorifies his deed by encasing a mile-high pile of dead bodies in concrete, creating the monument of the title. The huge numbers of people in the working classes and *lumpenproletariat* were a large factor in the fear of the middle classes; the sheer multitude was seen as potentially uncontrollable.

Although "anarchy' had long been associated with any attempt to order society which did not agree with that of the speaker, *Culture and Anarchy*[11] established a vision of society that equated anarchy with, in his words, the "populace." The chief characteristic of the populace, according to Arnold, is its desire to do whatever it likes—to indulge appetite like the decadent Romans rather than engage in the serious, disciplined work of institution building. Images of the riots in Hyde Park recur throughout the work, implying that the populace, when not firmly controlled by the minority, is violent and destructive. Common schooling is seen as a way to control the mob and preserve the artistic achievements of England; the lower classes and democratic rule are threats to everything that Europe has built. Arnold's narrative describes the threat not as the population itself, but the insufficient guidance of that growing population.

Arnold's equations of the lower classes with anarchy and the educated elites with culture becomes a key feature of discourses on social disorder throughout the rest of the century. In "Is Our Civilization Perishable?" J. A. Jameson (who answers the question of the title in the affirmative) finds both moral and political threats to the current order. Jameson first locates the moral threat:

> Mr Matthew Arnold has raised, none too early or too loudly, a warning voice against the prevailing tendency of French imaginative literature; he charges it with impurity . . . as a similar infection subdued the hardy virtues of the Roman commonwealth, making possible the immense ruin which befell it, so it may have rendered inevitable the awful overthrow at Sedan . . . the vice in the French novel consists in its perverted views of the sexual relations.[12]

Jameson finds the greatest political threats to civilization to lie not with monopolies and exploitative employers, but from the masses: "It is not, however, from the ranks of capital that the danger which we wish now to emphasize is to be apprehended, but from those who possess the physical force to compel obedience to any behest they choose to formulate—the vast laboring majority."[13] Jameson ignores the very real power of the propertied classes (with their hired agents, police force, and, as demonstrated during the 1877 strikes, the national guard and armed forces), instead focusing on inchoate potential power of the mob.

Many magazine articles of the time discussed the problem of how to control mobs in detail, especially in the immediate aftermath of working-class riots. Most of these were careful to stress that mob activity was isolated or inspired by unscrupulous agents, not a product of the social system or the basic morality of the common man. The *North American Review* from October 1885 pronounced that "Riots generally originate in crowded cities or in districts where the population is principally composed of operatives. They are due to two causes. First: the restlessness or peevish discontent of the working classes, who imagine that others are reaping large gains from their labor. Second: the plotting of demagogues."[14] Rather than suffer a repeat of the Strikes of 1877, when the government "suffered anarchy and pillage and murder to rule for days,"[15] the United States should educate working men about the true relations between capital and labor and drill the police forces to quash assemblies of working men that threaten to become riots. Capitalists in many cities took up collections and donated land so that the Federal Government could establish armories that would be used to suppress working-class discontent.

Writers in England were quick to applaud repressive measures in the United States. The *Fortnightly Review* of 1 March 1886, writing in response to a recent riot at Hyde Park that the author declares is worse than the one which inspired Matthew Arnold, offers the following prescription:

> There is no country in the world where overt resistance to the law is dealt with more firmly than in America. Every officer from the highest to the lowest acts in the name of the Commonwealth, and if the authority of the Commonwealth be defied, the only question is as to the amount of force needed to compel submission. This lesson must be learned here at home.[16]

One striking feature of the discourse surrounding the suppression of mobs is the social segregation which the writers assume; no one among their readers will ever be involved in a riot, or even have grievances similar to the working class. The "Commonwealth" is an institution that demands the obedience of the working classes, but does not speak for them. This social segregation, which was a social feature throughout the period, removed whatever check daily contact between classes had on the inaccuracy of class stereotypes and narratives. As the propertied classes spoke more and more to themselves, in a standard, authoritative language, the working classes developed their own discourse. As the discourses diverged, the fears of class struggle increased with the lack of interaction and were replaced by more and more outrageous narratives that sought to impose control over social groups excluded from the authoritative discourse.

One of the most prominent attempts to impose an authoritative order on the lives of the lower classes was made by Cesare Lombroso and his pupil, Max Nordau. Lombroso's writings were part of a tradition of sociological and psychological writings which attempted to apply the new disciplines to social and political problems; sociologists wrote books on topics such as secret societies and methods of social control, attempting to use the rhetorical power of science to comprehend social forces that seemed to escape more direct means of control. Lombroso's notion most relevant to the discorse of social disorder was "atavism," whereby "civilized" men could regress into savages either through the influence of a crowd or their own poisoned heredity. Groups of any kind could cause men to regress, he wrote, whether men on the street or in democratic assemblies:

> We have seen that it is not in the assemblage of a great number of men that the greatest wisdom and highest advancement is to be found. This ought to destroy the false notion born of a parliamentary atmosphere, which tends always to increase the number of those who shall deliberate upon the interests of the state. It is a mistake to lessen responsibility by dividing it up among undue numbers.[17]

The threat of democracy leads Lombroso to a study of anarchists and other "political criminals," where he finds evidence of hereditary abnormalities in revolutionists. The physiognomy of an individual is sufficient, argues Lombroso, "for distinguishing true revolution, always fruitful and useful, from utopia, from rebellion, which is always sterile . . . true revolutionists . . . have all a marvelously harmonious physiognomy"[18] while the Chicago anarchists show evidence of degeneracy. Thus science offered a way of working with the lower classes while fearing them; it is not the populace as a whole, but rather degenerate individuals within the working classes who incite revolts. This narrative repeats within scientific discourse the conspiracy theories that surrounded labor relations and the dreaded "walking delegate." Both ideas support the contention that individuals who publicly complain about conditions or encourage others to resist the social order should be suppressed quickly, lest their ideas spread like a contagion throughout the genetically weakened lower classes.

Max Nordau, a disciple of Lombroso's, directly connected his teacher's theories of atavism to the fate of Western culture itself with his book *Degeneration*.[19] In it, he connected degeneracy not only to political criminals and reformers, but also to artists and authors whose work, in Nordau's opinion, subverted social norms. This book, which created a brief sensation, drew clear lines between those forces that sought to maintain social order and those anarchical forces that aided the genetically suspect lower classes to increased political and economic power:

> Degenerates are not always criminals, prostitutes, anarchists, and pronounced lunatics; they are often authors and artists. These, however, manifest the same mental characteristics, and for the most part the same somatic features, as the members of the above-mentioned anthropological family, who satisfy their unhealthy impulses with the knife of the assassin or the bomb of the dynamiter, instead of with pen and pencil.[20] (vii)

This unholy alliance of unhealthy and extremist democracy, art which was offensive to conservative tastes, and the scientific label of abnormality created a vast conspiracy, an implacable enemy to conservative culture, which did not in fact exist. Although Nordau and Lombroso's work was discredited (and Lombroso himself had moved away from strict biological determinism by the early twentieth century), the caricature of the immoral artist or the anarchist continued to embody the low forehead, blank stare, and wild hair of the anarchist type, which carried fearsome cultural associations into the twentieth century.

The associations of anarchy with cultural disorder and the threat of the rising lower classes were encouraged by groups that opposed not only the anarchist agenda, but liberalism in general. Conservatives emphasized the leftists' roles as instigators of revolution and destruction by playing up violent acts committed by workers, activists, or the insane as "anarchical" while obscuring, distorting, or ignoring the ideological context that gave those actions their significance. Capitalists and advocates of increased institutional power on both the left and the right, engaging in social engineering of their own, could use the anarchistic narrative of revolution as a scapegoat for the social stresses caused by the alienation, displacement, and regimentation of their own agendas. For all of these groups, anarchism divorced from its language of social critique was useful as a dark mirror, an outside presence that instigated modernity's negative effects.

Being cast as symbols of the multitude, revolutionary anarchists achieved notoriety at the expense of becoming scapegoats to social fears. In the end, the fear of the multitude drowned out anarchist ideas. Anarchism came to stand for an motley hodgepodge of boogeymen. Cast as a threat outside reason, any disturbing social development or idea could be termed 'anarchistic'—from the absurdly simplistic redistributionary schemes Hyacinth Robinson envisions in *The Princess Casamassima* (1886), to simple murder and theft, to developments in science (Henry Adams describes developments in atomic theory as "anarchical" in his *Education*), to literature which questioned contemporary standards. Novels such as *The Angel of the Revolution* (1893) and *Hartmann the Anarchist* (1893) took advantage of the universal threat implied by anarchism to heighten the suspense of the narrative and encourage social repression. Even reform efforts which did no more than question current beliefs, such as universal education and women's suffrage, earned the epithet "anarchistic" from one writer or another.

As the strains of modernization undermined people's faith in social institutions, narratives of disorder and social chaos were adapted to the contemporary situation as a way of expressing these fears. Some writers expanded the symbolic threat of anarchism in order to inspire greater discipline, repression, and social order. Richard Savage's *The Anarchist: A Story of To-Day* (1894) discusses the efforts of a German anarchist to secure a rich American heiress' money in order to fund anarchist activity; he is thwarted through the efforts of a young man who is active in a local law-and-order league and who counsels never-ending vigilance against all disorder. The narrative of lower-class revolution and social decline is intimately associated with anarchism and informs the novels of the late nineteenth and early twentieth centuries in which anarchism is a major theme. In *The Princess Casamassima*, Henry James goes beyond the mere threat of revolution and identifies social decline in the seemingly irreconcilable differences between groups in modern society.

The Princess Casamassima and the Breakdown of Dialogue

Henry James's *The Princess Casamassima*[21] captures the dialogues surrounding the cultural changes of the middle 1880s. Inaccurate in its historical representation of the anarchist movement, the novel is nevertheless a moving dramatization of the anxieties that ran under the surface of the dialogues of the propertied class. The novel, which comes closer than any other James wrote to the lives of the lower classes and "the mob," uses the specter of anarchism to express the cultural fears of decline that gripped America and Britain in the late nineteenth century. James traces these fears

to the increasing segregation of society that allowed radically opposed ideologies to come into frequent conflict; Hyacinth Robinson,
as the site of these conflicting languages, destroys himself as a
warning of society's impending collapse.

The reputation of Henry James's *The Princess Casamassima*
has grown over the years despite its initial poor reception. *The
Princess Casamassima* represents, according to F. O. Matthiessen, Henry James's "most ambitious effort to treat political material."[22] For the novel, James left his accustomed leisure-class
settings in order to describe the revolutionary underworld of London, a world of well-meaning social workers, slumming aristocrats,
immigrant workers, and coldhearted revolutionaries; despite the
change in setting, the novel does reveal the same Jamesian fascination with character types and the interaction of fallible individuals
within larger social settings.

One dominant strain of criticism addresses the issue of the novel's historical accuracy. In his correspondence, James took some
pride in his research for the novel. Contemporary reviewers, perhaps reacting to James's previous career as a writer of genteel fiction, did not find the detail of the novel to be accurate or convincing,
however, and many critics have echoed that accusation.

Although it is clear that James had little direct knowledge of his
subject, many critics (led by Tilley's thorough monograph *The
Background of* The Princess Casamassima) have pointed to the numerous secondary sources he used in the composition of the novel
in order to give the novel what he hoped would be a semblance of
historical accuracy. Leon Edel describes James's self-conscious imitation of naturalistic research techniques, such as taking notes of
the speech patterns of London's lower classes. James himself had
been in the habit of walking the streets of London since his first
arrival in 1869. During one of these walks, he saw a young worker
looking, like himself, at the passersby, and he attributed his inspiration for the novel to this encounter. James supplemented his note
taking and his strolls with visits to prisons, a foray into the world of
the lower classes which led him to label himself "quite a naturalist"
in a letter. Despite that claim, Henry James's experiences of actual
working-class life remained limited; to make up for this deficiency,
James relied on the narratives of other writers to fuel his own imagination.

James supplemented the naturalistic methods of Zola and Balzac
with many literary precursors. The possible sources which James
used in writing *The Princess Casamassima* have been identified by
numerous critics. Most exhaustively, W. H. Tilley has traced most of

James's sources in his monograph *The Background of* The Princess Casamassima. According to Tilley, the novel overtly echoes Turgenev's *Virgin Soil*, which shares the plot in which a revolutionary son of a nobleman kills himself after he loses faith in the revolutionary cause. The works of Charles Dickens gave James a set of character types and narratives suitable for his depictions of working-class London.

In addition to literary precursors, Henry James relied on the London *Times* for his information about the nature and activities of anarchists. The anarchist movement, with its potent symbol of the dynamite bomb, had been adopted by the mainstream press as the symbol of every disorderly force in late Victorian England. On the Continent, there were several bombings (not all of which could properly be called the work of anarchists, but were nevertheless described as "anarchical" in the newspapers), and the Fenian Movement had succeeded in setting off blasts in England itself. In addition to the bombings of anarchists and others, the perceived stability of the social order was further undermined by working-class unrest (there were riots on in France, Italy, and the United States) and the seeming inability of the authorities to prevent this disorder.

Tilley has plotted the articles in the *Times* and the *Spectator* which would have supplied the language for many conversations among the leisure classes in England regarding the nature of the anarchist threat; he often repeats Henry James's assertion that the *Times* "was correctly held to represent the sentiment of the majority."[23] The relationship was actually much more complex. In its coverage of the anarchist movement, the *Times* did not so much represent the sentiment of the propertied classes as create a sentiment through selective reporting and give it substance through a set of mutually supporting narratives. Although there were several explosions set by members of the Fenian movement in England, there were in fact very few anarchist incidents in Great Britain; the *Times* created emotion from the general apathy of the English populace through sensationalizing those anarchist (and nonanarchist) bombings, riots, and assassinations in Russia, Germany, France, and Italy during the period.

Anarchism, as defined by the mainstream press in the 1880s, is almost devoid of political or economic significance. The calls for worker ownership of factories, increased local control, and greater individual liberty were all divorced from the anarchist message, and what remained were the fanatic writings of Nechaev and a portrayal of bombing not as a symbol of protest, but as an "outrage" (the

usual descriptive word in the *Times*, according to Tilley)—
something which, being "beyond rage," is beyond the realm of the
articulate and hence requires rejection, not understanding. Anything which might undermine the current social order was defined
as "anarchical," including increased rights for women and a relax-
ation of artistic censorship. Newspapers erased distinctions between the Russian Populists (inaccurately called "nihilists" as a
way of emphasizing their supposed destructive nature), Marxists,
individualist anarchists and communist-anarchists, blaming them
indiscriminately for any violent acts. By erasing distinctions, newspapers could turn local radicals into a greater threat to stability
through association. The virulence of this association explains the
eagerness of Fabians and other nonviolent radicals to disassociate
themselves from any taint of anarchism, even when their own ideas
(such as those of William Morris) were basically in line with anarchist thinking.

The label of "anarchist" was equated solely with destruction, a
negative "other" deprived of its own voice. In order to stifle discourse on the significance of the bombings, newspaper coverage
usually placed the incidents in an individual and social rather than
a political context. As a malady of modern civilization, anarchists
were made to mirror the very institutions they opposed through
elaborate conspiracy theories that attributed to the anarchists a secret power and rigid hierarchy out of Bakunin's most fevered
dreams. The bombs were taken out of the context of anarchist discourse and instead placed within a discourse of conspiracy, degeneracy and criminality, a sign of madness and the sickness of
modern civilization. The *Times*, far from simply reflecting opinion,
actively disseminated a particular narrative in order to bolster its
own group interest. Rather than seeing anarchists as small groups
united mainly by a distrust of the very powerful, centralized institutions which buttressed the current social order, the *Times* sees an
"international conspiracy, its murderous aims, [and] the fanaticism
of its members."[24] Following up reports of anarchist attacks with
calls for increased police power and coordination between national
governments, newspapers created a narrative justification for the
increasing powers of the nation-state and the increasingly international capitalist class which dominated that state.

Despite the frenzied narratives of outrage and conspiracy printed
in the *Times*, there were still many (especially the educated readers
of James's novels) who saw the anarchists as a varied group of
which only a minority were capable of truly violent action. Bakunin's secret societies, most of which existed only within his own

mind, were eagerly written about in the *Times* as "evidence" of a vast conspiracy, a centralized institution which would mirror the institutions it opposed. Later critics, including Lionel Trilling, are just as eager to believe in this narrative of conspiracy in order to justify Henry James's depiction of the anarchist movement. By insisting on proving the verisimilitude or the prophetic power of the novel, many later critics have missed the ambivalence and uncertainty which made the novel unsatisfying for many of James's contemporaries, even though James thought it one of his best novels to date.

The close relationship between the narrative of the *Times* and the cultural fears which lay behind this discourse encouraged Henry James to see the possibilities for self-expression within this story charged with fears of cultural decline, isolation, and revolution. James hoped that the silenced language of revolutionary radicalism that lies beyond the narratives of the London *Times* would give the novel its power: "the effect I wished most to produce was precisely that of our not knowing, of society's not knowing, but only guessing and suspecting and trying to ignore, what 'goes on' irreconcilably, subversively, beneath that vast smug surface" (48). Some critics point to the very tentativeness and mystery of the novel in its approach to its "revolutionary" material as a reason for its lack of popularity, despite the topicality of James's subject; however, this same indeterminacy and multiple layers of meaning give the novel a longer life than other, more monologic novels which deal with the theme of revolution.

James's reliance on such secondary sources as the London *Times* and the cheap pamphlets he could obtain (including, according to Trilling, Nechaev's *Catechism of a Revolutionary*) makes *The Princess Casamassima* a conflict between various languages and cultural narratives removed from actual history; the novel is not historically accurate, but it does demonstrate the interplay of narratives surrounding the issue of revolution in the 1880s. Critics such as Trilling, eager to vindicate James's historical verisimilitude, have too quickly substituted James's impression of events for the events themselves and have denied part of the complexity of the novel by doing so. Rather than factual history, the novel reflects the nightmare of revolution which had gripped the propertied classes in the 1880s in reaction to increasing social segregation, alienation, and the symbolic threat of bombings and working-class uprisings which occurred regularly during this time period. More significantly, the novel's protagonist, Hyacinth Robinson, is himself a battleground of competing narratives and languages. His suicide at the end of the novel betrays the gaps and silences in the discourses which James employs throughout the novel.

James's attempt to create a psychological study of the revolutionary milieu, like Hyacinth's attempt to fashion a coherent identity through the narratives at his disposal, is hampered by the monologic nature of his sources and the author's distance from the events themselves. Ultimately, *The Princess Casamassima* reflects the unreality of the anarchist "menace" and the conflicts of modernization which that menace was used to obscure.

The Princess Casamassima, forged from many mutually exclusive narrative voices, presents the reader with multiple interpretations as well. The language signifying anarchism occupies what might be called a "negative space" in the dialogues of the propertied classes: anarchists are outside the social order and come to stand for all the cultural nightmares which lurk in the narratives of those classes. The political nightmare of the loss of social control by the elites comes to signify all that lies outside human control, whether the perceptual uncertainties of an individual or the historical uncertainties of civilization as a whole.

The Princess Casamassima is a novel less about the anarchist movement as it is about the language which frames the anarchist movement and the ability of that language to influence individual perceptions and produce actions that warp society. James's anarchism, like James's elitism, communicates beliefs that are inconclusively supported by a text that ruthlessly undercuts perceptions. James writes a novel about his sources, and the novel becomes an enactment of the struggle to know reality through the maze of language and narrative which frames human perception. The novel depends upon the associative context of anarchism that his contemporary reader would possess: the uncertainties, the fears, and the strange vocabulary of revolutionaries underscore the stresses brought about by social segregation, the threats brought about by a seeming loss of consensus.

As the central figure in the novel and its main narrative presence, Hyacinth Robinson is the focal point for the novel's many conflicts. Most readers have identified Hyacinth's main characteristic to be his sensitivity—his ability to be influenced by his environment. Some critics have seen this as a strength (making Hyacinth into more of an artist or a version of James himself), while others have found this sensitivity to be a weakness (finding his oversensitive nature to be the reason he is unable to find an alternative to suicide at the end of the novel). When describing the origin of his idea for the novel, James describes "some individual sensitive nature" who could appreciate the fruits of civilization while living, for the most part, segregated from it. Miss Pynsent's first description of him is "now *ain't* he shrinking and sensitive?" (61). In the course of the novel, Hyacinth's sensitivity manifests itself as a complete openness to the languages, the narratives which surround him. This sensitivity to narratives would have been natural to Henry James and even more pronounced given the author's reliance on outside sources. Hyacinth's usefulness to the plot is his predisposition to be influenced by the conversations which surround him.

Most of Hyacinth's inner turmoil stems from the conflicts between those narratives which comprise the main strands of the larger cultural dialogue James includes in the novel. In order to emphasize the basis of characters' perceptions within structures of language, James often employs terminology from linguistic study or drama when describing people's beliefs regarding the social situation and the anarchist movement. This fixation on the level of language, rather than on a concrete "reality" within the novel, fits with the ambiguous position of anarchism within the cultural dialogue of the time. Hyacinth's role is to feel the full force of these narratives and to give them an emotional reality:

> What was most in Hyacinth's mind was the idea, of which every pulsation of the general life of his time was a syllable, that the flood of democracy was rising over the world; that it would sweep all traditions of the past before it; that, whatever it might fail to bring, it would at least carry in its bosom a magnificent energy; and that it might be trusted to look after its own. . . . With his mixed, divided nature, his conflicting sympathies, his eternal habit of swinging from one view to another, Hyacinth regarded this prospect, in different moods, with different kinds of emotion. (478)

Hyacinth's mind is in sympathy with the larger threat and promise of the modern age and the mass culture which that age has created. That cultural movement makes itself manifest to Hyacinth as a "syllable," as a part of language. Many critics have noted that crucial scenes within the anarchist movement are never directly reported: the interview with Hoffendahl and the note that calls Hyacinth to his mission are delivered only secondhand. The effect of this indirectness is to place the entire anarchist threat within the realm of narrative as opposed to concrete "reality"; all the reader knows of anarchism are the words of people who are caught up in the narratives themselves and may be playing a part.

Hyacinth's role is to respond to the narratives which are exchanged in the vast cultural dialogue. Lacking a strong identity himself,[25] Hyacinth faithfully echoes the tentative attitude of society on those strands which made up the "social question": a conviction that the more numerous poor would inevitably gain a voice in the government, combined with an ambivalence as to the effect their influence would have on a "civilization" inextricably linked to the propertied classes. Even Hyacinth's changes in opinion and "mixed nature" are emblematic of society as a whole, an aggregate of individuals of diverse backgrounds whose collective action appeared to swing from one extreme to the other.

Although James takes great pains to present Hyacinth with emotional depth, the character is in many ways simply the sum of the languages which engage in a dialogue within Hyacinth's own personality. Hyacinth Robinson is defined not as a type, but as the constant shifts of dialogue that constitute his being from one moment to the next. All that is required to change Hyacinth's personality is a strong statement or story; other characters even talk of "making" Hyacinth by telling him stories, as Mr. Vetch confesses to the Princess: "I made him, I invented him" (463); Mr. Vetch's tool was the story of his mother and father, a narrative which created associations of radicalism and distrust of aristocracy.

Many critics have described Hyacinth's parentage as having a Zolaesque determinism. However, within the context of the novel, the narrative of Hyacinth's parents is self-consciously developed by various people to frame Hyacinth within their own narrative preferences. Miss Pynsent, enamored of the aristocracy and fictions involving aristocratic characters, makes Hyacinth an illegitimate child of the aristocracy who may someday reclaim his birthright. She tells him of his noble father and censors the revolutionary story of his murderous mother. Pinnie has attempted to completely immerse Hyacinth in the penny-novel plot of the nobleman deprived of his birthright, and, when she is dying, Hyacinth recognizes the completion of the narrative (even as a fiction) to be the best gift he could give her: " 'I'll tell her my greatest relations have adopted me and that I have come back in the character of Lord Robinson.' 'She will need nothing more to die happy,' Mr. Vetch observed" (360). Although there is an element of condescending mockery in Pinnie's extreme devotion to cheap fiction, her attempt to order her life out of a given narrative is repeated by other characters in the novel, most notably Hyacinth himself, who avidly reads French naturalist novels (Zola's *Germinal* was published in 1885, just as James began writing *The Princess Casamassima*).

Mr. Vetch is not innocent of attempts to mold Hyacinth's nature.

When confronted with a dying wish from Hyacinth's mother to see her son, Amanda Pynsent asks Mr. Vetch—who at the time holds "blasphemous republican, radical views" (67)—for advice; he counsels her to take Hyacinth to his mother in order to help the boy understand his true relationship to society. It is not heredity, but the framing of the facts of his parentage within certain narratives, which defines Hyacinth's young personality: the constant reminders of his aristocratic heritage encourage Hyacinth to play the part of the fallen aristocrat; the violence of his mother's act convinces him that he will be forever cut off from that aristocratic world.

Hyacinth's mother is associated with rebellion as destruction because she is from France, the land of revolution and the Commune, the one place in Europe which has witnessed the destructive forces of the revolution. Her murder of an aristocrat (ignoring the fact that it was a murder of passion, not politics) completes Hyacinth's story of himself as a natural revolutionary. This radical background gains him acceptance into the group at the "Sun and Moon," where the fact that his mother killed an aristocrat passes for revolutionary credentials in spite of his command of an aristocratic accent: "he was *ab ovo* a revolutionist, and that balanced against his smart neckties, [and] a certain suspicious security that was perceived in him as to the *h* (he had had from his earliest years a natural command of it)" (282). In this situation, markers for belonging in either class narrative are somewhat superficial; the desire to include another within a group encourages the inhabitants of the Sun and Moon to find a way to enlist Hyacinth in their revolutionary discourse.

The radical opposition between his mother's narrative of revolution and the sentimental narrative of lost nobility that Pinnie has woven for Hyacinth threaten to rip Hyacinth apart. As he attempts to fashion his own identity from the narratives available to him, Hyacinth elaborates on his own mysterious parentage in order to present a fuller and more satisfying story of his grandfather, who was involved in the French Revolution:

> In other days, in London, he had thought again and again of his mother's father, the revolutionary watch-maker who had known the ecstasy of the barricade and had paid for it with his life, and his reveries had not been sensibly chilled by the fact that he knew net to nothing about him. . . . [H]e was reckless, and a little cracked, and probably immoral; he had difficulties and debts and irrepressible passions; his life had been an incurable fever and its tragic determination was a matter of course. (380–81)

Despite the few facts he has in his possession, Hyacinth creates a narrative of his grandfather out of the rhetoric of the anarchists ("the ecstasy of the barricade" reads directly from the Romanticized view of revolution) and the cautionary tales and stereotypes of radicals found in the mainstream newspapers. Although the young Hyacinth is thrilled by the passion and recklessness this invented story of his grandfather invokes, the negative images of the incompetence of radicals in business affairs and their insufficient emotional control undermine Hyacinth's faith in the revolution. The two narratives, from two separate groups in society, are irreconcilable; they describe the same events using different languages which carry different cultural assumptions.

Critics have seen the irreconcilability of Hyacinth's heritage as crucial to an understanding of his moral dilemma, but less attention has been paid to the fact that both horns of this particular dilemma are fictions—Hyacinth is in fact caught in the gap between two incompatible narratives of himself and two languages which do not engage in meaningful dialogue with each other: "He had evolved, long ago, a legend about his mother, built up slowly, adding piece to piece, in passionate musings and broodings, when his cheeks burned and his eyes filled; but there were times when it wavered and faded, when he ceased to trust it" (127). Caught between social worlds which are (for the most part) segregated, Hyacinth vacillates between Pinnie's conservative plot (which would promise him appreciation of aristocratic aesthetics as an amelioration of his hard life) and the revolutionary plots he learns from Poupin and Paul Muniment, which promise passion and revenge, respectively. Hyacinth embraces whichever plot offers the most stability and the greatest potential for coherent identity.

Early in the novel, Hyacinth finds greater stability and acceptance in the revolutionary aspect of his narrative heritage. Hyacinth is not the only person who owes his social position at the "Sun and Moon" to the part he plays in a revolutionary narrative. Poupin, a bookbinder who adopts Hyacinth as a son, also "owed his position at the 'Sun and Moon' to the brilliancy with which he represented the political exile" (284). It is Eustache Poupin, the refugee (despite repeated amnesties) from the Commune, who teaches Hyacinth the discourse and the narratives of the Revolution from the perspective of a true believer. Poupin lives almost completely within his language of the Revolution:

It was the constant theme of his French friends, whom he had long since perceived to be in a state of chronic spiritual inflammation. For them the social question was always in order, the political question always abhorrent, the disinherited always present. He wondered at their zeal, their continuity, their vivacity, their incorruptibility; at the abundant supply of conviction and prophecy which they always had on hand. (122)

Unlike Hyacinth, the Poupins can fashion a stable identity from their roles as exiles, however tenderly comical it may seem to an observer outside their discourse. The novel makes clear that it is in discourse, and not in reality, that the Poupins base their revolutionary zeal; Hyacinth does not learn how to fashion bombs, but how to fashion phrases from his French friends:

> Hyacinth knew their vocabulary by heart, and could have said every-thing, in the same words, that on any given occasion M. Poupin was likely to say. He knew that "they," in their phraseology, was a compre-hensive allusion to every one in the world but their people—but who, exactly, their people were was less definitively established. (123)

Poupin is nothing more nor less than his discourse, and that discourse has a relationship to actual events which is problematic at best.

The same disjunction between words and deeds which Eustache Poupin embodies is shared by the other "radicals" who gather at the "Sun and Moon" to complain about conditions and solace themselves with beer and talk of revolt. At times, the conversation is nothing more than a ritualistic repetition of phrases which used to carry some power, but only underscore the speaker's powerless-ness: "thumping the table and repeating over some inane phrase which appeared for the hour to constitute the whole furniture of his mind" (280). In contrast to the times when the promise of revolution seems unreal and mired in mere words are the times when the power of the narrative to inspire takes hold of Hyacinth, and he re-alizes the potential of revolutionary discourse to fashion an identity for him: "at these hours, some of them thrilling enough, Hyacinth waited for the voice that should allot to him the particular part he was to play. His ambition was to play it with brilliancy, to offer an example—an example, even, that might survive him—of pure youthful, almost juvenile, consecration" (283). The unreality of this dream is underscored by the use of drama as an underlying meta-phor—Hyacinth's participation will be understood on the level of fiction. The ambiguity of the anarchist political agenda (which con-sists of little more than outrage at the condition of the poor and a desire to destroy those who are not suffering within the context of James's novel) is made up for by a powerful emotional appeal which is mystical and idealistic in its nature. Hyacinth wishes to be "consecrated" through his acceptance of a revolutionary role, and the highest compliment paid to a revolutionary is to pronounce him "one of the pure." In this attitude, inspired by the potential for the revolution to give him a unified identity, Hyacinth is potentially useful as the "cat's paw" Vetch is worried he could be (467).

Despite their bluster, the denizens of the "Sun and Moon" are never going to create an actual revolution; their promise is only the "sun and moon" of the bar they meet in. The most incendiary member of the group (aside from Paul Muniment, whose ruthless silence makes him fundamentally different from the regulars of the pub) is Delancey, a man who, although it is never stated, may be a police spy. Delancey always carries a "pencil with which he was careful to take notes of the discussions carried on at the "Sun and Moon." His opinions were distinct and frequently expressed; he had a watery (Muniment had once called it soda-watery) eye, and a personal aversion to a lord. He desired to change everything except religion, of which he approved" (290). The main evidence for this suspicion comes from his habit of taking notes and a background vague enough to leave Hyacinth guessing as to his real occupation. His vague "personal aversion" would be a stereotypical cover for a police agent, and his personal idiosyncrasy (his approval of religion) could simply reflect the limits of what he would do "under cover." Just as the police often employed agents provocateurs to provoke violent acts in order to justify their own surveillance, so Delancey curses when the meeting breaks up with no action commencing: "There isn't a man in the blessed lot that isn't afraid of his bloody skin—afraid, afraid, afraid! I'll go anywhere with any one, but there isn't another, by G——, by what I can make out! There isn't a mother's son of you that'll risk his precious bones!" (294). Police detectives often tried to entice radicals to act rashly in order to arrest them; despite this encouragement, most English anarchists remained decidedly nonviolent.

Apparently, even the "pure" M. Poupin will no longer "risk his bones." For all his impressive rhetoric, Poupin is completely cut off from the realm of action. Mr. Vetch recognizes that Poupin is relatively harmless: "He isn't serious, though he thinks he's the only human being who never trifles; and his machinations, which I believe are for the most part very innocent, are a matter of habit and tradition with him" (467). In contrast to Poupin's verbose, almost playful, posturing, Paul Muniment represents a revolutionary who is deadly earnest.

Paul Muniment's defining characteristic is his silence. Hyacinth sees Muniment's refusal to engage in the discourse of the "Sun and Moon" as a source of Muniment's power, and Hyacinth eagerly fills in the blanks in Paul's character with wild ideas of conspiratorial power: "it was Hyacinth's belief that he [Paul] himself knew still better how asinine they were; and this inadequate conception supported, in some degree, on Muniment's part, his theory of his influence—an influence that would be stronger than any other on the day he should choose to exert it" (281). Paul self-consciously occupies the gap between the discourse of the revolutionary and the discourse of the larger world of actual politics and power, and, fittingly, that gap is represented by Paul's significant refusal to engage in the grousing and complaining which forms the general activity of the "Sun and Moon."

Muniment promises actions instead of words, and he directly contrasts his own approach to revolution with that of Poupin: "He has a sweet assortment of phrases—they are really pretty things to hear, some of them; but he hasn't had a new idea these thirty years. It's the old stock that has been withering in the window" (139). His metaphor from commercial discourse signifies his associations with efficiency and modernity that stand in violent contrast to Poupin's older, more Romantic rhetoric. Whereas Poupin voices an older understanding of the nature of revolution, Paul Muniment espouses a colder, more objectifying understanding of the revolutionary impulse. Whereas Poupin embraces the noble gesture, Paul says,

> A man's foremost duty is not to get collared . . . If they succeed in potting you, do as Hoffendahl did, and do it as a matter of course; but if they don't, make it your supreme duty, make it your religion, to lie close and keep yourself for another go. The world is full of unclean beasts whom I shall be glad to see shoveled away by the thousand; but when it's a question of honest men and men of courage, I protest against the idea that two should be sacrificed where one will serve." (289)

His calculations leave Poupin cold, but they reflect a more implacable revolution, a revolution for its own ends, such as Nechaev outlined in the *Catechism of a Revolutionary*. Interestingly, they also echo industrial rhetoric of mass production and efficiency. The calculation of costs and benefits emphasizes an economy of terrorism and omits the spiritual motivation; for Paul, you do your duty for the sake of doing your duty and go about it in as businesslike a manner as possible. Paul's revolution is very much in keeping with the spirit of the industrial capitalism of his age. Art has no place in Paul's world.

Paul is a chemist (although not associated with bombs) who has permanently stained hands; he does not feel the guilt which this image implies. Whereas Poupin stridently voices his allegiance to "the people," Paul "moved in a dry statistical and scientific air in which it cost Hyacinth the effort of respiration to accompany him"; he finds emotional appeals "unbusinesslike" (391). Although his means are quite obvious, his goals are shrouded in silence; for Hyacinth, who has been buffeted by contradictory voices, Paul's silence appears to hide plans beyond his own limited understanding.

The Princess Casamassima is also attracted to the stories that Hyacinth can relate, although Hyacinth's ideas are little different from those to be found in any fashionably radical social circle. When he asks the Princess why she has summoned him, she replies:

> "Well, you have general ideas."
> "Every one has them to-day. They have them in Bloomsbury to a terrible degree. I have a friend (who understands the matter much better than I) who has no patience with them; he declares they are our danger and our bane. A few very special ideas—if they are the right ones—are what we want." (198)

In this conversation, Hyacinth adopts some of Paul's mystery: the promise of some future action, as yet unnamed. Paul is distinguished from others who simply discuss revolution by his lack of patience with discussion and his menacing "few very special ideas." The few ideas which Paul shares with Hyacinth, however, are vague and ill-formulated at best. Paul's goal was "to frighten society, and frighten it effectually; to make it believe that the swindled classes were at last fairly in league . . . [despite the fact that] they were not in league, and they hadn't in their totality grasped any idea at all" (292). Terrorism, for Paul, is nothing more than the construction of a fiction which could frighten those in power, in order to gain power himself. Anarchism, based in fictions, has as its goal the propagation of other fictions.

The anarchist movement in *The Princess Casamassima* is more a shared narrative delusion than any reflection of social reality. This delusional quality makes the Princess's fascination with radicalism even more dubious, because she feels that these revolutionaries are more "real" than the aristocrats with which she had formerly associated. To undercut this romanticized notion of the revolutionary, James has Hyacinth lie about the movement when asked about it:

> He had said, indeed, more than he had warrant for, when she questioned him about his socialistic affiliations; he had spoken as if the

movement were vast and mature, whereas, in fact, so far, at least, as
he was as yet concerned with it, and could answer for it from personal
knowledge, it was circumscribed by the hideously papered walls of the
little club-room at the "Sun and Moon". (251)

Just as Hyacinth derives some strength of identity from his revolutionary heritage among the patrons of the "Sun and Moon," he also
gains some authority with the Princess by exaggerating the threat
of revolution and the power of conspiracy (much as Bakunin and
other anarchists did). Although many other conservative narratives
involving anarchists go to great pains to deny the reader's skepticism regarding the power of the anarchist movement, James takes
no special pains to provide concrete details of actual anarchist conspirators. In fact, he never includes details of a great anarchist conspiracy at all, in contrast to the numerous details of everyday life
which fill the novel. The anarchist conspiracy is more a function of
discourse and belief than a concrete political threat.

Even the great anarchist Hoffendahl exists more as a character
within a conspiracy novel than a real human being. The reader is
never given a glimpse of Hoffendahl or any of his language (even
his note to Hyacinth comes through Schinkel), and everyone who
discusses him, from the Princess to the patrons of the "Sun and
Moon," treat him as a kind of holy mystery, a person made tran-
scendent by the role he plays within the narrative of revolution.
Poupin recites his credentials: "one of the purest martyrs of their
cause, a man who had been through everything—who had been
scarred and branded, tortured, almost flayed, and had never given
them the names they wanted to have" (288). He is telling the others
at the "Sun and Moon" a story, reinforcing the values of fortitude
and perseverance in pursuit of social change which they all pledge
themselves to (no matter how far their actions fall short of that
pledge). Hoffendahl's fame, it appears, rests on an incident which
no one except Poupin and Muniment remember, and which he
claims was never reported in the mainstream press: "Was it possible they didn't remember that great combined attempt, early in the
sixties, which took place in four Continental cities at once and
which, in spite of every effort to smother it up—there had been editors and journalists transported for even hinting at it—had done
more for the social question than anything before or since?" (288).
Hoffendahl's power, like Poupin's position at the "Sun and Moon,"
rests on his ability to fulfill a role within the narrative of revolution,
and the willingness of others to accept his role in the narrative.

For Hyacinth and the Princess, the desire to believe leads them both to embrace the narrative over concrete reality. When describing his visit to Hoffendahl, Hyacinth says "I have seen the holy of holies," to which the Princess replies: "Then it *is* real, it *is*, solid? . . . That's exactly what I have been trying to make up my mind about, for so long" (330). The Princess had met Hoffendahl before and found him a striking personality, but had not come to believe in the larger revolution. Because she believes Hyacinth to be the "real thing"—a real member of the working classes, as opposed to the shadowy, mythical figure which is Hoffendahl—she believes him when he spins his tale of the worldwide conspiracy. Given Hyacinth's own ignorance regarding the extent of the revolution, and his willingness to exaggerate for the Princess, her faith in him is ironic; now that he has a role as someone pledged to die for the cause, Hyacinth is more interested in exploiting the role in order to gain admittance to the aesthetic world of the aristocracy from which he has been shut out than he is in furthering the revolution.

The Princess opens the door, and a windfall inheritance enables Hyacinth to go to Paris. While in Paris and Venice, Hyacinth ignores the letters of introduction from Poupin to various radical acquaintances and instead engages in a dialogue with the architecture of those cities. For one whose identity has been caught in the tumultuous conflict between incompatible social languages, the stable, opulent reality of the buildings offers a welcome respite. Whatever the wrongs committed by the inhabitants of these rich houses, the houses' very existence justifies the role of the rich in Hyacinth's eyes. Here, Hyacinth realizes "not the idea of how the society that surrounded him should be destroyed; it was, much more, the sense of the wonderful, precious things it had produced" (382). The feelings which had been awakened by his stay at the country home in Medley are confirmed, and he embraces, to the extent he is able, the role which Pinnie had crafted for him when he was young. In an allusion to Matthew Arnold's *Culture and Anarchy*, a book which informs much of the grander social vision of James's novel, Hyacinth imagines himself in the role of "some clever young barbarian who in ancient days should have made a pilgrimage to Rome" (387). Hyacinth still accepts the coming revolution, but he finds himself drawn to the stability represented by the history and architecture that he associates with the aristocracy.

When Hyacinth returns to London, he is caught between two narratives: the story of Hoffendahl's authority as symbol of the revolution, and the narrative of cultural achievement which finds a concrete expression in the architecture of Paris. Each narrative has a claim on his own tenuous identity, and they need not be incompatible—many people espoused a belief in the coming fall of civilization while embracing the aesthetic stance of the aristocracy. Mildred Hartsock has observed, regarding the two pulls on Hyacinth's identity, that "Hyacinth could have said 'No' to Hoffendahl without equating that rejection of violence with a betrayal of the poor. He did not have to assume that social change ineluctably means annihilation of cherished values".[26] The dilemma, therefore, is not between the rich and the poor; rather, it is between culture and anarchy, between the aesthetic heritage of Europe and the rising power of the masses, regardless of specific politics. At this point in the novel, James switches from predominantly political language to an aesthetic discourse.

Hyacinth still recognizes the injustice and suffering which the current social system heaps upon many, but he finds the art produced by the "happier few" to balance out that suffering. The threat that Hoffendahl poses is the threat of the masses, of an economics of mass production which devalues art:

> He would cut up the ceilings of the Veronese into strips, so that every one might have a little piece. I don't want every one to have a little piece of anything, and I have a great horror of that kind of invidious jealousy which is at the bottom of the idea of redistribution. (396–97)

The threat of the revolution is primarily a threat to the aesthetic life; Hoffendahl would destroy art and replace it with material distribution. This fear translates the fear of anarchism into the fear of mass culture. The businesslike brutality of Muniment and Captain Sholto's objectifying gaze of Millicent Henning only confirm the transformation from the older aesthetically satisfying social order into a culture of mass production, controlled by those who conform to Arnold's caricature of the "populace," like the patrons of the "Sun and Moon," who "proclaimed their opinion that the only way was to pull up the Park rails again—just pluck them straight up" (280). The novel has collapsed the narrative of anarchist revolution back into the general cultural fear of the numerous members of the working classes.

Even the noble discourse of the revolution that had inspired Hyacinth earlier in the novel boils down to mere envy. The source of the older discourse of revolution, Poupin, cannot appreciate the beauties of Paris without coveting them for the "people":

> [Poupin] "Ah yes, it's very fine, no doubt," he remarked at last, "but it will be finer still when it's ours!"—a speech which caused Hyacinth to

turn back to his work with a slight feeling of sickness. Everywhere, everywhere, he saw the ulcer of envy—the passion of a party which hung together for the purpose of despoiling another to its advantage. In old Eustache, one of the "pure," this was particularly sad. (405)

Hyacinth's sadness is more complex than it appears, however, because so much of his own identity has been based in the narrative of revolution. When he was barred from enjoying the great works of aristocratic culture, he happily joined in the call for revolution; now, finding a more secure identity by associating himself with art, he tries to reject his earlier emotions by attributing them to Poupin, the Princess, and the whole language of the revolution. Poupin's use of language is questioned, down to individual words, as Mr. Vetch declares "The way certain classes arrogate to themselves the title of the people has never pleased me. Why are some human beings the people, and the people only, and others not?" (462). Hyacinth's conversion is itself expressed in terms of language: "when one had but lately discovered what could be said on the opposite side" (553). Hyacinth has not only changed his mind; he has also learned a new language.

Hoffendahl's authority has been completely undercut by the time Hyacinth's fearful summons comes. Schinkel, delivering the letter from Hoffendahl, comes to the Poupin's. Madame Poupin, rebelling against the order, asks "who is Hoffendahl, and what authority has he got?" Her husband reminds her that "he has no authority but what we give him; but you know that we respect him, that he is one of the pure, *ma bonne*," and Schinkel, who is relishing his new role as intermediary within the anarchist conspiracy, adds to the impression of Hoffendahl's authority in order to enhance his own: "certainly, there is no compulsion . . . It's to take or leave. Only *they* keep the books" (552). Hyacinth's reaction to this argument is to refuse to talk about it, to remove the order (and the self-destruction it implies) from the realm of dialogue into silence. Hyacinth disentangles himself from the language that previously had defined him by refusing to employ that language. If Hyacinth is the location of a dialogue between revolution and privilege, then the language of revolution has become excluded from the dialogue, just as the popular press refused to engage in a debate with the revolutionists.

Hyacinth's identity has not been resolved, however. As he comes home from the Poupin's, Hyacinth finds Mr. Vetch waiting for him; Mr. Vetch compliments him on his work. This reminder of his working-class status, combined with the crisis which his promise has placed him in, shows Hyacinth that the world of the aristocracy is not really open to him, either, despite his facility at book-binding. Vetch appeals to his memory of Pinnie, and Hyacinth, lying with supreme impudence because his words are no longer grounded in any concrete reality, swears by her memory not to "do their work" (565). After the Princess has decisively rejected the aristocratic life which Hyacinth craves, he feels his newfound identity undermined yet again: "he had a sense of his mind, which had been made up, falling to pieces again" (582). He finally appeals to the only part of his life which appears to be beyond mere language: his relationship with Millicent Henning and the reality of the body. Sadly, even she has been co-opted by the marketplace; Captain Sholto, who "imitated a real [purchaser] better than our young man" (585), gazes at her and wordlessly dismisses Hyacinth to his death.

Hyacinth's sensitivity is actually a kind of nullity, by which he is constantly defined by the narratives which surround him. The three dominant social discourses, as described in the novel, are irreconcilable: the bored aristocracy dreams of a self-annihilating revolution, and the workers revel in the promise of power which the revolution holds out to them, but neither discourse opposes the silent commercialism and objectification of the modern world. The revolutionaries, according to James, are ushering in a world not of justice, but of commerce; the world of the democracy will follow the objectionable developments of commercial America. Hyacinth's suicide is the logical outcome of the radical disjunction of these discourses and the breakdown of dialogue itself. Arnold's philistines have the last word, and the populace (Schinkel) and the aristocracy (the Princess) can only stand in mute witness.

NOVELS OF ANARCHIST REVOLUTION IN THE 1890S

The same fear of a revolution rising from below which motivated Matthew Arnold and Henry James is the common theme linking *Hartmann the Anarchist, The Angel of the Revolution*, and *The Anarchist: A Story of To-Day*,[27] which were published just as anarchist "propagandists by the deed" were entering their most active period in France and England. Ravachol's bombings had transfixed the newspapers in March of 1892, and the revenge bombings would continue through 1894 with bombings in London. The end result of these acts of terror was a strengthening of the repressive measures used against anarchists; after 1894, only sporadic acts of terrorism were committed, and many of these (such as the assassination of McKinley in 1901 which led to the suppression of anarchism in the

United States) were only tenuously linked to the anarchist movement itself. However, the social disintegration which these isolated terrorist acts symbolized led these authors to play against the fear of anarchism and at the same time offer their readers a way to contain anarchism, a counternarrative which promised to limit the threat of revolution which anarchism came to symbolize.

Hartmann the Anarchist, *The Angel of the Revolution*, and *The Anarchist: A Story of To-Day* all try to contain the threats associated with anarchism (the ills of modernity: overcrowding and immigration, rapidly advancing technology, and a sense on the part of the elites of an erosion of institutions and a loss of control) by placing anarchism within some other, more dominant, context. As with the journalistic coverage of the movement itself, the writers' first step was to redefine the cause of anarchism; none of these works allows a sense of economic and social injustice caused by authoritarian institutions to stand as the primary motivation for its anarchist characters; instead, personal revenge, race loyalty, and basic greed become the spurs which lead some down the anarchist path. By "exposing" the more basic causes of anarchism, each author can then propose a solution that addresses other social and political concerns, promising increased social stability if a particular course of action is adopted. Dealing with the anarchist "threat" becomes a kind of wish fulfillment, allowing each writer to envision a world freed of the threat of the mob through increased social control.

Despite their shared cultural moment and subject matter, each of these three books approaches anarchism with radically different agendas and generic expectations. *Hartmann the Anarchist* is an example of the "mad genius" plot, in which an obsessive genius, ignored by society, builds a flying death-machine for a secret group of London anarchists; only after he has caused massive chaos and the death of his own mother does he realize the hopelessness and vanity of his actions, and he commits suicide by destroying the machine. *The Angel of the Revolution* also tells the story of an obsessive genius who builds a flying machine for the secret, international Brotherhood of Terrorists, but, rather than the fear of the mob, the novel details the threat posed by other ethnic groups to the "Anglo-Saxon race." What distinguishes the Brotherhood of the novel is not a tendency toward violence and anarchy, but rather an iron discipline and regimentation; the anarchist movement becomes a proto-fascist vehicle for a paranoid fantasy of racial superiority. The Brotherhood (actually a front for a secret plan to create an Anglo-Saxon world order to fight the despotism of Russia) manipulates the great powers of Europe into a destructive world war, which defeats the Tsar of Russia and his French allies, unites Europe, and beats back an attack by the Moslems to the South. Although the two previous novels are science fiction, *The Anarchist: A Story of Today* goes to great lengths to establish its claims toward realism; the novel, constructed around the conventional story of plotters after a rich heiress's wealth, warns the reader of the dangers of anarchism and unstable economic elites and argues for the creation of law-and-order leagues among the propertied classes to defend their position against the greedy and envious agitators of the mob.

In each case, a pathological fear of revolution and social decline motivates each novelist, and each novel offers the promise of a regimental and racially pure social order as a reward. Anarchism becomes a symbol, standing in for those aspects of modern society which disturb each writer and therefore increase the fears associated with anarchism. The lack of dialogue between anarchists and the general public and the social disorder created by rapid technological and economic change left a vacuum which novels such as these rushed to fill.

HARTMANN THE ANARCHIST AND THE DANGERS OF THE MOB

E. Douglas Fawcett's *Hartmann the Anarchist, or the Doom of the Great City*[28] magnifies the destructive threat of anarchism by giving a secret cell of anarchists a secret weapon—a flying machine which could rain destruction down upon people on the ground while being nearly invulnerable to counterattack. By giving anarchists a destructive power which no one at the time possessed, Fawcett could demonstrate the futility of attempting to change society through force. The novel's narrator, a reform socialist on the Fabian model, learns the dangers of revolution and the inherent viciousness of "the mob" that anarchists would unleash on London.

Although the narrator is described as sympathetic to radical goals, *Hartmann the Anarchist* takes great pains to argue for centralized control by the elites as the key to solving the problems of the mob. The novel, set in the year 1920, is told by Stanley, a young man of independent means who has had some taste of literary success and is running for Parliament as a moderate socialist. His views have not served him well; the conservatives, becoming more and more reactionary as social problems become more and more dire, want only more repression; on the left, revolutionary extremists accuse him of being halfhearted in his desire for change and advocate revolution. Early on in the novel Stanley states his belief in a top-down reform of society, controlled by the educated classes. He is a committed socialist, but firmly against the chaos which revolution promises: "By all means, I argued, have a revolution if a revolution is both a necessary and safe prelude of reform. But was it really necessary or even safe?" (6). His love interest, Lena Northhampton, the intelligent daughter of an old-style Liberal, agrees with his moderate politics. Stanley even reassures his prospective father-in-law that, "once elected to Parliament I am prepared to stand by any Government, Tory or Radical, in supporting the cause of social order. We contend that should revolutionary socialists or the anarchists initiate a crusade in the streets, they must take the consequences of their temerity" (23). Social change must be done under the guidance of an elite, the narrator argues, and should not be left to the impassioned masses. Stanley's vision is a socialism that aspires to bring everyone into agreement with the propertied classes: "I hated revolution, and I equally hated the pettiness of a sordid socialism. We must not, I contended, see the graces of high life, art, and culture, fouled by the mob, but the mob elevated into a possession and appreciation of the graces" (17). Stanley embodies the paradox of the upper-class socialist, working for reforms which would benefit a class he looks down upon culturally as "the mob." The whole need for reforms is grounded not in an idea of general justice, but in the need for equitable distribution in order to maintain social order.

Through an old friend, Burnett, Stanley is taken aboard a flying machine built by a famous anarchist named Hartmann. Hartmann, an isolated and embittered mechanical genius who had fallen under the influence of a radical German named Schwartz (building on the association of sinister radicals with Central Europeans), had been thought dead since a failed attempt to blow up the German Minister's carriage killed about sixty people near Westminster Bridge about ten years earlier. Instead, the genius had solved the problems inherent in heavier-than-air flight by inventing a very light, very strong alloy. Giving an anarchist control of a flying machine filled with bombs, guns, and burning petroleum becomes a way of exaggerating the threats of the anarchists to the furthest imaginable extent, as well as playing on fears that technology has passed humanity's ability to effectively control its use. The device of a flying ship was not a new one in science fiction or fact, and heavier-than-air flight was one of the scientific preoccupations of the late nineteenth century. At the same time, anarchists such as Johann Most were writing paeans to dynamite, proclaiming it a gift of science toward the liberation of the masses because it increased the

destructive power which an individual could easily carry on his or
her person. The ultimate failure of this ploy to change society becomes an argument that even extreme terrorism is unable to make
a lasting change in society and can even cause a reaction opposite
to its intended effect; because terrorism does not work, anarchism
is wrong.

The argument that anarchist terrorism is incapable of effecting
an anarchist revolution, in its historical context, is a form of straw
man; anarchists were never deluded into thinking that a few bombs
in themselves would bring about social change. However, within the
novel, the anarchists seriously believe they can change society, despite their minority status, through violence. In a conversation with
Burnett, the anarchist, Stanley denounces propaganda by the deed
from an elitist perspective: "it converts no one, strengthens the
hands of the reactionaries, and, what is more, destroys useful capital" (11). Nevertheless, Burnett contends that the anarchists' newfound destructive power can bring about the ruin of civilization and
a Rousseau-inspired state of nature despite the fact that their
followers are but a tiny minority: "suppose, for instance, that the
leaders of these few thousands came to possess some novel inven-
tion—something that—that made them virtual dictators to their
kind" (12). Within the novel, the anarchists are divorced from the
economics and liberty and instead stand for an extremist and autocratic nihilism, seeking only destruction. In this way they echo the
mob, shortsighted and controlled by emotion.

The autocratic appeal to brute force that forms the undertone of
anarchism as defined in this novel is exemplified by the design of
Hartmann's flying machine. Similar to most fictional flying machines of the period (such as Jules Verne's clipper of the clouds), its
basic design resembles that of a sailing ship, complete with a deck,
with rotors in the place of sails. The interesting features of this ship,
however, are the protections that surround the control areas:
"amidships there stood a small circular citadel, evidently the
stronghold of the captain. Here were mounted three or four cannons
of the quick firing sort" (77). The captain is shut off from the fanatic
crew through the guns, and the captain is the only one who has access to the controls and engine of the ship; even the leader of the
anarchists does not trust his followers. The design of the ship assumes the premise of the author: the mob must be controlled by
some central authority for any society to function.

Like any mob, the anarchists, even the formerly civilized Burnett,
become more and more brutal as they sense their growing power.
From the beginning, they are recruited from the most violent dregs

of society. Hartmann describes them: "My crew are enthusiasts, Mr. Stanley; nay, if you like, fiends of destruction. Every man is selected by myself. Every man is an outlaw from society, and most have shed blood. They burn to revenge on society the evils which they have received, or, given the appropriate occasion, would receive from it" (81). The crew of anarchists are bloodthirsty ruffians, belligerent when they have the upper hand, but cowards otherwise; they are the embodiments of the popular conception of the mob given the power of science, "the vices and powers of man brought into common focus" (182). The plan for the flying machine is to use it to terrorize London and give the anarchists of London an opportunity to incite a general revolution which would leave the city in ashes and bring about the downfall of civilization; the airship causes destruction which would have "glutted to the full the morbid aestheticism of a Nero" (202), alluding to Gibbon's argument on the fall of the Roman empire.

The novel's basic conflict is between social change controlled by the educated elites (represented by moderate socialism) versus social change dictated by the rude mob (anarchism). The anarchist's violent actions strengthen the right: "a vigorous reaction had taken place . . . the conflagrations were partly checked, while the anarchists and rioters were being driven mercilessly from the streets with bullet and cold steel" (187–88); the anarchists are routed with none of their goals achieved, and Hartmann's own mother dies during the riots. Disconsolate at this last severance of his ties to humanity and facing a mutiny from his crew, Hartmann destroys himself by blowing up his airship. The narrator's position is vindicated, despite the fact that the terrible events (and his marriage to Lena) have led him to withdraw from the public life. The excesses of the anarchists have deprived the moderate socialists of at least one supporter.

The novel directly shows the dangers involved in the idea of revolution and the hopelessness of achieving constructive change by means other than the steady work of elitist reform. Anarchism, defined within the narrative as an ideology of destruction, will always be a minority movement and will never have the power to effect the desired overthrow of civilization. Anarchism is a completely negative force which threatens the work of moderate reformers who wish to increase centralized power and control it for social good; the novel echoes the distance which reformers sought to put between their own work and the taint which has been applied to anarchists.

THE ANGEL OF THE REVOLUTION AND A REVISED APOCALYPSE

Like *Hartmann the Anarchist*, which was published in the same year, *The Angel of the Revolution*[29] involves a flying machine in the hands of a secret international terrorist brotherhood. *Hartmann the Anarchist* uses the device of vast technological power to expose the limitations of the revolutionists, but *The Angel of the Revolution* transforms the anarchist movement into a secret organization bent on fighting Russian despotism and initiating an Anglo-Saxon world order. Far from being agents of anarchy, the terrorists in Griffith's novel are more disciplined and orderly than the governments which they manipulate; the anarchist movement becomes a secret twin to the international corporations which were expanding the economic influence of Britain and America, promising even greater discipline and order than the market can provide. *The Angel of the Revolution* becomes a pathological fantasy of racial superiority, seeking to contain the threats of social and technological change with protofascist means.

Like *Hartmann*, the flying machine of *Angel* is built by an obsessive scientist, Richard Arnold. In keeping with the novel's theme of Anglo-Saxon superiority, the genius capable of inventing a flying machine is English. At the beginning of the novel, he is poor but not politically motivated; he is befriended by a fellow Englishman who happens to be a member of the inner circle of an international secret society known as the Terrorists, who have been responsible for several assassinations of Russian officials (the novel includes many "newspaper clippings" of background events; the novel, although set in the future, includes the discourse of present-day journalism). The Terrorists are assassins within the overall conspiracy known as the Brotherhood, which has millions of members throughout the world, all organized into cells of ten men and operating under strict secrecy and discipline; members of the Brotherhood are active in Parliament and the London police force. Arnold is taken to a meeting of the inner circle to demonstrate a model of his flying machine, where he meets the beautiful Natasha, the "angel of the revolution," daughter of the mysterious Natas (Satan spelled backwards), who is the leader of the Terrorists. Arnold falls in love and agrees to build a flying machine for the Terrorists.

Griffith builds on earlier attempts to order the so-called anarchist conspiracy by granting to radical groups an absurdly grand capacity for organization and discipline. The Terror, which assassinates government officials and manipulates the policies of the European powers, is the power behind every group that wants to change or overthrow a hopelessly corrupt contemporary society: "that which is known to the outside world as the Terror is an international secret society underlying and directing the operations of the various bodies known as Nihilists, Anarchists, Socialists—in fact, all those organizations which have for their object the reform or destruction, by peaceful or violent means, of Society as it is presently constituted" (32). Unlike such organizations in the real world, the Brotherhood is characterized by total allegiance to the mastermind, Natas, and powers of organization and information gathering which makes it nearly omniscient. Natas's plan is to allow the nations of the Earth, built on injustice and vanity, to engage in a cataclysmic world war that will weaken them sufficiently for the Brotherhood to take control. Although such a confrontation is seen as inevitable, the Brotherhood has been delaying such a confrontation because their own power was not sufficient to allow them to dictate terms after the war. Having an unstoppable weapon such as a flying machine, the Brotherhood could turn the tide of battle in their favor and complete Natas's plan. Although the newspapers say that they would instill anarchy, the Brotherhood would actually replace the anarchy of contemporary society with a centralized government.

Using the terrorists' seemingly unlimited resources, Arnold quickly builds a flying machine along the lines of Verne's "clipper of the clouds." The ship is completed just in time to rescue Natasha, who has been captured in Russia and is being sent to Siberia, where she will be forced to be a consort to some savage official of the tsar. The ship, which has a practically unlimited range and the capability of traveling a mind-boggling one hundred and twenty miles per hour, quickly rescues Natasha and has time to destroy a Russian fortress along the way. This successful test allows the Brotherhood to build a fleet of airships just as the European powers are sliding into war, with Russia, France and Italy siding against England and Germany. The alliances build on the writer's underlying racist argument: it pits the German and Anglo-Saxon "races" against the inferior Slavs and Mediterraneans.

The war goes badly for the English and the Germans, primarily because of the inherent indecisiveness of the English parliamentary system. After losing a crucial vote, the prime minister is forced to dissolve the government and hold a general election:

> The deplorable crisis which immediately followed was the logical consequence of the inherently vicious system of party government. While the fate of the world was practically trembling in the balance, Europe, armed to the teeth in readiness for the Titanic struggle that a few weeks

would now see shaking the world, was amused by the spectacle of what was really the most powerful nation on earth losing its head amidst the excitement of a general election, and frittering away on petty issues of party strife the energies that should have been devoted with single-hearted unanimity to preparation for the conflict whose issue would involve its very existence. (139)

In the place of party strife, Natas and his chief assistant, Alexander Tremayne (a member of the House of Lords), would teach Europe the follies of war through the terrible lesson of modern warfare, then destroy the governments of Europe which are based on militarism. Curiously enough, the leader of the anarchists is a religious man, who calls himself "the instrument of vengeance upon this generation, even as Joshua was upon Canaan" (145) and predicts that Tremayne will build a new order to replace the old one which Natas will destroy. This reassures the reader that the terrorists offer, not anarchy, but a superior form of order based on Anglo-Saxon dominance. Natas, the Russian Jew who will be the destroyer, asks Alexander Tremayne "would it not be a glorious task for you, who are the flower of this splendid race, so to unite it that it should stand as a solid barrier of invincible manhood before which this impending flood of yellow barbarism should dash itself to pieces?" (146). The novel transforms a loose collection of secret societies and popular movements into a secret machine of Anglo-Saxon racial superiority, identifying the Brotherhood as the institution which will unite the English-speaking peoples and rule the world with wisdom and justice.

The bulk of *The Angel of the Revolution* describes the course of the war, which it describes repeatedly as "Armageddon." The Russians and French, using dirigibles to drop bombs without fear of retaliation, destroy the German armies and lay siege to London. The Brotherhood, which has replaced a corrupt American plutocracy with a dictatorship in a nearly bloodless coup (a popular move in the United States, the novel describes), aids Britain on the condition that the current government abdicate in favor of the Brotherhood. The Brotherhood, aided by the millions of secret agents in the British, French, and Russian armies, destroys the invading forces with ruthless, regimented efficiency. The tsar, all of his troops killed, is sent to work in the mines of Siberia; all the European powers are disarmed, and the Anglo-Saxon federation rules the continent, just in time to beat back a renewed Muslim invasion; the lovers are united, and peace reigns under the benevolent dictatorship of Tremayne.

The Angel of the Revolution transforms the fears of revolution and anarchy into a secret force that promises increased order and racial dominance for Griffith's English readers. The reforms which Griffith mentions are reminiscent of Henry George's single tax ideas (municipal control of rents, for example), which had some notoriety at the time; more significant is the fact that the supposed "anarchists" are more orderly and authoritarian than even the tsar. The threat of revolution and anarchy is swept away by Griffith's racist utopia of Anglo-Saxon superiority; however, the novel is in keeping with the time in its call for more discipline and order, rather than less, as a way to deal with the threats of increased technology and immigration. *The Angel of the Revolution* represents one extreme of xenophobia and imagined order in the face of a changing world.

SAVAGE'S *THE ANARCHIST: A STORY OF TO-DAY:* A "REALIST" CALL TO ARMS

Both *Hartmann the Anarchist* and *The Angel of the Revolution* address the problems which anarchism symbolized through the mode of science fiction; Savage's *The Anarchist: A Story of To-Day*[30] paints anarchism as a immediate problem by including facts from actual history in its story of an anarchist attempt to seduce a rich heiress in order to use her money to finance a campaign of destruction in the dangerously unstable United States. Alarmist and sensational in tone, *The Anarchist: A Story of To-Day* offers a reactionary prescription against anarchy in two parts. First, Savage celebrates an idealization of the British landed aristocracy that fosters a greater social stability than mere money can confer. Second, Savage advocates the enforcement of class distinctions through armed law-and-order leagues working with the police.[31]

The novel's conservative agenda is served through the overall plot as well as the numerous speeches lauding social stability and decrying the anarchist menace. The basic plot is straight out of romantic convention: an innocent woman, heir to millions of dollars, is the target of fortune hunters who want her fortune for their own. Luckily, clear-sighted men of her own class and community (a childhood friend, in this case) help the heiress avoid what would be a fatal mistake and expose the shady pasts of the fortune hunters. The basic message of the narrative is an argument for upper-class solidarity: women should not go to Europe in search of a husband because of the dangers inherent in the project, and it is better to marry where you know people and their history. Richard Savage wrote many novels with this same basic premise; in this narrative, it is the author's direct cultural and political commentary that invites the audience's interest.

In his author's preface, Richard Savage wanted to impress upon his audience the accuracy and timeliness of his narrative. "The story of active anarchism is a chronicle of the present time" (3), he writes, asserting a kind of journalistic realism for his novel. Alluding to the bombs and assassinations which the newspapers lumped together as radical and anarchical, Savage warns his readers that "this red propaganda has crossed racial and national dividing lines, and watching the troubles of the weaker governments for propitious moments—anarchism has emerged from the shadows of midnight conspiracy and now fights boldly in the open!" (3). Following the lead of Schaack and other right-wing conspiracy theorists, Savage describes anarchism in his narrative not as a small number of agitators, radicals, and cranks, but rather as a vast hierarchical conspiracy, with leaders, resources, and a sinister agenda which represents a real threat to society.

As the threat grows, Savage argues, women must be as informed about the threat as men, because anarchism "needs money, skilled and plausible emissaries, and must, on the line of its battle against society, deal with the life of women—with the schemes of the 'salon'—with active political effort and with all the priceless interests it would destroy" (3–4). The material wealth on which he assumes his female readers rely is directly threatened by anarchism, and he hopes, through this novel, to educate women on the nature of the threat. He also is direct in his proposed solution: "The octopus feelers of an insane revolt against all law which guards Private Right are stealing to-day through every avenue of human life. Organized cosmopolitan repression will be the stern answer of the civilized world to the dark creed of destruction" (4). Savage adds fortune-hunting anarchists to the list of threats to which every young woman must take heed as she enters the world of society; on a more direct level, he is educating affluent young women on the nature of their economic position and encouraging their roles in a project of cultural stratification and repression.

Every element of the basic narrative in *The Anarchist: A Story of To-Day* is related to some development in contemporary society. The villains are the anarchists, who wish to abuse the liberty of the United States in order to overthrow the proper rule by the elites in favor of mob rule. The anarchists are aided in their task by a variety of social ills that are traced to pernicious German ideas of the new school: socialism, materialism, and especially ideas of women's rights. Bent on revenge and fantasies of destruction, the anarchists of the novel, inspired by Bakunin, will stop at nothing to overthrow the government of the United States (which is seen as weaker than European governments because of its hesitancy to resort to repression[32]) and cause massive destruction throughout the world. The secret anarchist conspiracy which threatens all is opposed by the most stable, conservative forces in society: those who are inspired by Britain's ideal of landed aristocracy and wish to instill a similar sense of class stability in the United States in order to prevent unrest at home and the departure of women and money to the more stable European countries. Each element is called into service to fill out the narrative of improper seduction.

The novel's opening firmly places the narrative within the context of the anxiety over the numerical power of the working classes and the threat which they become when seen as an abstract, monolithic whole. Hartley, the self-made millionaire and father to the beautiful and intelligent Evelyn Hartley, looks over his emerald lawn to the toiling millions below, described in breathlessly hyperbolic prose: "wealth's luxurious citadels reared their stately fronts along the famed avenue, but in far distant streets, crowds of men, roughly clad, with labor's drooping shoulders and sullen tread, trooped on or off shift . . . it was an object lesson in 'Environments.' They were results en masse!" (11–12). The specter of the faceless, rude masses, made mechanical and threatening by the nature of their labors and their sheer numbers, makes the stately mansions of the more fashionable districts possible.

Savage's scene connecting the fates of the rich and the poor alludes to a stock position of radical economists: the causal link between wealth and poverty and an admission of the dehumanization of labor in an industrial system are both contained in the image. Building on the social Darwinist conventions of capitalist biography, Savage distinguishes the entrepreneurs and business leaders from mere middle men by celebrating the leaders' superior natures. He describes Hartley in luminescent terms: "There was not a softened shade on the bronzed cheek of this apostle of work and syndicated energy!" (14). Hartley, however, has a heart condition from his own hard labor when younger; his background in the working class and his successful rise out of that class characterize him as one who has succeeded on American terms, based on superiority of character rather than social position. Unfortunately, his years of hard work have taken their toll, and, as the novel opens, he is draft-

ing his will with the loyal family lawyer, Fox, in full knowledge that
he has not long to live.

Fox, the lawyer, comes across as somewhat alarmist early in the
novel, but is justified by events as the novel progresses. He is com-
fortably rich, but has not lost his cunning, and he is gifted with more
than usual farsightedness in matters of money and property. Fox
reminds Hartley of the destructive potential of the "sullen crowds"
in America's recent past and urges Hartley to invest in European
government bonds in order to safeguard his fortune from the coming American anarchy:

> "I urge you to divert a portion of this great inheritance destined for your
> child to England, France, and Germany for investment in government
> funds! You and your fellow millionaires forget flaming Cincinnati,
> sacked Pittsburgh, and great New York under mob rule! The poison of
> anarchy is daily infiltrated through the industrial stratum! " (30)

The mob, led by anarchist agitators and abetted by a "press free to
the point of license" (32) and an apathetic upper class, only requires a few strong leaders in order to bring about a social revolution.

The very fluidity of American culture that allowed Hartley to
amass his fortune will make it easier for the anarchists to destroy
it if it stays in money-mad America. As part of his effort to make
the novel as realistic and immediate as possible, Savage recites a
list of recent anarchical events which have tested the powers of
American government:

> The Chicago Haymarket affair, the death of Lincoln and Garfield, and
> other untoward events of the past prove how quickly black clouds may
> form in our clear sky. The New York draft riots demanded the return of
> an army corps from the field! The elements of *disorder* are as potent as
> the elements of *order*. There is a free-and-easy lawlessness in the South
> which is appalling. It is not vitally dangerous because finally checked by
> a superior class, the landowners, the political rulers! But the transient
> character of our daily institutions becomes daily more apparent. (170)

American institutions are too easily influenced by the mob to be a
check on popular revolt; stability is possible only when the superior
class dominates political life (as in the agrarian South, according to
Savage). The situation only gets worse as "blocks of alien laborers,
aggregations of foreigners, disturb our labor market and throng our
cities" (216); the dregs of Europe, the lazy, the vicious, and the dis-

contented, are allowed to come to America, and the unfixed American institutions are unduly influenced by them.

The only antidote for the increasing threat of the masses is a strong, institutional governing class, according to the novel. Fox tells Hartley that "Old Britannia will make the last stand against the Red Spectre, thanks to feudal land laws and a strong aristocracy!" (31–32). The time for liberty has passed, the novel argues; what is now needed is a retrenchment designed to protect the positions of those who have accumulated wealth. Otherwise, the wealth created in America will depart for more stable locales. The writer creates a Britain which exists only in fiction or in Thomas Carlyle's rendition of the Middle Ages—one in which everyone is happier because they recognize and accept their place within the larger scheme of things.

The flight toward more stable parts of the world is already occurring where American women are involved, and Evelyn Hartley simply joins the trend when she goes to Europe to travel and possibly find a noble husband to complement her vast inheritance. Although American men are more dynamic, they must devote all their energies to earning money in order to maintain their station; Europe's hereditary aristocracy, who are secure in their positions regardless of the fortunes of the market, represent, according to Savage, a security which American men cannot match. American women "throw themselves so eagerly into the arms of foreigners . . . because they realize the absolute hollowness of the pretense of a settled American society . . . the women have caught the advantages of marriage into a permanently graded European society" (44). Superior women, the key to any society's success, are leaving America because of the unstable nature of its class system.

Savage depicts aristocracy as an inherently superior social system for the rich and poor alike. Commercial culture leads to envy and alienation because it appears to be based on mere money; aristocracy, according to the novel, ensures that those who are naturally superior rule for the benefit of all:

> The only difference I can see is that the English aristocrats' rank is owned and cherished by all. The community calmly accepts the gracious sovereign's ennobling touch! In the United States the successful plutocrat makes his own crown, puts it on himself, and wears it in defiance of public reprobation or personal envy! The intangible fabric of British civic structure seems to be sacred, as a whole, to prince and peasant! (185)

The novel goes to reactionary extremes in order to give affluent Americans a class consciousness of their own and a desire to make permanent the social order which was emerging from the gilded-age economy. According to the doctrines of social Darwinism, the rich were the fittest; Savage is simply arguing that the superior minority must make sure that the numerous, envious mob will not threaten those who have won life's struggle. The frustration lies in most Americans' refusal to see anarchism as a serious threat and a general preference for economics over politics in the upper classes.

Another import from Europe also threatens the American plutocracy. The upper classes do not resist the mob in part because of the pernicious teaching of German idealism, which preaches materialism, atheism, and the inevitability of revolution. A Cardinal warns the hero, the young American Philip Maitland, "Do you know where Spinoza, Hobbes, Locke, lead to? Pure atheism! And whither does the idealism of Kant, Fichte, Schelling, and Hegel tend? Toward the anarchy which the civilized world is being drawn by this materialistic current in the face of your boasted intellectual freedom!" (90–91). Blinded to the true nature of the anarchist threat, the upper classes do not support the vigorous crackdown on radicals which Savage feels is necessary: "Instead of vigorously applauding the punishment of would-be murderers of the State, a storm of approval meets the unwise pardoning in a Western State, of men who would have been interned for life, in any cool community" (218). This is a specific reference to the pardon of the surviving Haymarket defendants by Governor Altgeld, which occurred in the year before the publication of the novel. Altgeld's idealism allows menaces to society to continue their work. Later in the novel, Savage asserts a causal relationship between the encouragement given anarchy by the pardon and the death of the former mayor of Chicago; the anarchist threat is immediate, and modern notions of liberty and rights only encourage it on its path of destruction.

The threat posed by modern doctrines is personified in Carl Stein, the anarchist of the title, who makes Evelyn vulnerable to an anarchist seducer by tutoring Evelyn in newfangled German doctrines. Overhearing Stein's lectures on women's emancipation to Evelyn, Fox laments "on what road does he lead out that fearless neophyte? She has passed out on the sea of modern unrest, feverishly acquired knowledge" (25). Stein tries to indoctrinate Evelyn in the methods of materialism, and her teachings make her reckless, fair game for the young anarchist which Stein uses to capture her fortune.

In order to fit anarchists into his fortune-hunting plot, Savage has the main anarchist, Stein, receive his orders directly from Bakunin while the latter was on his death bed. Bakunin orders Stein to work to overthrow America, because of American society's fatal weaknesses:

> In America there is but one engine of power—Gold!—There is no actual repression there! The tyranny is of the plutocrat alone! Without money, you can never fight the battles of the cause in America! Go there, my best disciple! Your talents will lead you into higher circles! Let your objective point be *one* great fortune! If you, Carl Stein, can find one golden heap unguarded, pour out its yellow flood in action! Money is the ammunition of your battle there! The stolen dollars, robbed from the toiler, may be, in your hands, the grape-shot of a last forlorn stand! (50)

Savage's characterization of the anarchists as purely destructive echoes the defamation which built on the refusal of some anarchists to outline a positive vision of society and instead concentrate on removing the authoritative structures which kept the current society in place. Savage makes the threat more particular by having the "Apostle of Destruction," Bakunin, single out the United States as an easy target for anarchist subversion. Built on money alone, America can just as easily be destroyed with money, according to Savage's version of Bakunin. Stein's desire for a fortune allows him to fulfill his part of the fortune-hunter plot, and a romantic young Pole, Victor Oblonski, is young and handsome enough to play the suitor for the anarchist.

Of course, a hero comes to save the young woman from this presumed horrible fate and to demonstrate right thinking for the reader. Philip Maitland, a friend of Evelyn from childhood, reminds Evelyn of her duties to her native country and class. Maitland himself has spent several years in Europe, but Fox awakens him to his patriotic duty: "From an American standpoint, the absenteeism of our leading young men, the slavish adoption of the English idea, and the abandonment of their country, is cowardly social treason" (235). Maitland discovers that Oblonski has previously married a gypsy and saves Evelyn from a disastrous marriage and likely assassination. Evelyn learns the importance of American women recognizing their crucial roles in maintaining social stability: "The American women of to-day have as much at stake in the anarchistic issue as the men. They must in every way defend the family tie and home. Sustained in the fight against anarchy's terrors, and all corruption *by our women*, the right will prevail! *There can be no higher standard in the community than the hearts, lives, thoughts, and code of its best women!*" (365). By treating the woman's role as preserver of social order in heroic terms and depicting the anarchists as such base cowards, Savage creates a reactionary role for his female readers and gives repression a moral sanction. Savage casts female common sense in political terms—inherently conservative and authoritarian.

The solution to the anarchist threat, according to Savage's novel, is a combination of enlightened care for the less fortunate and severe repression for any who threaten the social order. According to the novel, Europe is already taking such measures, which will produce a new wave of anarchist immigration to the United States: "Naturally, cool repression, intelligent measures, will drive every cowardly dynamiter in the world to your shores, and these fellows, in the face of your loose government, your trifling army, your skeletal national guard, will carry on their damnable trade of terrorism, demoralization, and destruction" (357). In the face of this threat, America, too, needs to adopt its own institutions of repression. First, the press should not be allowed the license to undermine faith in social institutions: "The great newspaper of the future will be the trusted ally of the state, a true voice of the people—at once arbiter, referee, educator . . . a general public opinion, properly called out by calm and disinterested journalistic appeal, is the soundest verdict of a civilized people!" (346). The "calm and disinterested" press will educate the masses in the rightness of oligarchy and maintain social order by defusing, rather than pandering to, the mob's passions. The upper classes themselves will organize into "law-and-order leagues" which will help the police and the militia to crush any riot before it has a chance to spread. In addition, charity, when guided by the wisdom of a superior class, can help produce social stability: "Not spasmodically, not with sudden fancy to guide, but in a broad continuous general plan to help, lift, aid and better all those around you! This and only this generally adopted all over our land—a live moral effort to raise, and purify, and better, political, moral, and social life, will prevent a sudden, vicious and widely spread attack on wealth as an unprotected element!" (366). In this idea, Savage anticipates the corporate charity of Andrew Carnegie; it is a form of palliation which reinforces the right of the wealthy to control all aspects of society. Philip Maitland's election to Congress on the strength of his militia service (he foils Stein's attempt to assassinate Evelyn) augurs well for the ability of America to repress its radicals successfully and preserve social stability at all costs.

The Anarchist: A Story of To-Day is outrageously reactionary when read 100 years later, and its advocacy of severe repression in the interests of capitalism anticipates the worst excesses of fascism and corporate domination of news media in our own century. Anarchism represented the fear of disorder at the very heart of modern society that produced such emotional extremes; the fear of anarchism justified the erosion of liberty and the increased power of the state that occurred in the early years of the twentieth century.

The fear of the mob which lay at the heart of anarchist fears easily led to such extreme fantasies, of which the airships of *Hartmann the Anarchist* and *The Angel of the Revolution* are only small examples. The most extreme fantasy which was constructed out of these fears of anarchy was the anarchist conspiracy itself; writers such as Savage and Griffith built up the disciplined, hierarchical threat of a secret anarchist conspiracy in order to justify their own desires for increased power to combat the menace of the mob. As has been demonstrated by the Haymarket Trial, the belief in a conspiracy often trumped the facts: the anarchist "movement" was at best an informal collection of individuals, never very numerous or powerful; the true power lay in the expression of fear by the propertied classes.

4

Industrialism and Utopia

THE LATE NINETEENTH CENTURY WITNESSED MANY FORMS OF UTOPIAN NARrative. Fantastic novels by writers such as Bellamy and Morris are the most obvious examples of the desire to imagine new social arrangements that many in the period felt, but the utopian urge was also manifest in the many panegyrics to technology and corporate endeavor. Increasing economic centralization was described as the key to improved living conditions in utopian terms, and the leaders of these new economic institutions were often cast as heroes. The focus on the individual masked some of the contradictions inherent in this capitalist ideology, while the focus on material advances allowed supporters of corporate dominance to use the authority of science to bolster their own authority. At the same time, other writers were attempting to enlist the discourse of science to their own cause, including one prominent anarchist, Peter Kropotkin. In the end, anarchists came to symbolize a lost possibility for social organization, one usually rejected as inadequate or relatively powerless against the capitalist juggernaut.

Many groups had a stake in the debates over social and economic organization that raged throughout the late nineteenth century. Marxists, capitalists, socialists, progressives and others recognized that society was in a crucial period of self-definition, as evidenced by the popularity of utopias and other novels which dealt directly with social issues. As with most debates, it was not so much individual arguments that effected the greatest social change as it was the initial choice of language (and their associated narratives) that dominated that debate. Proponents of corporate capitalism were able to straddle the inherent contradictions between order and freedom in their own ideology through the construct of social Darwinism, modified to include a kind of hero worship of great capitalists as ones who were successful in this social competition. Many of the opponents of corporate capitalism accepted parts of this argument even Socialists and Marxists, who opposed capitalism, were in favor

110

of increasing centralization and saw society through a narrative of competition. By favoring decentralized, non-authoritarian cooperation, anarchists worked against the dominant discourse in almost every way and consequently were shut out of the debate on social organization. Nevertheless, the anarchist played an important role in novels as a foil (although usually an ineffective one) to the triumphant capitalist, showing that the idea of individualism could obscure the increasing lack of power which individuals had in the emerging economic system.

The success of the corporate model depended on several factors. The corporation responded effectively to the technological forces created in the industrial revolution because, through its division of labor and centralized control, it modeled the mechanical technologies that it sought to bring under effective control. The corporation preserved the interests and power of the upper and upper-middle classes: not only did it offer a way for numerous individuals to pool their resources for profit, but the corporation also offered a way to control the labor of the lower classes and was the institutional expression of the bourgeois goals of material success and economic power. On a pragmatic level, corporations grew step by step, and individuals understood them through existing metaphors and language. This step-by-step approach to greater social control enabled the corporation's advocates to argue that the corporation fulfilled the practical needs of many different social groups in terms suited to each group. By the late nineteenth century, advocates of the corporate model used statistics to paint a convincing picture of increasing material well-being, justifying a further expansion of corporate power.

Despite the flexibility and the widely trumpeted economic benefits of corporate centralization, the social changes related to the advance of the corporate model produced resistance from many classes that did not directly benefit from these changes. In both America and England, the pre-industrial professional classes resisted the encroachment of this new economic class, and the laborers created by the factory system demanded a more powerful role in economic decision making and a greater share of the economic benefits of the new system. The older professional and educated classes, which had been the upper-middle class before industrialization, felt threatened by the power of corporate leaders and middle managers in the expanding commercial culture. Every class experienced the increased alienation that comes with advanced capitalism, and the crowded urban centers from which factories recruited their workers, combined with the increasing economic and social segregation that characterized urban culture, produced much social tension. The conflicts between these groups and the growing capitalist and managerial classes manifest themselves culturally in a variety of reform, social, and labor movements.

For many supporters of the emerging corporate order, the solution to the ills produced by increasing industrialization, competition and centralization was further industrialization, competition and centralization. Any change attempted from outside the market—whether from government or social consideration—was defined as outside the realm of permissible discourse. The language of corporate capitalism which dominated nineteenth-century economics was socially closed; conservatives insisted that any discussion of economic issues that did not wish to be banished as "radical" occur within their discourse, which was imbedded with their own ideology and assumptions. A crudely deterministic social Darwinism formed the core narrative of this corporate language.

Social Darwinism was more than the phrase "survival of the fittest"; it was a complex of narratives that supported a conservative ideology. Its main idea was the converse of the Darwinist catch phrase: those who succeeded were the fittest. The reasons some individuals prospered and others failed had nothing to do with the workings of society, because the marketplace was a faithful mirror of the process of natural selection; therefore, failure lay entirely with the individual character. To interfere with the marketplace, even rhetorically, was anathema. Social Darwinism achieved widespread acceptance among the elites because it confirmed their superior positions in society and was grounded in a scientific language that avoided the controversies of religious belief. It obscured the injustice and repressive social controls of society by focusing attention on individuals rather than institutions and held out a promise of success for those who had sufficient drive and talent.

Advocates of corporate organization translated their narratives from naturalist discourse into other social languages. In America, the defenders of the newly emerging corporate order redefined the civic language of American democracy to be congruent with social Darwinism. William Graham Sumner championed definitions of liberty and equality that were limited to economic rights within the new industrial economy. Biographers built the successful entrepreneur into the hero of this new materialist era, expanding the scope of capitalist language into everyday life. Other writers sought to understand corporations through the image of the successful individual entrepreneur and make others aware of the extent of corporate power and abuse. Robert Herrick's *The Memoirs of an American*

Citizen and Frank Norris's *The Octopus* sought to describe in fiction the complications and potential for abuse present in the evolving corporate economics, as well as the individuals who controlled those institutions.

The rhetoric of individual competition obscured the capitalist reliance on force to preserve an expansive notion of property rights. For the conservative capitalists of the time, the government's main function was the preservation of capital—the investments and rental properties that insured that capitalists would control the lion's share of industrial production. Popular support for this action was created by equating those tools and institutions with the more everyday notion of property for personal use. Any questioning of this expansive definition of property was either suppressed or redefined as common theft. Anarchists, who opposed hierarchical power on general principles and were especially opposed to the power represented by investment property, were opposed to corporate organization on every issue and were consequently either excluded from the dialogue or had their positions distorted into nonsense by shifting the concept of property from one realm to the other. For example, the anarchist critique of slumlords was twisted into the notion that anarchists were mere thieves who wanted to throw everyone out of their own houses.

Some anarchist theorists, most notably Peter Kropotkin, were fairly well-known,[1] but few anarchistic ideas received an impartial hearing. Kropotkin attacked social Darwinism at its scientific roots in *Mutual Aid*,[2] but could not break the dominant rhetorical position that conservatives held the debate. Even when reformers proposed less incendiary ideas, such as credit unions or community ownership of factories, the proponents were careful to eschew any connection with anarchy. William Morris's utopia *News from Nowhere*,[3] which rejects industrialism altogether in favor of community-based crafts, depicts a decentralized, nonauthoritarian society even as it lampoons the follies of individualist anarchism. Most people understood anarchy to mean lawlessness, an understanding that its critics encouraged; in the popular mind anarchism combined the disorder of threatened revolution or degeneration with the destruction of individualism associated with communism.

The anarchist thinker, describing exploitation and misery where others depicted progress and material wealth, was in a curious position in the battle of assumptions and languages that surrounded the advance of corporate capitalism. The increased efficiency, material wealth and power which corporate organization promised were widely celebrated, and the anarchist's call to return the genie to its bottle generally was ignored by the many who stood to gain materially from the new economy. The corporation had swiftly become a fixture of modern society; for the most part, it did so by claiming that nothing had changed.

THE LANGUAGE OF NATURAL LAW

Although they relied on government force when necessary, the advocates of corporations succeeded in changing society because they convinced many individuals from all classes to adopt the language and therefore the assumptions of corporate capitalism. The main rhetorical ploy used in this argument was the argument based on "natural law," an assertion that corporate organization was perfectly in agreement with the other workings of the universe and therefore was inevitable. Despite the present hardship, corporations promised a capitalist utopia. This rhetoric cast dissenting voices into the realm of the unnatural and the nonsensical—one could no more demand justice from the economy than one could demand that gravity be abolished.

The persuasive power of this rhetoric was based in a language that had already achieved widespread authority because of its utility: the rhetoric of science. This adaptation of the rhetoric of physics to sociology was accomplished by Smith and Ricardo, who created a vision of a mathematical economy of consumers and producers and abstracted out of the equation any social or ethical concerns. Society was defined as a set of autonomous individuals who interacted freely according to principles of natural law. Their mathematical description of an economy would become the root of capitalist "laws."

In order to create a place for themselves in the cultural discourse, the supporters of corporate power subverted key phrases from established discourses and reduced those ideas to fit within their own linguistic framework. The advocates of corporate advancement spoke the same words as others in their society but shifted the metaphorical context. The "rights of man" were reduced to a right to material property; being "created equal" simply meant that everyone had, in theory, the same right to gain property. Rather than describe their efforts as a revolution in social organization, the advocates of corporate capitalism claimed that corporate hierarchies were a logical development from widely held assumptions about the nature of the universe.

The corporation was granted the same legal status as the individual. However, this legal metaphor obscures the significant differences between the corporation and the economic individual of classical economics. Corporations are uninhibited by local norms, undiminished by inheritance taxes, and able to combine the wealth and labor of many individuals to the benefit of a few. Through a trust or a monopoly, the leader of a corporation could hold more power than any civic leader could ever hope for. The corporation, based in individualist economics, shattered that framework by its sheer scale, dwarfing individuals and whole communities and overwhelming human norms with the abstractions of the marketplace. Even as it effected a revolution in social organization, the corporation claimed that the workings of industry were natural and therefore could not be changed by political regulation or intellectual theorizing.

Dialogue on economic issues was to be restricted to those who held the same assumptions as the corporate leaders. In the lead article of the January 1896 *American Journal of Sociology*, "Business Men and Social Theorists," C. R. Henderson summarizes the position of businessmen by quoting "an able and upright manufacturer":

> "The relation between capital and labor is one of the many questions in the comprehensive science of political economy, and as such is a purely business matter. Philanthropy has nothing to do with it, nor has religion or sentiment, any more than they have to do with astronomy or the law of gravitation. . . . and the sooner the whole matter is taken out of the realm of sentimental philosophy and placed on the bed rock of simple, practical business common sense the better. . . . All that legislators and editors and preachers and philanthropists can do is to educate people that they may be able finally . . . to pass out of these turbulent and obscuring mists of ignorant and selfish struggle into the clear light of universal law and justice."[4]

The only possible solution to the social problems caused by capitalism is to educate people in the language and ideology of the capitalist class—"practical business common sense"—and to accept the corporate order as a natural law with the same unquestionable authority as a planetary orbit. This rhetorical ploy is crucial to the expansion of capitalist hegemony; the language of capitalism claims total authority on questions of production and distribution of material goods.

From this secure base in economic theory, advocates of corporate expansion could translate other discourses into capitalist terms and exclude other groups from the debate. Many writers adopted this ploy, such as Albion Small, an editor for the *American Journal of Sociology*, who writes in an article titled "Sanity In Social Legislation": "I will confine myself for illustration throughout this paper to the labor question. What is true of the labor question . . . is true of all desired social progress."[5] The language of political economy imposes a host of unspoken assumptions on the subject. By framing debates in the language of economic theory, defenders of laissez-faire capitalism could employ their rhetoric of natural laws against supposed artificial meddling with the market by radicals.

The advocates of corporate capitalism, through their narrative of natural law, created a language that ignored nonmonetary concerns and silenced radical calls for social justice (for instance, by justifying the refusal of many capitalists to supply pensions or health care to their workers as untoward interference in the workings of "survival of the fittest"). The debate is framed as an issue of monetary greed rather than altruistic justice, blunting dissent by promising a future in which increased material wealth made such issues moot, or by playing up stories of the poor as violent or worthless and encouraging hero worship of the successful capitalist.[6]

THE STRUCTURE OF THE CAPITALIST UTOPIA

William Graham Sumner and other advocates of capitalism embraced a definition of freedom grounded in economic language. For most of American history, this term had an uneasy ambiguity between those who saw freedom in religious or spiritual terms and those who saw it as a purely economic concept. By limiting the concept of freedom to the economic license to buy, sell, hire and fire as one pleased, the advocates of corporate order could mix metaphors from the natural world and the world of machines to obscure the inherent contradictions between social order and individual freedom within their ideology. By describing the "dis-order" of the marketplace as an industrial "system" or mechanism, defenders of capitalism placed the economy outside of individual or social control. Despite its status as a natural force, propagandists promised that industrial beneficence would eventually outgrow the miseries of its early stages and blossom into a materialist utopia.

The metaphor of corporation as mechanism echoed the general fascination with machines in the nineteenth century. Smith and Ricardo had already extended the mechanistic metaphor to economics, and numerous political philosophers also applied it to the very structure of government. By applying this metaphorical description to the corporation, the corporation laid the groundwork for the claim that this new system was not new at all, but simply the application of familiar principles to a common situation. In this case, it was not principles so much as metaphors that the new organization shared with its predecessors.

The metaphor of the machine was familiar to the middle-class audiences to which these descriptions were aimed. By describing the corporate enterprise as a mechanism within the larger mechanism of the "free market," advocates of corporate organization were associating their interests with technology and science and, by extension, with narratives of orderly progress toward future bliss. The conception of the market, characterizing competition as a nearly ideal system for determining the usefulness of people rather than a destructive dog-eat-dog world, made use of another scientific discourse, that of natural selection. In this metaphor, the economy was seen as part of the natural, rather than the social, world; economic changes could be equated with forces of nature, both equally beyond human control. Finally, the metaphor of corporation as a tool or machine used by individuals allowed capitalists to appropriate the language of individual rights and place it within a purely economic and materialist context, preserving the sacred phrases of American politics, but changing their meaning.

These metaphors work in several ways. The corporation was a metaphorical application of mechanical concepts to human behavior. On an obvious level, corporate organization simply employed the concept of division of labor combined with economy of scale. On a deeper level, the development of the corporation mirrors the profound and subtle division between operators and tools, working on several levels of abstraction. On the factory floor, the tools and operators are literal—men work the machines. The manager, however, could view the workers and their machines as one unit—a large machine—that he directed; the chairman, a man supposedly endowed with tremendous energy and vision, could understand each factory as one tool that he controlled. Although individuals exerted control at each level of the organization, the whole machine, it was claimed, could only be understood by experts and exceptional men. [7]

By elevating corporate self-interest into a system based on natural laws, defenders could build on the promises of other technologies. As the metaphorical extension of the promise that new inventions gave the people of the nineteenth century, the current industrial system was associated with many of the same rosy possibilities. Paul Monroe states the common argument that the present "system" will outgrow its attendant ills as the individuals who control capital become more morally advanced, shifting attention from the institution to the individual. Monroe quotes Herbert Spencer as a way to reinforce the assertion that the current social ills are the responsibility of individuals, not the system: "It must be admitted that the practicability of such a system depends on character. Throughout this volume it has been variously shown that higher types of society are made possible only by higher types of nature; and the implication is that the best industrial institutions are possible only with the best men."[8] This claim accomplishes two goals: first, it echoes the racist argument that those of northern European heritage are morally superior to individuals of other races, and, second, it makes any attempt at reform beyond the level of the individual impossible. To illustrate this claim, the writer details the conditions at a National Cash Register plant in Dayton, Ohio, as an example of the benefits possible under the current industrial system, when that system is combined with sound moral principles.

The factory described is, first, aesthetically pleasing; the whole enterprise seems to be lifted out of George Bernard Shaw's *Major Barbara*. The grounds have been designed by Frederick Olmstead; the interior colors are determined by a committee of female employees. Not only does the factory not resemble a factory, it has design features that would be welcome in a middle-class home. More important for the author is the fact that "the merits of the institution can only be appreciated after a thorough investigation, and a realization of the scientific treatment given every phase of the work. For there is a system so well perfected that it may well be distinguished as 'scientific.'"[9] The system is run by committees of workmen and administrators, quite similar to the structures which in the late twentieth century fall under the label of total quality management. Suggestion boxes, company newsletters, and conventions including all employees of the company are but some of the innovative features that National Cash Register uses to bring together the interests of the employer and the employed. Careful records of applicants and employees guarantee that the best candidates are employed, and on-the-job training and hygiene (each employee is expected to take at least one bath each week, on company time) ensure a healthy work force.

National Cash Register gives special attention to the treatment of female employees. Monroe applauds the operators of National Cash Register for the "solicitude [which] is shown for their moral and intellectual as well as their physical welfare." The women work shorter hours than male employees for the same pay. They begin

work fifteen minutes after the men and depart fifteen minutes earlier, to catch an earlier tram and reduce contact with the male employees. "Perhaps the one feature which, more than any other, has
won for this establishment the epithet of 'incipient socialism' is the
noon luncheon furnished to all female help at the company's expense."[10] According to the author, this paternalistic expense is justified by the increased productivity of the women.

In other ways, too, the factory might be regarded by contemporaries as socialist. Since the entire town is dependent upon the success of the factory, the owners take a vital interest in the well-being
of the community as a whole. "The company's landscape gardener
has general oversight of the streets, lawns, and park places of the
entire community." Prizes are awarded for the best-landscaped res-
idence. The improvement in the community's appearance "is adequately expressed in the change of the name of the community from
Slidertown to South Park"[11]; the corporation has succeeded in moving factory workers into a middle-class sensibility.

The author saves the best points for last: this approach to industrial management has transformed the normally contentious labor
force into a group that expresses their thanks to National Cash Register. The author quotes a proclamation by the Dayton Trades and
Labor Assembly:

> Believing that our fellow-workmen, as a rule, are eager to rise above
> mere shophands, and that every effort made by the manufacturers of
> the city to better the condition of their employees should be properly
> recognized . . . we recognize the progressive spirit prevailing in their
> management, and would point them out to other manufacturers as wor-
> thy of imitation.[12]

Here, then, is a solution to the Labor Question, and one which "in
no essential, save that of superintendence, is the present factory
system changed; only modified as a just appreciation of the responsibility of an employer would dictate." Industrialism can also incorporate the more radical socialist movement into its fold. "A
prominent German socialist, after visiting the factory, remarked:
'That is all I mean by Socialism.' And what is more to be emphasized, in the present day, is the fact that 'it pays' from the standpoint of the employer."[13] One can be a socialist and realize a profit
at the same time; the approval of the presumably radical yet unnamed German socialist confirms that enlightened capitalism can
incorporate the best elements of socialism without renouncing the
benefits of competition, centralization, and the profit motive.

Of course, the egalitarian rhetoric of the previous passage flies in the face of most people's market experiences. In fact, people are not equal and benefit from market processes unequally. Despite these obvious inequalities, the fact that the market encompasses everyone is a sufficient argument for its essentially egalitarian character, argues a *New York Times* editorial:

> There are infinitely varied degrees of industry, of skill, of ability to employ means to ends, of command over instrumentalities and agencies, and hence the widely different rewards and gains that are acquired through the part taken by different men in these industrial processes. They are controlled by inevitable laws, which work on the whole, beneficently, and attempts to interfere with them by legislation can only prove disastrous.[14]

The fact that some people profit from "instrumentalities and agencies"—corporate mechanisms—far more than others is not a cause of antagonism, but simply the natural result of the same process that allows these people to accumulate wealth in the first place. Rather than being a cause for divisiveness, this editorial would have the inequality of wealth be a cause for celebration, since it is a sign that the system is working "in accord with natural laws." Everyone is united by the marketplace, and all human activity should be conducted under its language and logic.

By the logic of the marketplace, it is competition and the inequality of wealth that produces the greatest good, not equality. The very inequality of wealth becomes the best means to help the poor:

> It is for the interest of the poorest laborer that competition should be free, and that energy, skill, and accumulated capital should be able to secure their advantages. Otherwise, there would be no incentive to the development of the most powerful agencies in promoting industrial activity.[15]

The assumption of this editorialist is that the only possible path of industrial progress is through increasing centralization of capital. Because workers are dependent upon corporations for employment and every producer is an equal part of the vast mechanism of production, workers should support the conditions that allow for the unfettered accumulation of capital. Because the worker will get some small share of the wealth produced by industry through working, the worker should help the people who control money increase their share of that wealth.

Although it may seem nonsensical to ask workers to defer their own interests to those of their employers, the logic imbedded in market language encouraged these priorities. As the previous editorial shows, it was taken for granted in the 1870s that any further economic expansion would be accomplished only through the framework of corporate finance. Advocates of the corporate dominance of the American economy (which included the *New York Times*, most federal politicians, and the Supreme Court) saw corporations as providing crucial services and technological advances to the American economy which in turn justified advancing corporate wealth and power. Many would claim that there would be no economic expansion (and related growth of the United States as a world power) outside of the corporate framework; economic expansion, although uneven in the short term, would inevitably lift all boats.

Understanding the world through a language of materialist progressivism, many newspaper editorials confidently proclaimed that no socialism could prosper in the United States because of the unique conditions of the country. "Socialistic theorists profess to find in American society the germs of a struggle as intense as that which underlies the surface of things in England and France. Practical people know that the assertion has no solid foundation."[16] Although Europe may choke under an ossified hierarchy of classes, America was a land of open opportunity. The *New York Times* describes the United States's economy in these terms:

> We have no privileged class, and no class doomed hopelessly to labor. The capitalist of today was a working man ten years ago; hard work, and skill, and thrift, and judgment have made him what he is. And the road he trod to fortune is open to the whole body of working men.[17]

Since any industrious person is theoretically capable of becoming wealthy through the devices of capitalism, advocating any other means of advancement is suspect at best. "When, therefore, a man mounts a platform and harangues them to be an oppressed and injured class, we may be quite sure he is a demagogue."[18] These messages—that the ambition of the poor could be fulfilled through capitalism and that the conditions in Europe were incomparably worse than the situation in the United States—was particularly urgent during the days of the Paris Commune, when the propertied classes witnessed a potential revolution of the poor.

Even as moderate reformers were attempting to convince the leaders of business that engaging in "socialistic" or "paternalistic" practices was good business in the long run, most employers used the language of the marketplace to limit their relationships with employees to the strict terms of contract. Just as no one should be forced to buy unwanted merchandise or be forced to pay more when a product was available at a lower price, so employers (thought of in this discourse as individuals, not combinations) should not have their freedom to hire, fire, and negotiate wages limited in any way. To these business leaders, any talk of economic justice was simply clouding workers' minds with pie-in-the-sky dreams which made them discontent without showing them that the only way to improve themselves was individually, through the competitive system.

THE INDUSTRIALIST AS CAPITALIST HERO: ANDREW CARNEGIE AND ELBERT HUBBARD

Although a corporation was a legal and contractual framework that accumulated the wealth, effort, and logistical skill of numerous individuals, the individual who led the corporation was, according to the descriptions of the time, its animating genius and its human face. The identification of the corporation with the individual who led it allowed the corporation certain rhetorical advantages by substituting a human symbol for various corporate institutions, which eased the integration of corporate structures into society. Economic fortunes would be discussed in terms of the individual, implying that any success or failure was necessarily the result of personal genius or dissipation; the role of changing corporate institutions could be obscured and therefore shielded from criticism.

The metaphor of the corporation as a living individual allows advocates of the corporation to claim rights with the same words that many Americans had already accepted, but give them an exclusively economic emphasis: the "natural" rights amounted to unlimited freedoms to buy, sell, hire and fire as one pleased. Since the corporation was an individual by statute only, the language of capitalism focused attention away from the corporate effort and toward the individual who was held to be solely responsible for the accumulation of wealth that the corporation represents.

Many metaphors preserve the focus on the individual while acknowledging the group endeavor that the corporation represents. The head of the corporation could be seen as a "captain of industry" (to use a military metaphor) or, by critics in the United States, as a "Robber Baron" (reminiscent of the practice of some later European nobles of charging tolls on roads through their small fiefdoms and attacking those who would not pay the toll). The principle of metonymy was nearly always operative: the various parts of a corporate concern were nearly always identified with the top officers of that corporation.

This metaphor created the possibility of ad hominem attacks on the corporation in the person of the chair. Usually, these attacks were as simple as using the head of the corporation to represent the institution in editorial cartoons. On a more literal level, the anarchist Alexander Berkmann sought to end the Homestead Strike in Pennsylvania by attempting to assassinate Henry Frick, the manager of the Carnegie Steel Works there.

Often, the leaders of great corporations were depicted as warriors in biographies and, like Prince Hal in *Henry V*, were excused for their coarseness on the grounds of their background as soldiers in the competitive marketplace. C. R. Henderson explains the resistance that many business leaders have toward sociologists in this way:

> It would be strange if the "captain of industry" did not sometimes manifest a militant spirit, for he has risen from the ranks largely because he was a better fighter than most of us. Competitive commercial life is not a flowery bed of ease, but a battle field where the "struggle for existence" is defining the industrially "fittest to survive."[19]

In the United States and Great Britain, the heroes of the age with the most widespread acceptance were still military heroes. As part of the expansion of materialist rhetoric, supporters of the emerging capitalist order naturally sought to create for economically successful figures the same popular esteem which military leaders enjoyed.[20] Employing the language of competition which the natural sciences, economics, and militant nationalism have in common, many writers sought to portray the successful industrialist as a hero for all segments of society.

The successful entrepreneur, like all heroes, achieves his significance within a particular discourse. The heroic position of the businessman is grounded in a corporate materialism that aggressively asserts its claims to encompass the material life of society as a whole and to provide boons for all members of society. For the young and the poor, the role of successful businessman promises rewards to individuals who will serve the capitalist class through self-discipline, hard work, and a desire to invest earnings to increase available capital for corporate concerns. The capitalist claims the allegiance of the laborer by his prodigious ability to "provide work" (seen as essential to both dignity and survival) to those

dependent on capital for their livelihood. For the established middle
and upper classes and the emerging managerial class, the capitalist
hero promises increased material wealth from increased production and logistical efficiencies and increased stability by embracing
the social structure of the established elite.

Several tropes occur repeatedly in the biographies of heroic capitalists. In keeping with an emphasis on the self-made individual, the
role of the parents is often minimized; parents' contributions are
usually either the encouragement to save or the negative example
of drunkenness and profligacy. The young hero first learns the
value of hard work and then learns the language and related priorities of capitalism, usually with the help of some mentor figure. Often
this mentor sets the hero up with his first investment. The hero is
credited with the ability to determine a good investment from a bad
one and the first investment is a crucial step in the capitalist hero's
development. Finally, the hero is usually depicted as pursuing his
capitalist goals even after he has made a fortune, thus justifying
capitalist claims of inherent beneficence. At each stage, the emphasis of the story is on the individual merit of the hero; the successful
industrialist is seen as an exemplar against laziness and excuse-
making, and for ambition, thrift, and sobriety.

Elbert Hubbard takes special care to describe the childhoods of
his subjects in ideological terms in his series *Little Journeys to
the Homes of the Great*. Written for a younger audience, Hubbard
preaches to his readers a complete faith in the marketplace and
total devotion to hard work. When parents are mentioned, they are
valued for their ability to teach the wisdom of thrift and self-discipline. The mother is often singled out for special praise in this role,
echoing the established worship of maternal self-sacrifice prevalent
in middle-class literature. Often, the father is portrayed as only a
middling success, or as a negative example, showing the son the
value of determination and hard work by being unambitious and
lazy. Hubbard describes Astor's father as simply a butcher
"through an extreme case of atavism."[21] As a boy, H. H. Rogers
(who would become the President of Standard Oil) was taught by an
economical and practical mother. He worked many odd jobs, including renting out his skates to other boys for money. He made his first
money by delivering groceries, a business in which he was a pio-
neer; Hubbard justifies Rogers's wisdom by the fact that his father
thought it a bad idea, but his more practical mother recognized its
genius.

Following the narrative conventions of the genre, Alderson's *Andrew Carnegie: The Man and His Work*[22] stresses Carnegie's hum-

ble beginnings, discipline, and devotion to hard work. One often repeated story regards a class in which the young Carnegie was asked to repeat a proverb from the Bible. "When it came Andrew's turn he stood up and boldly proclaimed, 'Take care of your pence, and the pounds will take care of themselves.' This was not quite orthodox, but it illustrated how the famous maxim had been drilled into the lad's mind by his mother."[23] As well as demonstrating the young Carnegie's early education, the episode also demonstrates the displacement of a religious rhetoric with the language of the marketplace which can be traced back to Franklin's *Autobiography*. Just as Hercules had mastered wrestling as an infant, and Jesus of Nazareth could dispute theology with the elders of the temple almost as soon as he could walk, so Andrew Carnegie had learned the wisdom taught through the language of the marketplace while a young boy.

As a young adult, the heroic capitalist is devoted to learning the language and ideology of the business community rather than receiving a college education. Sometimes, the hero begins as a manual laborer, demonstrating his superior capacity by doing the work of labor as well as capital; however, the hero's superiority usually makes this stage quite brief. For example, Carnegie moved from a job in which he monitored a steam boiler into the telegraph business where, by moonlighting and studying in his spare time, he earned the attention of his superiors. In each situation, the key ingredient is the natural genius of the hero for understanding the potential wealth in a given situation and acting ambitiously and decisively.

The success of the hero is always due solely to the hero's genius and not to inherited wealth, luck, or the timely aid of others. A fictional capitalist observes "that many men lack capacity for the wise direction and organization of their own labor . . . others possess qualities of mind and character which fit them to be leaders or masters of the industry of others."[24] That unnamed capitalist begins a partnership with a local cobbler: he provides the cobbler with a shop, materials, and a salary, and they divide the profits from the shoes he produces equally. The shoe shop is a success and takes on other workers to meet the demand, and the capitalist reinvests his money in other enterprises, which also create employment: "thousands of men have been employed in connection with these enterprises, and hundreds of them enabled to become in their turn employers and organizers of labor." Through a lifetime of work, "the little straggling hamlet in which the young man began his business life has become a handsome and important town, with seven or eight thousand inhabitants, most of them operatives employed in manufacturing industries."[25] The individual capitalist is solely responsible for this success, according to the article.

Philip Armour's early life is a prototype of the capitalist mindset. As a youth, Armour was in California for the gold rush. However, "this very sensible country boy figured out that mining was a gamble . . . he decided he would bet on nothing but his own ability. Instead of digging for gold, he set to work digging ditches for men who had mines, but no water." He quickly moved from using his own labor to contracting out the work, paying his employees less than he himself received. Hubbard admiringly states, "it was all a question of mathematics. In five years Philip Armour had saved eight thousand dollars."[26] Carnegie's superintendent, Thomas Scott, offered Carnegie an inside deal on an investment, which gave Carnegie his first taste of investment success: "This small transaction was destined to prove the forerunner of a long series of gigantic deals."[27] In both employment and investment, the emphasis is on the hero's personal responsibility for his fortune; he has earned the favors of jobs and inside investment deals through his own talents and, although luck may have played some small role, it did not play a decisive one. This reflects the individualist rhetoric of corporate capitalism: success is not the result of a system favoring some at the expense of others; it is the sole result of individual merit.

The military hero was an important figure in late nineteenth century America, and corporate biographies often took pains to justify their subjects' actions during war. This task was complicated by the widespread war profiteering that occurred during the American Civil War and the Spanish-American War. Most biographies of business leaders portray the decision to earn money rather than fight as an heroic act, justified by the need for the hero's talents of coordination of production in the war effort.[28] Carnegie, never a physically active person, was not a soldier; his job was to supervise the network of railways and telegraphs that provided logistical support. In this capacity, "he manfully stuck to his post, working indefatigably night and day."[29] Moreover, "although he did no fighting, he was the third man wounded in the war. A telegraph wire which had been pinned to the ground, upon being loosened sprung up suddenly and cut a severe gash on his cheek, but he did not allow the injury to affect his duties. He was present at several battles, and at Bull Run was one of the last to leave the field."[30] Working through a wound establishes Carnegie's strength, despite his stature; being one of the last to leave when Union forces were routed demonstrates a courage superior to many actual soldiers. The characteristics that make Carnegie a successful businessman are portrayed as identical to those that make an effective soldier: perseverance, courage, and clearheadedness. The Roman ideal of civic and military service was fulfilled by the heroic businessman who created wealth and improved the lives of the entire community.

Having demonstrated his worthiness on the battlefield and in the marketplace, the heroic capitalist builds his corporate empire. After achieving his fortune, he continues to work tirelessly and exploit every possibility. This continued economic activity also justifies the system of capitalism itself and the claim that the businessman provides benefits to society through his economic actions alone.

The capitalist of the biographers fulfills the heroic pattern described by Joseph Campbell in *The Hero with a Thousand Faces*; a special individual, he has withstood trials and brought benefits to his community. For this very reason, criticism of prominent capitalists was seen within this discourse as mean-spirited and unreasonable. Hubbard derisively summarizes Upton Sinclair's exposé of the practices of Armour's packing company as follows:

> Upton Sinclair scored two big points on Packingtown and its Boss Ogre. They were these: First, the Ogre hired men and paid them to kill animals. Second, these dead animals were distributed by the Ogre and his minions and the corpses eaten by men, women, and children. It was a revolting revelation. It even shook the nerves of a President, one of the killingest men in the world, who, not finding enough things to kill in America, went to Africa to kill things.[31]

Hubbard encourages us to laugh at the effete hypocrisy of people who are offended by the packing trade and instead admire the genius of the man who invented an industry. Of the later scandals involving sales of spoiled meat to the government, Hubbard mentions that the accusers committed suicide, and a commission of officers found the charges to be without foundation. However, the slander did its damage: "Here were forces that Philip Armour, as unsullied and as honorable as Sir Philip Sidney, could not fight, because he could not locate them."[32] Armour passed away, dying but not defeated. To his last he had been a capitalist.

Another capitalist that Hubbard must defend against the attacks of writers is H. H. Rogers, the man behind the Standard Oil Company. Hubbard introduces his sketch by claiming "those who did not like him usually pictured him by recounting what he was not. My endeavor in this sketch will be simply to tell what he was." What he was, according to Hubbard, was a typical American—"his fault, if fault it may be, was that he succeeded too well."[33] When under attack, the corporate leader was defended as being a normal, even typical individual, contradicting the biographer's insistence on the entrepreneur's superiority.

The polemic intent of the capitalist biographer was often very clearly stated by juxtaposing the reasonableness of the capitalist with the spiteful rhetoric of the radical, as in this passage from "The Career of a Capitalist":

> This account is merely true. It describes the life of a quiet, humane gentleman,—one who has been most useful to his fellows, who has aided in the development of whole regions of the country, and who, I am sure, never knowingly harmed any human being. And yet this man, according to the teachings of those who pretend to be the best friends of the laboring man, is an enemy to society, an oppressor of the poor and of all who toil.[34]

This passage juxtaposes two languages: the language of gentility and civic service that the middle-class readers of the *Atlantic Monthly* have already adopted as their own against the alien rhetoric of the demagogue and agitator. The capitalist's biographer, by using the language of civic-minded professionalism to describe the actions of his model capitalist, convinces his reader of the truth of his statements by adopting their language. The capitalist is simply using his natural gifts to benefit society, and his possessions are simply the natural reward for the exercise of his uncommon talents. Against the "disorganizing elements and tendencies in our society," the capitalist encourages efforts to educate workers of the truth found in economics; in other words, teach the language of the capitalist class to everyone, so that they may understand the world in the same manner.

Although such rhetoric convinced many members of the middle class, the working class, which experienced first hand the pernicious effects of capitalism, were not so easily convinced of the entrepreneur's superiority or the beneficence of the marketplace. As criticism of capitalist practices mounted, writers would bolster the entrepreneur's heroic claim by emphasizing the subject's innocence with regard to the ravages of the industrial system. In his biography of Carnegie, Alderson acknowledges the differing opinions regarding Carnegie as an employer. "On the one hand he is looked upon as a man who has violated in practice all the excellent theory which he has written on the subject; and, on the other hand, it is asserted that he has done everything possible for his work-people compatible with the maintenance of his business in the face of fierce competition."[35] Both options contain some compliment to Carnegie as an individual. In the discussion of labor strife, Alderson presents three common justifications which are rooted in the language of capitalism: first, that market forces, not individuals, are responsible for low pay or harsh conditions, so that complaining about conditions at the bottom of the market hierarchy is the equivalent of complaining about the weather; second, that the benefits which accrue to the community as a whole from the wise administration of the great capitalist outweigh the hardship of the rank-and-file employees; and third, that any violence or strife is the result of shadowy "agitators." Although the capitalists' success is due solely to his own merit, his failures are the responsibility of all but himself.

The capitalist also justified himself to society as a whole through public (and often publicized) charitable acts—endowing public libraries, funding pensions for worn-out workers, and building public swimming pools, for example. Through these actions, capitalists adopted themselves to the established language of Christian charity, making the benefits they theoretically bestowed more tangible and immediate. This narrative of philanthropy, which justified charity by the language of capitalism by speaking of it as "investment," played an important role in the ascendancy of corporate institutions in society.

One of the primary authors of this corporate philanthropy was Andrew Carnegie. Although he was pursuing success according to a capitalist standard, Carnegie was uncomfortable with the discord which existed between materialism and the Presbyterian doctrines of his youth. He reconciled the two languages through which he understood his life by creating his own *Gospel of Wealth*.[36] The very title is emblematic of the two languages of the treatise, Christianity and materialism. Unlike many of his contemporaries, Carnegie was not satisfied with the ideology that proclaimed that any investing or work of economic expansion was inherently beneficial to society as a whole, with no thought or obligation required by the wealthy. Carnegie, in the *Gospel of Wealth*, proclaimed the rich to be "trustees" of society's wealth, positions that they had earned through their demonstrated superiority in attaining that wealth. He then proceeded to systematize charity as he had systematized production and management, overseeing the dispersal of his wealth with the same ruthlessness and self-confidence with which he had conducted its amassing.

In his essay "The Problem of the Administration of Wealth," Carnegie attempts to reconcile his faith in the "law of competition" with his recognition of the spiritual ills of capitalism. Because of industrialism, "the poor enjoy what the rich could not before afford."[37] The price of this increased material wealth is an increased difference between the rich and the poor; however, Carnegie argues that this, too, is beneficial in terms reminiscent of Hyacinth Robinson in *The Princess Casamassima*: "It is well, nay, essential, for the progress of the race that the houses of some should be homes for all that is highest and best in literature and the arts and for all the refinements of civilization, rather than that none should be so. Much better this great irregularity than universal squalor."[38] Both of these benefits Carnegie traces to the inevitable effects of the "law of competition," which, according to capitalist ideology, is responsible for all progress in human history and is indispensable for future progress as well, since it "ensures the survival of the fittest in every department."[39] Although Darwin dealt with species in his work, the grafting of individualism onto evolutionary theory gives support to the idea that those who succeed do so solely because of their superiority.

Carnegie declares competition to be the cornerstone of civilization; anyone who questions this order of things, as many critics of his *Gospel* did, is attacking civilization itself:

> The Socialist or Anarchist who seeks to overturn present conditions is to be regarded as attacking the foundation upon which civilization itself rests, for civilization took its start from the day when the capable, industrious workman said to his incompetent and lazy fellow, "if thou dost not sow, thou shalt not reap," and thus ended primitive Communism by separating the drones from the bees.[40]

The right of the businessman to maximize profit grows from this first act of individualism, and progress is dependent upon giving these superior men the free play to exercise their rare talents. The talents required by "the manufacturer who has to conduct affairs upon a great scale" are proven to be rare by the law of supply and demand, since "it invariably secures enormous rewards for its possessor."[41] That these persons are often in a position to set the price for their own services is obscured by the abstraction of natural law.

After the businessman has earned his fortune, Carnegie argues, the next ambition of the successful businessman should be to exercise his talents in charitable fields by effectively administering his wealth: "the man of wealth thus becoming the mere trustee and agent for his poorer brethren, bringing to their service his superior wisdom, experience, and ability to administer, doing for them much better than they would or could do for themselves." The form this charity should take, so as to not pauperize the recipient, is "to help those who will help themselves."[42] Through this system, individualism and competition will have a free reign, but any of the poor who wish to improve themselves will have ample resources.

The idea that charity, as practiced in its older form, is pernicious is a common one in the narratives of social Darwinism. In his *Little Journeys*, Hubbard describes what he terms " 'Hubbard's Law,' or the Law of Altruistic Injury. This law provides that whenever you do for a person a service which he is able and should do for himself, you work him a wrong rather than a benefit."[43] Hubbard constantly criticizes charity workers as greedy to get their hands on the money which the great businessmen have earned the right to dispose of themselves: "these philanthropists do not realize that, for the most part, they are plain grabheimers from Grabville. And all of their pious plans for human betterment have their root in the desire for personal aggrandizement."[44] The charity work of the great businessman is to give opportunity, not charity; to help only those who are able to help themselves. According to Hubbard, great progress is made when the language of business and the genius of the individual businessman controls philanthropy. In fact, "The big things of the world are always done by individuals. One-man power is the only thing that counts. The altruistic millionaire is the necessity of progress—he does magnificent things, which the many will not and cannot do."[45] Far from being a sign of a system which is unjust, vast accumulations of personal wealth signify a progressive civilization to Hubbard.

Alderson, of course, finds the idea of the individual entrepreneur as symbol of progress to be a conception of the highest order, "approving of Mr. Carnegie's businesslike methods in the distribution of wealth."[46] This is the rhetorical key to Carnegie's rationale: *The Gospel of Wealth* is a formula for applying the language and accompanying values of capitalism to charitable practice. The marketplace seeks to encompass yet another realm of social exchange, replacing the language of charity derived from the Gospels themselves with a combination of Malthus and capitalist optimism.

Carnegie's many donations, always through foundations or agreements for continued support by those who benefit, earned him the respect and admiration that his business pursuits did not. Carnegie the industrialist was feared for the immense power he had over the lives of people and the ways in which he used that power; Carnegie the philanthropist has been remembered as the benefactor he wished to be. Carnegie Steel may be almost forgotten, but

Andrew Carnegie's name is written on hundreds of library corner-
stones and foundation reports.

PARADISE THROUGH CAPITALISM:
RADICAL REIMAGININGS OF THE CAPITALIST UTOPIA

Nearly all of the dominant cultural narratives of the late nineteenth century—nationalism, corporate capitalism, and progressivism—encouraged an increasingly centralized, hierarchical society.
Although the anarchists were opposed to this agenda on nearly
every front, other radicals, more in step with the dialogue of the
time, argued that increasing centralization would eventually produce a more just society. Marx, the Fabians, Bellamy, and Morris
all imagined a future in which the corporation would increasingly
dominate, then become an institution which would work for the benefit of all, rather than the few. Morris's *News from Nowhere* (1891)
is especially interesting in its polemic moment: the utopian romance
criticizes both anarchist individualists (who were taking over the
Socialist League of which he was a member) and Bellamy's centralized corporate nationalism (which he also had criticized in a scath-
ing review). Despite the avowedly Marxist revolution that brings it
about, Morris's utopia, based on local control and consensus, is essentially communalist-anarchistic.

Many writers imagined alternatives to the steady advance of commercial industrialism. Many of these alternatives took for granted
the increasing centralization of society and imagined ways in which
that centralization could be used to promote social justice. In this
way, the reformers were working in concert with the capitalism of
the time. Coming out in favor of centralized order also allowed other
leftists to distance themselves from the anarchists, who were increasingly slandered in the press as advocates of disorder for their
terrorist propaganda and their desire to abolish centralized power
structures. Marxism in particular encouraged the centralization of
everything—political and economic power—in the hands of the
state, and the Fabian socialists worked for municipal control of
basic utilities and other expansions of centralized power as part of
their reform agenda. The Marxists and Fabians worked to increase
the power of the government to counterbalance corporate power,
hastening the centralization of corporate structures.

Among literary utopias, Bellamy's *Looking Backward*[47] envisions the increasing centralization of corporations taken to its logical extreme. In the novel, the mergers and trusts that were growing

at an alarming pace during Bellamy's day eventually combined into one giant corporation that ran the entire economy. Rather than assume absolute power for itself, this giant corporation was peacefully taken over by the government that then ran the corporation for the benefit of all. Each citizen is employed by the corporation, which structures everyone's life. Government is handled by bureaucrats and retired workers, while everyone else lives by a system of rewards and demerits. Pneumatic tubes distribute goods from the centralized warehouses to the charming, middle-class neighborhoods where everyone lives. It is a radically structured world; like Marx's dictatorship of the proletariat, one power controls both the political and economic spheres of society. Bellamy's utopia sparked a brief sensation and inspired clubs in both the United States and Britain which attempted to effect his vision. William Morris, however, detested the world of Bellamy's imagination.

In a review for the *Commonweal*, Morris rejected Bellamy's utopia as too regimented: "a machine life is the best which Bellamy can imagine for us on all sides; it is not to be wondered at then that his only idea of making labour tolerable is to decrease the amount of it by means of fresh and ever fresh developments in machinery."[48] What attracted Morris to radical social theories was not the fantasy of controlling society, but rather the ancient promise of creating a golden age, in which the emotional needs of human beings were fulfilled through spiritually rewarding labor. What attracted him to Marxism was not the dictatorship of the proletariat, but the classless society afterward; unlike Marx, he saw the revolution not as a means to industrialize society, but rather to renounce the dehumanization of industrialization.

While writing *News From Nowhere*, Morris was distancing himself from the anarchist wing of the Socialist League. Michael Holzman writes that "when readers of *Commonweal* saw the opening lines of *News from Nowhere* on the front page of the January 11, 1890 issue, they knew that Morris was making a major (and last) statement concerning the anarchist faction that had taken over control of his league."[49] By 1890, accusations of anarchism were commonly used to tar the reputations of all other radical movements, and many leftist organizations were distancing themselves from anarchists in order to avoid guilt by association; Morris's condemnations of anarchism follow the lead of Marx, who ousted the Bakuninist faction from the International in 1871. Morris also had reservations about anarchist theory. Morris's argument with anarchist theory was the weakness of its decision-making mechanism, as well as the anarchists' firm stance against all institutions, including trade unions. The extreme individualism of some anarchists meant, according to Morris, that a small minority could destroy any consensus and consequently no communal work would be possible. This was ideological purity carried, in Morris's view, to the point of silliness, and it impelled him to abandon the League which he had worked hard to build up.

The revolution which brings about Morris's utopia is decidedly Marxist. In the face of capitalist exploitation and government repression, the workers of nearly all wage-paying occupations form one grand union. This union succeeds in winning reforms, but the conflicts inherent between the capitalists and the union lead inexorably, in an escalating, dialectical fashion, to a revolution, in which the workers persevere in the face of a divided capitalist class. The only allusion to anarchists during the description of revolution is a mention of the fear of dynamite as a justification for the soldiers to fire on workers[50]; anarchists encourage resistance to the revolution rather than hasten it. Morris does not deal with the transition from revolution to utopia except to say that, gradually, people realized what would make them happiest; the people who lead the revolution gracefully step aside once the fighting is over. It is the unified stand of the working class that succeeds in carrying the revolution, not the spontaneous anti-authoritarian revolution which requires no planning for which the anarchists hoped. This criticism of anarchism would not have been lost on Morris's readers.

Morris's criticism of anarchism is evident from the opening lines of *News From Nowhere*. He describes the composition of a group that is discussing the nature of society after the revolution: "there were six persons present, and consequently six sections of the party were represented, four of which had strong but divergent anarchist opinions" (1). Despite the vociferous debate, the narrator is unable to recall any of the arguments on the subway ride home. The debate in which none of the anarchists can agree with each other is pointless; all these differences of opinion amount to nothing.

Despite his criticism of anarchism as a means of bringing about the revolution, Morris nevertheless found the idea of noncoercive, locally based social groups appealing, and this anarchistic idea serves as the basic form of organization in his utopia. Guest, the main character, discusses social administration with Hammond, an historian of the future. The custom of the small, local units of administration in *News From Nowhere* is to propose something at one meeting, vote at the next meeting, and act only when a clear majority has agreed on the course of action. Morris skirts the problem—an intransigent minority—by having his utopian factions be as well-behaved and reasonable as William Godwin could hope for; it is unreasonable to persist in a minority opinion, so the minority will gracefully give way. To attempt to order society through pure individualist anarchism is laughable:

> "There is something in this [system of administration] very like democracy . . ."
> Said he: "The only alternatives to our method that I can conceive of are these. First, that we should choose out, or breed, a class of superior persons capable of judging on all matters without consulting the neighbors; that, in short, we should get for ourselves what used to be called an aristocracy of intellect; or, secondly, that we for the purpose of safeguarding the freedom of the individual will, we should revert to a system of private property once more. What do you think of those two expedients?"
> "Well," said I, "there is a third possibility—to wit, that every man should be quite independent of every other, and that thus the tyranny of society should be abolished."
> He looked hard at me for a second or two, and then burst out laughing very heartily; and I confess that I joined him. (76)

Pure individualism, in which every person is completely independent of everyone else, runs so contrary to Morris's vision of human nature that it does not even merit serious consideration. Although this kind of individualism was extreme even for an anarchist (Kropotkin, for example, argued in favor of local communities similar to the ones Morris describes), several members of Morris's League had argued such a position, which Morris thought contradicted the pressing need for collective action in order to prepare for the revolution.

Despite his insistence on a Marxist revolution and his hatred of Bellamy's ideas, Morris is motivated by an ideal of society which rejects industrialization in favor of individual craftsmanship and rejects the authority of a central institution in favor of local control, to the point that the inhabitants of his utopia cannot remember what the "national" in "National Gallery" means and consequently have one in nearly every community.

In *News From Nowhere*, Morris expresses an optimistic view of human nature. Given the right system of rewards and education, people want to work and to live in cooperative communities. Morris's optimistic opinion of human nature was radically at odds with the social Darwinist narrative, which stressed the competition between individuals and the basic desire to avoid work as inherent parts of human nature. In addition, Morris's anti-industrialism was anachronistic in its opposition to material progress, however well-reasoned his position may have been. Peter Kropotkin, anarchist and scientist, would attack the narratives which justified capitalism directly in order to convince readers that the optimistic view of human nature was justified by science, and that anarchism could be more than a laughable dream.

KROPOTKIN'S *MUTUAL AID* AND THE ATTACK ON SOCIAL DARWINISM

In the newspapers of the day, conservative writers rejected radical opinions by employing the language of natural law. In America, William Graham Sumner rejected any notion of justice or morality in social concerns as mere Romantic sentiment, and in England Thomas Huxley eagerly applied Darwinian concepts to all social institutions. One major anarchist writer, Peter Kropotkin, chose to challenge the claims of the capitalists on their home turf, scientific discourse. In *Mutual Aid*[51] (1890–96), Kropotkin presented an alternative understanding of natural selection; he depicts examples of communal behavior in both the animal kingdom and human history and challenges the social Darwinist's emphasis on individual survival.

William Graham Sumner attacked radicalism at its roots in an optimistic vision of human nature. Like many of his contemporaries, Sumner sees in history evidence of a deterministic natural law which equates progress with increasing authority and centralization. Conditions are as they are because the laws of the universe have made them so; chief among those laws are economic forces of supply and demand and the human need for material goods. Nonmaterial needs are rejected in Sumner's thoughts as mere superstitions or delusions. In a series of articles for the *Independent* published in 1887 and 1889, Sumner attacked Rousseau's notion of the noble and free savage. Rousseau and other enlightenment philosophers created the concept of the noble savage by

> abstracting one after another the attributes of the civilized man, until a sort of residuum was obtained . . . [Rousseau] took the notion of the red man as European travelers had described him before the middle of the eighteenth century, and, having rounded off the notion with some poetical additions, he went on to make his deductions as to civilization.[52]

In contrast, Sumner claims that he is building on scientific research into the actual conditions of primitive man. For Sumner, the native

American "is far back in civilization when regarded from the standpoint of civilized man; but if he is regarded with reference to the real and ultimate origin of society, he is very far on up the scale." Native Americans have many organizational technologies that allow them to exploit the land that at the same time constrict the liberty of the individual to "do as he likes," in an echo of Arnold's phrase. The noble savage, according to Sumner, would have found the modern conception of liberty meaningless, because all of that savage's energies would have been devoted to earning a living. Freedom of choice is only possible when one has earned some material security, and that security only becomes possible at more advanced stages of social organization. Advanced social organization, although it gives the civilized man "a measure of liberty under the natural conditions of life," also "form[s] bonds which create duties and obligations which constrain liberty."[53] All human historical development, in Sumner's depiction, is an advance of social and technological abilities to extract human material needs from nature at the cost of increasing individual discipline; this discipline is preferable, however, to the harsh struggle for material existence outside civilization and its institutions. While other writers glossed over the inherent contradiction between individual freedom and social order, Sumner mounts the argument that order is preferable, and that conservative thinking is the driving force behind civilization.

The eighteenth-century social philosophers and their nineteenth-century anarchistic descendants repeat the same erroneous fiction that liberty to do as one likes is a "natural right," and the sheer numbers of the lower classes that are primitive enough to be swayed by such arguments present a real danger which must, to echo Matthew Arnold's argument, be met with education. "The eighteenth-century notions of liberty and equality have passed into the most cherished faiths of the nineteenth century. That notion of liberty is an anarchistic notion. It is the conception according to which liberty means unrestrainedness, emancipation from law, lawlessness, and antagonism to law."[54] The very notion represents a slippery slope, because "it is supposed that the Anarchists carry it to some exaggeration, but there is no apparent rule for drawing the line to discriminate error from the truth."[55] The danger lies in following abstract conceptions rather than concrete social science, in a philosophy based in "Romanticism" rather than reason.

In fact, Sumner argues, there is no liberty apart from security of property: "liberty and property go together, and sustain each other in glorious accord." It is this true liberty which anarchists in particular threaten. "Anarchists and nihilists, accepting the notion that liberty is all strength, elevate revolution to the highest function as a redeeming and reforming force; to destroy and tear down becomes a policy of wisdom and growth . . . everything which has grown as an institution is an obstacle to that ideal of primitive poverty and simplicity confused with liberty."[56] This passage echoes Bakunin's famous saying, "the urge to destroy is also a creative urge," as well as the disastrous policy of propaganda by the deed which some anarchists adopted as their own in the 1880s; Sumner's use of the specter of violence against property transforms the anarchists into a group which worships brute force and attempts to cast all humanity into a Hobbesian savagery. Ever the pessimist, Sumner updates Hobbes's own vision of a basically depraved human nature by placing it in the language of materialism and the natural laws of the marketplace, which force human beings to progress almost despite themselves.

Anarchism's optimism about human nature can be clearly seen in the writing of Peter Kropotkin, the most widely published anarchist writer of the late nineteenth and early twentieth centuries. Trained as a scientist, Kropotkin attempted to place anarchism on the same rhetorical footing as capitalism by revising the capitalist interpretation of Darwin in his book, *Mutual Aid: A Factor of Evolution*. Kropotkin's analysis of the shared social nature of all human endeavor aligns nineteenth-century anarchism with other criticisms of economic individualism and capitalism. Kropotkin attempts to refute the social Darwinist idea of competition among individuals as the primary mode of progress by arguing that cooperation among individuals within species is at least as important to progress, if not more so. Just as Huxley, Sumner, and others portrayed a consistent pattern from the world of animals to the historical development of human social institutions, so Kropotkin tries to show a consistent pattern of mutual aid in both the natural world and in human social development.

Mutual Aid was written in response to an essay by T. H. Huxley published in the February 1888 issue of the *Nineteenth Century*.[57] This article, "The Struggle for Existence," combined a Hobbesian vision of human nature with a Malthusian vision of natural selection that was a popular intellectual position at the time. Like other animals, primitive human beings in their small family groups were forced to compete with each other for life's necessities: "the weakest and stupidest went to the wall, while the toughest and shrewdest, those who were best fitted to cope with their circumstances, survived" (332). However, at some point in human prehistory, people banded together. "The first men who substituted the state of mutual peace for that of mutual war, whatever the motive which impelled them to take that step, created society" (332). There is no obvious reason to have a society, since society, which impels human beings to control their natural impulses, has to work against "the deep-seated organic impulses which impel the natural man to follow his non-moral course" (332). Like Freud and others, Huxley believes human beings to be naturally pathological and only tenuously held in check by social institutions. The same social institutions which create peace carry the seeds of their own destruction; as Malthus theorized, populations increase to exceed the capacity of their food supply, so that even in advanced societies the struggle of each against all for survival is inevitable. This narrative bolsters a conservative ideology by shifting the balance between freedom and order in favor of order by defining the universe as overwhelmingly deterministic. The challenge of government—the only purpose of which is to preserve some semblance of peace and property—is to prevent a critical mass of people from being plunged into such despair that revolution results: "The animal man, finding that the ethical man has landed him in such a slough, resumes his ancient sovereignty, and preaches anarchy; which is, substantially, a proposal to reduce the social cosmos to chaos, and begin the brute struggle for existence once again" (335). This argument expands the metaphor of anarchism as atavism to the entire human race. In Huxley's world, the only alternative to savage economic competition is anarchy and starvation; the only real solution is a combination of technical education and improved sanitation in the poorer urban areas, to give those who are not doomed to fail through vice a chance to rise.

Like Sumner in the United States, Huxley in England used scientific discourse, which has wide authority, to bolster the language and ideology of individualistic capitalism. Ricardo and Smith's concept of the atomistic economic individual is combined with the neo-Darwinian concept of individual competition as the mainspring of the social mechanism. In this model, the government's role is simply to preserve an order which allows individuals to accumulate wealth, property, and power; an attempt to manipulate these natural forces toward more "moral" ends would be doomed to failure. This argument caught members of the more traditional middle class in a dilemma: they could reject the scientific discourse in which terms this argument had been couched, or they could reject the language of civic responsibility that permeated their religious discourse. The advocates of individualistic capitalism presented a resolution for this dilemma in the claim that these natural forces had a beneficent effect; people could pursue their individual interests and benefit society at the same time. Poor and miserable people existed because of individual failings, not policy or greed.

Most anarchists appealed to people for whom these more established discourses had already lost currency; for a desperate and dispossessed audience, the appeal of blood, revenge, and revolution is understandable. In *Mutual Aid*, Kropotkin argued his vision of communitarian anarchism by re-signifying the quasi-scientific narratives which Huxley, Sumner, and others had used to buttress the arguments of laissez-faire capitalists.

Kropotkin was aware of the shift of meaning which individual capitalists had effected in discussions of Darwin and of the ways in which this intentional misunderstanding of Darwin affected other discourses. Although careful not to dismiss the effects of individual effort and individual greed in both human behavior and social institutions, Kropotkin argues that the contributions of the many have been systematically undervalued in literature and history in favor of the story of the few, so that vital contributions to human prosperity were forgotten in favor of hero worship. Kropotkin saw that many common behaviors were not motivated by desire for individual gain so much as an awareness of common suffering; society itself was dependent upon people acting from communal, not selfish, motives.

This voluntary mutual assistance is instinctive, Kropotkin argues. The impulse to mutual aid is impossible to eradicate because it is both an innate human impulse and the best strategy for coping with the environment. In the animal world, the successes of creatures who employ techniques of mutual aid are evident: bees, ants, and herd animals are all successful despite their individual weaknesses. The keys to this non individualistic success are the cooperative and intellectual capacities of the creatures involved:

> While fully admitting that force, swiftness, protective colours, cunningness, and endurance to hunger and cold, which are so often mentioned by Darwin and Wallace, are so many qualities making the individual, or the species, the fittest under certain circumstances, we maintain that under *any* circumstances sociability is the greatest advantage in the struggle for life. Those species which willingly abandon it are doomed to decay; while those animals which best know how to combine, have the greatest chances of survival and of further evolution, although they may be inferior to others in *each* of the faculties enumerated by Darwin and Wallace, save the intellectual faculty. (57)

Kropotkin sees this principle at work everywhere; he first came to understand the concept while looking for evidence that the battle for survival was a battle between individuals of the same species. Kropotkin found that the battle for survival does not always go to the species with the best individuals; often, the species best able to adapt and thrive does so through cooperation and mutual aid.

When survival in the environment depends upon cooperation, self-seeking at the expense of others is at best an eccentricity and quickly develops into a pathology. Observing bees, Kropotkin comments on the interaction between the forces of mutual aid, which dictate that individual bees should work together for the common benefit, and individualism, which encourages each bee to seek out her own fortune at the expense of others if necessary:

> We thus see that anti-social instincts continue to exist amidst the bees as well; but natural selection continually must eliminate them, because in the long run the practice of solidarity proves much more advantageous to the species than the development of individuals endowed with predatory inclinations. The cunningest and shrewdest are eliminated in favour of those who understand the advantages of sociable life and mutual support. (17–18)

This passage replies to individualists who would argue that collectivism is a slippery slope which inevitably destroys individual variation and initiative. In keeping with his overall project, Kropotkin argues that natural law enforces the importance of collective over individual fortune. The advantage which sociability confers to a group of individuals is so great that selfish individuals are naturally culled out—not by other bees, but by the periodic lean times of a given climate.

Crucial to Kropotkin's refutation of the social Darwinists is a rebuttal of Malthusian doctrines of population growth. Whereas Malthus saw the food supply of a given area as a constant and the growth of a given population to that maximum as inevitable, Kropotkin emphasizes a climate's variability as a determining factor of population size. Populations do not automatically rise to consume the theoretical maximum food supply, because that supply is never constant:

> We have good reasons to believe that want of animal population is the natural state of things all over the world, with but a few temporary exceptions to the rule. The actual numbers of animals in a given region are determined, not by the highest feeding capacity of the region, but by what it is every year under the most unfavorable conditions. (69)

The greatest threat to individual survival is not other individuals, but weather and illness. Populations will take years to recover from harsh winters, periodic droughts, plagues, and climactic changes that occur over time. In addition, animals will usually strive to avoid harsh competition by relocating or altering their food supply over time. Kropotkin uses the example of North America: the expanding population of horses and cattle did not starve the existing herbivores, so clearly the plains were capable of feeding a much greater population than was there originally. Through this argument, Kropotkin shifts the focus (and larger significance) of Darwinism from the celebration of powerful individuals to the collective struggle against environmental conditions.

Only occasionally do populations strip the ability of the climate to sustain their numbers. This does not lead to improvement of the species (as the social Darwinists would argue), but rather the weakening of all members of the species:

> If natural selection were limited in its action to periods of exceptional drought, or sudden changes in temperature, or inundations, retrogression would be the rule in the animal world. Those who survive a famine, or a severe epidemic of cholera, or small-pox, or diphtheria, such as we see them in uncivilized countries, are neither the strongest, or the healthiest, not the most intelligent. No progress could be based on those survivals—the less so as all survivors usually come out of the ordeal with an impaired health. (73)

Malthus's world never progresses, because the factors which determine one's odds of surviving a calamity are not identical to those which bring progress. The very harshness of the competition he describes would weaken all members of a population and reward not those best able to compete under normal conditions, but those who were merely able to survive the calamity through fortune or endurance.

When Kropotkin observes behavior in nature, he does not find keen competition among individuals. Rather, he finds the opposite: "better conditions are created by the *elimination of competition* by means of mutual aid and mutual support" (74). The way of nature is to avoid competition when possible, through storage of food, hibernation, migration, and expansion of territory. "And when animals can neither fall asleep, nor migrate, nor lay in stores, nor themselves grow food like the ants, they . . . resort to new kinds of food—and thus, again, avoid competition" (75). Whereas the social Darwinists find competition to be the law preached by nature, Kropotkin finds its opposite. Nature, he says, preaches cooperation among individuals to reduce the threat of natural variability, which is the chief threat to populations.

Kropotkin's naturalism, like that of the social Darwinists, lies not in describing nature, but in creating a metaphor for guiding human behavior. Human beings, Kropotkin argues, are no different from other social animals in their strategies of surviving in the natural world.

Kropotkin transfers his naturalistic observations into a prescription for human society. By observing the nonhuman world and the record of human development, Kropotkin and Huxley both assume they will find some essential concept of humanity that will serve as a persuasive guideline for human behaviors. However, Kropotkin and Huxley's assumptions lead them to widely different interpretations. Because the only human institution that exists outside the state in modern times is the family, Huxley and others assume that the only alternative to the state is the family unit; therefore, they conclude, primitive human beings must have lived in isolated families. In an echo of Sumner's critique of Rousseau's abstract vision of primitive man, Kropotkin claims that Hobbes' and Huxley's vision has little beyond arbitrary ideology to support it:

> It may be remarked at once that Huxley's view of nature had as little claim to be taken as a scientific deduction as the opposite view of Rousseau . . . Rousseau had committed the error of excluding the beak-and-claw fight from his thoughts; and Huxley committed the opposite error; but neither Rousseau's optimism nor Huxley's pessimism can be accepted as an impartial interpretation of nature. (5)

Kropotkin (with many citations from archaeologists to support his position) argues that social technologies predate physical technologies. "At a time when men were dwelling in caves, or under occasionally protruding rocks, in company with mammals now extinct, and hardly succeeded in making the roughest sorts of flint hatchets, they already knew the advantages of life in societies" (80). The key to human survival, then, has not been the gradual expansion of technology, as Sumner argues, but the same original cooperative impulse that allows bees and ants to thrive while more individualistic species have declined. "Sociability and the need of mutual aid and support are such inherent parts of human nature that at no time of history can we discover men living in small isolated families, fighting each other for the means of subsistence" (153). Human beings naturally prefer cooperative local communities as a part of the instinctual desire to render mutual aid.

Kropotkin's history of Europe is a history of peaceful settlers clearing forests, tilling land, and wishing only to be safe from the roving bands of plunderers who were a peripheral, if dangerous, part of life. In fact, "the very peacefulness of the barbarians, certainly not their supposed warlike instincts, thus became the source of their eventual subjection to the military chieftains" (155). By raid and plunder, the roving warriors could deprive men of the means of making the land productive (such as cattle and iron for plows). The peaceful barbarians, driven to starvation, would then accept servitude, working the land and exchanging the food they produced for the warlord's protection. The warlords began to accumulate wealth by reducing others to poverty, as all wealth has been created throughout history, according to Kropotkin.

This premise raises an objection: if human beings originally lived in happy anarchistic villages and only by force accepted feudal servitude, why did they come to accept the authority of kings and, later, nations? Kropotkin argues that the early arbitrators of disputes gradually began to assume the rhetorical authority of law. Over time, the judicial and executive function was usurped by the king, and people who had once been free and peaceful were now under the nominal dominion of a feudal ruler. Through a process of reification, what was once temporary and man-made became permanent and ordained.

This process was resisted at times, most notably by the free cities of medieval Europe. Kropotkin sees the rebirth of voluntary cooperative behavior—the revolt against the clerical and feudal lords which occurred spontaneously—as a prototype of an anarchist revolution. This time of free cities was itself a utopian time, argues Kropotkin:

> They had covered the country with beautiful sumptuous buildings, expressing the genius of free unions of free men, unrivaled for their beauty and expressiveness; and they bequeathed to the following generations all the arts, all the industries, of which our present civilization, with all its achievements and promises for the future, is only a further development. (163)

Kropotkin locates the central tenets of guild-based social organization in the free association of equals voluntarily engaged in common pursuits. In the guild, every member was equal, and every member was pledged to the aid of his fellows. Instead of having agents of the feudal lord as judges, the members of the guild would elect judges out of their fellowship; the guilds, Kropotkin avers, prospered because they served the basic human needs of union and support without depriving the individual of personal authority and initiative.

His grand claims for these cities and their supposedly nonauthoritarian social structures form a bridge between the animal societies and human ones and are a key part of his communalistic argument.

Kropotkin picks several facets of the economic operation of free cities as a way of criticizing the capitalistic social organization of his own time. He notes that " 'Production' did not absorb the whole attention of the Mediaeval economist. With his practical mind, he understood that 'consumption' must be guaranteed in order to obtain production; and therefore, to provide for 'the common first food and lodging of poor and rich alike' was the fundamental principle in each city" (181). To secure adequate supplies for all, most cities forbade the selling of goods to retailers before they had reached the common market and been available for some specified time. Even after a shopkeeper bought goods, he was limited to an "honest profit" from the goods he wished to resell. In many cases, the city itself would buy goods from neighboring towns for the benefit of all citizens. The medieval city was more than a political union; it was a society of mutual aid and support which joined the social and economic life of the town without depriving citizens of their freedoms in a bureaucratic manner.

This golden age of association ends, according to Kropotkin, through a combination of the unscrupulous machinations of the feudal lords, who had based their power in the castle and lands outside of the cities, and the refusal of the cities to expand their society to the surrounding rural areas on which they depended:

> Instead of looking upon the peasants and artisans who gathered under the protection of his walls as upon so many aids who would contribute their part to the making of the city—as they really did—a sharp division was traced between the 'families' of old burghers and the new-comers. For the former, all the benefits of communal trade and communal lands was reserved, and nothing was left for the latter but the right of freely using the skill of their own hands. (218)

In this way, what had been a free association of individuals bound by geography and common goals had become a state, using law to protect the power of a minority at the expense of others. Within the cities was a growing population that had little allegiance to the city because its participation in the life of the city was limited by law. Blinded to the importance of cooperative endeavor by their greed, the decadent cities were eventually subdued by the kings.

Kropotkin claims that the rise and fall of these cities exemplify the power of ideas over people. The old ideas of "self-reliance and

federalism, the sovereignty of each group, and the construction of
the political body from the simple to the composite" were changed
through the preaching of "the students of Roman law and the prel-
ates of the Church," who held that "salvation must be sought for in
a strongly centralized State, placed under a semi-divine authority;
that one man can and must be the savior of society, and that in the
name of public salvation he can commit any violence" (220). The
people put their faith in governing institutions rather than in themselves, and "the very creative genius of the masses died out" (221).
Although what Kropotkin terms the "Roman idea" of the central,
bureaucratic state is still in hegemony, he finds the idea of mutual
aid still alive, and with his eternal optimism looks for the coming of
a new model of humane social organization.

So long as the language of natural law had hegemony, the vast
expansion in corporate structure and power could be defined as
simply a natural progression, outside human control. These concepts reinforced one another: the way in which individuals succeeded through the mechanism of the corporation justified its
existence in terms of natural law, although it was the expansive notion of private property defended by the state which allowed individuals to accumulate great power. It was an age which celebrated a
heroic ideal of classicism in its architecture and in its language, and
the "Roman ideal" which Kropotkin decried was effectively used to
celebrate the triumph of capitalism. The ability to share in this triumph was one of the chief reasons for the corporation's social success within the expanding middle class. The means by which a
young man of the middle classes could share in corporate glory
were defined by the numerous biographies of prominent capitalists
(such as those of Elbert Hubbard) which were written at the time.
Many writers instinctively used the anarchist as a foil to this trium-
phalist narrative of capitalism.

THE GREAT CAPITALIST IN FICTION: THE OCTOPUS AND
THE MEMOIRS OF AN AMERICAN CITIZEN

Fiction writers did not ignore the powerful symbol of the individualist, entrepreneurial hero in their works. By taking the capitalist
out of his element, however, American writers such as Frank Norris
and Robert Herrick could demonstrate the power as well as the in-
adequacies of this vision of heroic humanity through a language
outside the discourse of business. In *The Octopus*[58] Frank Norris
focuses on the innate superiority of the individual who governs the

impersonal forces of the marketplace and the wh_
oirs of an American Citizen[59] Robert Herrick strips _ne Mem_-
ism of the capitalist down to the bare bones—the gras_ividual_-
ambition that lay at the heart of the narrative of the succ_moral
talist—and shows how forces outside themselves make, a_api-
sionally almost break, entrepreneurs.   _a-

Norris's project in the "trilogy of the wheat" (of which *The O_
pus* is the first book) is to trace the path of the wheat from its plan_
ing in California, through its market transfer in Chicago, to its
consumption in Europe. By telling the story of humanity's use of
natural bounty, he demonstrates what he believes is the interaction
of human activity with ultimately beneficent natural laws. Norris
embraces the language of materialist economics, and his characters
can either accommodate themselves to the deterministic laws of
natural supply and demand, or selfishly overreach and risk destruction by those impersonal forces. Although some critics have seen in
The Octopus a traditional romantic exaltation of the agrarian over
the industrial, Norris is well aware of the capitalistic nature of
large-scale agriculture. Through Presley, the idealistic artist-figure,
Norris guides the reader from a romantic naiveté regarding the me-
chanics of capitalism, through a hostile reaction to the institutional
forces of the corporation, and finally to a distanced faith in the beneficence of the market forces as a part of natural law. Presley's
conversion comes during an interview with the great capitalist Shelgrim, who controls the railroad that acts as the arteries and veins
of the vast corporate machine.

The tension of *The Octopus* is not so much between ranchers and
railroad managers as it is between individuals and the natural
forces that they seek to exploit for their individual gain. Donald
Pizer has observed that this moral ambivalence seems contrary to
an assumed romantic attitude on Norris's part. Donald Pizer argues
that the ranchers seek to exploit the land, and the railroad seeks to
exploit the need for transport; neither has a monopoly on virtue.
"The ranchers and the railroad fail to realize the omnipotence and
benevolence of the natural law of supply and demand which deter-
mines the production and the distribution of wheat. Both groups
greedily exploit the demand for wheat, the first by speculative "bo-
nanza" farming, the second by monopoly of transportation" (159).
According to Pizer, Norris disapproves of the shortsightedness that
transforms natural bounty into human misery, but is fascinated by
individuals who strive to combine the forces of nature and the machinery of the market.[60] The shift in focus away from the story of the
successful individual to the story of challenges posed by the larger

ι parallels the rhetorical shifts made by Kropotkin in
envi, d.
Mu, terconnectedness of the modern world, both through na-
rd its metaphorical analog, the market, is a recurrent theme
be Octopus. On a symbolic level, Norris relates the rhythms of
'human world to the natural rhythms of the wheat's growth
ycle; more fascinating are the technologies that integrate this production into a worldwide market of supply and demand. All the
ranchers in the San Joaquin valley have market tickers in their offices, which relay the going price of wheat on the Chicago exchange.
When the market is active, the ranchers will sit and monitor the rise
and fall of the value of their harvest: "At such moments they no
longer felt their individuality. The ranch became merely part of an
enormous whole, a unit in the vast agglomeration of wheat land the
whole world round, feeling the effects of causes a thousand miles
distant" (54).[61] The ranchers occupy a place between the grindstone
of nature and the wheel of the worldwide marketplace.

While the ranchers facilitate the growth of the wheat and feel the
effects of commodity traders half a continent away, the Pacific and
Southwestern railroad supplies the transport which this system demands. In the mixed metaphors of mechanistic natural forces which
Norris employs as a framework for his story, the railroad is as much
a part of the mechanism of the wheat as the ranchers are. The railroad itself is described in a complex metaphor:

> The whole map was gridironed by a vast, complicated network of red
> lines marked P. and S. W. R. R. . . . . a veritable system of blood circula-
> tion, complicated, dividing, and reuniting, branching, splitting, extend-
> ing, throwing out feelers, off-shots, tap roots, feeders—diminutive little
> blood suckers that shot out from the main jugular and went twisting up
> into some remote county, laying hold upon some forgotten village or
> town, involving it in one of a myriad branching coils, one of a hundred
> tentacles, drawing it, as it were, toward that centre from which all this
> system sprang.
> The map was white, as if all of the color which should have gone to
> vivify the various counties, towns, and cities marked upon it had been
> absorbed by that huge, sprawling organism, with its ruddy arteries con-
> verging to a central point. (289)

The railroad first overlays the map as a technological artifact—a
"gridiron"—only to quickly become the circulatory system for the
organism that is California. However, this circulatory system is also
parasitic; the railroad withholds the necessary life force from the
outlying regions that depend on the railroad for survival. Norris de-

scribes an organism in which the heart is holding the arms and legs hostage, acting as both a life-giver and a parasite. This metaphor accurately captures his ambivalence toward the railroads: they are an essential part of the global market system of modern capitalism, but their natural (and legally bolstered) monopoly makes them powerful enough to exploit all the other agents in the market. Although all the ranchers are human beings with faults and vices, the owner of the railroad seems to transcend mere humanity.

Shelgrim is the mysterious individual behind the monopolistic Pacific and Southwestern Railroad of *The Octopus*. The corporate giant and owner of the Pacific and Southwestern rail road is "a giant figure in the end-of-the-century finance, a product of circumstance, an inevitable result of conditions, characteristic, typical, symbolic of ungovernable forces" (104). The creation of a market on such a scale creates a demand for men who are larger than life, and, in the mechanism of capitalist economics, every demand creates a supply. Norris repeats the panegyrics to the genius of those who run large corporations, as Presley is humbled by the penetration of a man who saves the job of a drunken clerk, then criticizes Presley's own poem based on a French painting. Presley is overwhelmed:

> No standards of measurement in his mental equipment would apply to the actual man, and it began to dawn on him that possibly it was not because these standards were different in kind, but that they were lamentably deficient in size. He began to see that there was a man not only great, but large; many-sided, of vast sympathies, who understood with equal intelligence, the human nature in an habitual drunkard, the ethics of a masterpiece of painting, and the financiering and operation of ten thousand miles of railroad. (574–75)

Despite his superhuman greatness, Shelgrim makes Presley believe that he is subject to the same forces which govern the ranchers in the San Joaquin valley; the railroad is a force of nature. "The Wheat is one force, the Railroad, another, and there is the law that governs them—supply and demand. Men have only little to do with the whole business" (576). Shelgrim cannot control the road, any more than the ranchers can control the wheat; as far as the exploitation and the violence, Shelgrim advises Presley to "blame conditions, not men" (576). Despite his natural sympathy with the workers and ranchers, Norris's use of language that has been defined by capitalists leads to the illogical conclusion that no one is responsible. There is no reasonable cause for the ranchers' resistance to the railroads; the railroad must be run according to the logic of the financial markets, and it is only the poor understanding of the ranchers that leads them to violence. The rhetoric of natural law, combined with the force of personality invested in the individual who symbolizes the railroad trust, transforms a human institution—the market—into something that operates outside of human control. Ironically, the mechanism of the market is more important than the people who created that market, and whose needs it ostensibly serves.

Nevertheless, Norris tries to find some alternative to this universe of inhuman natural forces of supply and demand. Opposed to Shelgrim and his grasping, ever voracious trust is Cedarquist, the benevolent industrialist. Like Andrew Carnegie, Cedarquist tries to combine a faith in the market with an older humanistic moral sense. Although Shelgrim is constantly portrayed as an invisible hand manipulating events, Cedarquist is active in the social life of the community and is concerned about the welfare of communities around the world. Cedarquist personally organizes a shipment of wheat to Indian communities that have been racked by famine. This charity also serves a business interest, as Cedarquist hopes to create a new market for California wheat in the East, circumventing the railroad monopoly of transport to Europe. In this way, the forces of supply and demand will, in the long run, naturally counteract the exploitation of individuals. Monopoly, although successful in the short term, ultimately runs counter to the law of supply and demand. By arguing that the market will naturally correct these abuses without outside interference, Norris echoes the faith of some moderate antitrust activists in the benevolence of the god of the market.

Norris, although believing in the ultimate beneficence of the market in the abstract, provides little hope for reform of the monopolies that the market creates. While Cedarquist is sending wheat to India, Mrs. Dyke, driven to wander the streets of San Francisco after being dispossessed by the railroad, dies of hunger.

If the trust triumphs, then the dispossessed will be more attracted to the violence of anarchy, Norris warns. Even in this novel, the anarchist is invoked as a threat of a nihilism which capitalism insists lies outside the limits of civilization. Egged on by the anarchist bartender Caraher and their own sense of desperation, both Dyke and Presley engage in acts of individual terrorism against the railroads. Dyke, a former engineer who has been fired by the railroad, tries to become a hop farmer, only to have the railroad raise the rates to transport hops past the level at which he could make any profit. He then becomes a train robber and is hunted down; his wife and daughter are left to starve in San Francisco. Presley, distraught over the railroad posse's murder of several ranchers during a showdown near an irrigation ditch, listens to the violent rhetoric of the bartender and then throws a pipe bomb into Berhman's home; Behrman is unhurt. Neither action produces any meaningful change. Norris uses these incidents to denounce revolutionary violence as pointless:

> Caraher was nonetheless an evil influence among the ranchers, an influence that worked only to the inciting of crime. Unwilling to venture himself, to risk his own life, the anarchist saloon-keeper had goaded Dyke and Presley both to murder; a bad man, a plague spot in the world of the ranchers, poisoning the farmers' bodies with alcohol and their minds with discontent. (620)

Anarchism, as conventionally portrayed within the discourse of the capitalist market "system," has only destructive possibilities. The anarchist is portrayed as an individual coward, unwilling to take responsibility for his actions as well as those actions he inspires others to commit. The echoes of the Haymarket verdict resonate in this passage, as Caraher is found guilty of murder for his violent words against the railroad trust. These individual attacks against corporate power are quixotic and dangerous. The anarchist saloon-keeper reinforces the perception of anarchist philosophy as a refuge for poor losers in the great marketplace competition.

Although violence may be unable to solve the social and moral problems that arise out of the workings of the marketplace, Norris does see the threat of violence as a warning and a call for reform. While eating with Gerard, a vice president of the railroad, Presley has a vision whose details mimic the descriptions of capitalists in the anarchist press:

> All these fine ladies with their small fingers and slender necks, suddenly were transfigured in his tortured mind into harpies tearing human flesh. His head swam with the horror of it, the terror of it. Yes, the People *would* turn some day, and turning, rend those who now preyed upon them. It would be "dog eat dog" again, with the positions reversed, and he saw for one instant of time that splendid house sacked to its foundations, the tables overturned, the pictures torn, the hangings blazing, and Liberty, the red-handed Man in the Street, grimed with powder smoke, foul with the gutter, rush yelling, torch in hand, through every door. (608–9)

The language of revolution bursts into the small conversation of the rich; like a scene from the French Revolution, the abstraction of "the People" will destroy this civilization, taking the good and the bad together. Norris, who accepts the premise that the only possibility of progress is through the "laws" of capitalism, accepts its corollary: any deviation from capitalism will destroy the good in society as well as the bad. Violence is no answer, but the monopoly, which works against natural market forces to benefit a few individuals, will produce this violence as a natural counterreaction if the trust is not reformed.

Having accepted the language of the world that proclaims the institutions of corporate capitalism to be both natural and inevitable and rejected the language of revolution that allows for the possibility of a world constructed along different ideals, Norris has forced himself down a blind alley. The narratives of his chosen discourse show little relief from the grind of the monopoly, and, in keeping with the conservative rhetoric of the time, liberty in a political and moral sense can only be destructive. By accepting the conservative rhetoric of individualism and natural law, Norris has ruled out any form of cooperation except the hierarchical, authoritarian, capitalist-dominated corporation. Norris's only escape is an older American discourse, the civic pride of the older middle class, as a means to harness the forces of the market for social good rather than individual gain. Norris has little faith in a language that does not recognize the overarching power of the market, and he sees such change coming slowly, if at all. Meanwhile, Lyman Derrick, the railroad's man on the Railroad Commission, is now a candidate for governor; the corporation exerts control over the civic institutions as well.

Although Norris embraces the positivism implied in the language of natural law to supply his otherwise bleak picture with optimism, the Chicago writer Robert Herrick was too disgusted with the workings of the market that surrounded him to hold such faith in the working of the marketplace. In *The Memoir of an American Citizen*, Herrick parodies the cult of success that grew around the often repeated narratives of entrepreneurial biography. Herrick's successful businessman is no superhuman titan, such as Shelgrim in *The Octopus*. Herrick's businessmen are small-minded, grasping men, content to bleed as much wealth and power as they can out of a system which they may find disturbing, but never question. Far from being the product of individual prowess, Herrick's businessmen make their money through corrupt business practices, favoritism, stock watering, and knowing when to squeeze those who are in their power. It is a world of getting and spending, a world in which traditional values of integrity and justice are shoved aside for the pursuit of material success.

Robert Herrick, a Boston native who lived in Chicago for thirty years, was never comfortable with the monstrous, commercial metropolis that Chicago became during the late nineteenth and early twentieth centuries. In a series of novels set in Chicago, he explored that rough-and-tumble world with a conscience reminiscent of Nathaniel Hawthorne's. *The Memoirs of an American Citizen*[62] tells the rags-to-riches story of Van Harrington, an Indiana farm boy who begins as a tramp in Chicago and ends by taking the Senate seat he has bought with the money he has earned from various trusts and holding companies. Herrick tells his story through the words of the grasping and spiritually shallow businessman; Harrington is the type of man who has a twinge of pity for the Haymarket anarchists whom he is asked to judge, but still delivers the guilty verdict that will please his employers and further his career. He is a capitalistic success because he knows how to use people to further his own driving ambition and is content with life on the surface, material level; the cost for his individual success is an inability to love or be loved and a paucity of skills for nonmonetary endeavors. Although Herrick has Harrington speak for himself in the *Memoirs*, the author makes obvious his contempt for the American attempt to raise self interest to a universal beneficent principle.

Herrick makes effective use of the common tropes of businessmen's biographies in *The Memoirs of an American Citizen*. Just as biographers of the great entrepreneurs demonstrate their subject's childhood grasp of business principles, so do our earliest stories about Van Harrington satirically confirm his own business sense. As a child, Harrington stole some peaches from the orchard of the Judge who had owned the mortgages of the entire town of Jasonville. He was caught and forced to work to pay the fine for trespassing. During this time, Harrington made an important realization:

> While I was sweating on that farm I saw the folly of running against common notions abut property. I came to the conclusion that if I wanted what my neighbor considered to be his, I must get the law to do the business for me. For the first time it dawned on me how wonderful is that system which shuts up one man in jail for taking a few dollars worth of truck that doesn't belong to him, and honors the man who steals his millions—if he robs in the legal way! (22)

Harrington's conclusion parodies the paeans to hard work and saving which fill the biographies of Carnegie and Armour; this summary of business practice echoes the rhetoric of Pierre Proudhon, Johann Most, and others. Anarchists decried the government's role in protecting the property of the rich as a form of theft; the future capitalist, Harrington, sees this state of affairs as an opportunity.

After he has been spurned as unworthy by his childhood sweet-heart and run out of Jasonville, Harrington tramps to Chicago and is accused of stealing a purse. Poverty is grounds for suspicion in Chicago, a city described by Herrick's contemporary Henry Blake Fuller as "the only great city in the world to which all of its citizens have come for the common, avowed object of making money."[63] Everyone, from the established meatpacking magnate to the clerk who has scrimped together 100 dollars, hopes to become a success in the rough-and-tumble markets of Chicago. In Harrington's case, the usually tough judge listens to his story, and the story, combined with the admission by his accuser, Sarah Gentles, that she did not think he stole her purse, gets him freed with a one-dollar loan from the judge.

Harrington finds a boarding house and begins work in a local su-permarket. He soon manages the deliveries for the market and uses that connection to become acquainted with some of the larger meat-packing firms. When the grocery appears to be in trouble, he aban-dons his first employer and quickly gets a job with the firm of Henry Dround. At the firm, he is trained by the manager, Carmichael, in all the tactics and tricks necessary to maintain a profitable busi-ness: how to squeeze suppliers, how to bribe the city council to ex-tend railway spurs to your warehouses, and how to protect the parts of the city which you consider to be your "territory" while sur-reptitiously expanding into the areas in which your competitors dominate.

Like Andrew Carnegie, Van Harrington makes his first successful investment by taking advantage of inside information. Following the narrative of businessmen's biographies, Harrington puts aside most of his salary—around one thousand dollars in savings—and waits for his big chance. Just as he considers following one of the ques-tionable "tips" of an acquaintance who works as a clerk in the office of a broker for the Chicago Board of Trade (which is to buy pork before Strauss, the biggest packer in town, buys the price up), Har-rington glances at a letter to his manager, Carmichael. The letter, from a broker, shows that Carmichael has recently sold pork. Har-rington guesses that Carmichael, who has contact with Strauss's corporation through his work monitoring the trade agreements with other packers, has some inside information. At lunch, he takes out all of his savings and sells pork short. After a month, pork prices drop, and Harrington makes four thousand dollars on his initial in-vestment. "Somehow, I seemed to forget how I had learned the right tip, and thought of myself as a terribly smart young man" (59). Despite his ride on the coattails of richer market manipulators, he understands himself in the context of capitalist individualism; any success reflects the superiority of the individual, not the workings of favors or random chance.

Harrington has one good idea in the meatpacking trade: take the regular sausage and package it more nicely, transforming it into a "premium" kosher sausage that will sell more quickly. Although this idea gets him promoted to a manager in Dround's firm, the company doesn't act on the idea because of Dround's anti-Semitic fastidiousness. With his new investment income, Harrington buys control of a struggling kosher butcher's operation outside Chicago and, delivering through Dround's supply chain, begins to make money with "Duchess" brand sausage. In 1886, a mere nine years after he has come to Chicago, he already owns a company and has several successful investments. He owes his success not to improving the standard of living, but to deceptive advertising.

In 1886, the McCormick strike becomes yet another crisis in the conflict between capital and labor. The strike becomes a common subject in the discussion around the boarding house. "We were all on the same side then, I guess—the side of capital; there was enough for all of the good things in life, we thought, if only the men would stop kicking and keep at work" (62). Harrington, as a person who has profited in his own small way because of the capitalist system, readily adopts the language of materialism and capitalist progress to defend the rich. His fellow boarder, lawyer, and close friend, Slocum, is sympathetic to the strikers: "so long as they respected the laws he was with them in their struggle to get all they could from their employers" (62). Harrington's position is now reversed: whereas the boy in Indiana had chafed as the law punished him for questioning the property rights of another man, the young manager now saw which side he was on and could offer little sympathy to the workers.

As the strike becomes violent, several boarders—including some women who live at the boarding house—go to witness the commotion. At the Haymarket Square, they are disappointed to find

> only some hundreds of men who were speechifying from a cart. It didn't look very lively . . . suddenly, so Slocum said, there was a shout from somewhere behind them:—
>
> "The police! Look out for the police!"
>
> In the rush that followed, Slocum and Grace were jammed back by the press and separated from the others. He remembered only a little of

what happened those next moments. And what he did remember didn't tally with the stories that were told later at the trial. (63)

One woman, Hillary Cox, is grazed on the cheek by a bullet. At the same time that the Haymarket tragedy is occurring, another woman, Lou Pierson, is attacked by a plant manager, Renshaw, who then simply drops her by the curb at the boarding house. When Slocum tries to get the man to stop, Renshaw violently pushes the lawyer out of his carriage.

> As Slocum helped me carry the girl up the steps, he said:—
> "That's who Renshaw is. A bit of a bomb would be about the right thing for him!"
> Generalizations, I have learned, are silly things to play with. But there are some experiences of a man's life which tempt him to make them. It was only a mere accident that the man who was Lou Pierson's companion in the cab that night had taken a prominent part against the striking workmen. But when, later, I was called upon to sit in judgment on some hot-headed fools because they, in their struggle to get an eight-hour day, fomented strife, my thoughts would go back sourly to this example of the men I was expected to side with. (65)

In Herrick's vision of Chicago, there is very little difference in moral character between those who have money and those who are striking in hopes of getting more. Both are equally capable of cowardice and selfishness; only the widespread worship of Success ensures that those who are able to get some money will stand by those who already have it. The hero worship of the rich and powerful (and the possibility of joining that elite) is the chief appeal of capitalism for the noncapitalist. Although they may not be worth such sacrifice on a personal level, Harrington recognizes that he must side with the powerful if he hopes to become powerful himself; integrity and honor have little currency in this market.

The Haymarket anarchists are put on trial amid a newspaper-generated panic: "from what the papers said you might think there was an anarchist or two skulking in every alley in Chicago with a basket of bombs under his arm . . . it was all a parcel of lies, of course, but the people were crazy to be lied to, and the police, having nothing better, fed them lies" (66). The rich men of the city, sensing in this the potential for riots on a wider scale, set up a fund of money to suppress the anarchists with an iron hand: "this famous trial of the anarchists was engineered from the beginning by prominent men to go straight" (69). Dround, always active in public matters, sits on the grand jury and takes a lead role, much to the concern of his Irish manager, Carmichael, who wishes he would let others take the heat for the anarchists while Dround quietly made money.

Harrington, along with other presumably loyal managers, is called to the jury. He realizes that this is an opportunity to demonstrate his loyalty, but Carmichael jokingly reminds him of the danger: "you mustn't mind finding a stick of dynamite under your bed when you go home from the trial" (70). Herrick depicts Judge Gary as an advocate for the prosecution, eagerly impaneling biased jurors and leading them to the conclusion he wanted. During the trial, "His Honor made the law—afterward he boasted of it—as he went along. He showed us what sedition was, and that was all we needed to know" (73). The machinery of capital is pressing down on the defendants and the outcome of the trial is a foregone conclusion.

The anarchists themselves are portrayed as a motley bunch. "Two were stupid; three were shifty; but the other three had an honest glow, a kind of wild enthusiasm, that came with their foreign blood, maybe. They were dreamers of wild dreams, but no thugs!" (73). Harrington realizes the true purpose of the trial—"a struggle between sensible folks who went about their business and tried to get all there was in it—like myself—and some scum from Europe, who didn't like the way things were handed out in this world" (74). As with the real trial, the "foreignness" of anarchism is an important aspect of the threat it poses; the anti-immigrant feeling obscures the equation of "sensible folks" with businessmen that is embedded in the language of capitalism. The fact that the police had killed more people than the anarchists had ever killed is also immaterial; these men must be made an example of to prevent further riots. At this point, Harrington realizes that "life was for the strong, all there was in it! I saw it so then, and have lived it so all my life." (75). Harrington identifies with the strong—the rich—and that identification makes him feel more important. By the next day, as he prepares to resume his work with the firm, he almost thinks that he single-handedly saved Chicago from being blown up—every success becomes an individual triumph, regardless of the part others play in it.

Later in life, when he goes to one of his factories to coordinate the breaking of a strike, he gets attacked by an anarchist. Harrington engages the anarchist in conversation and manages to convert the murderous striker into a docile fellow by expounding his philosophy. About revolutionaries, Harrington says "if by any luck you should do away with all my kind, your own men would take to robbing you on a big scale as they now do on a small one" (160); he convinces the anarchist of "the gospel of man against man" and, as the anarchist meekly leaves the plant, concludes that "he wasn't a bad sort of fellow, only easily excited and loose-minded" (171). In the end, the anarchists presented little threat; the rich successfully exerted their power over the public discourse before such radicals could create a following. [64] Once this small threat has been dispensed with, the populace of Chicago is free to return to getting and spending.

As he rises in the firm, Harrington learns to play by rules more brutal and corrupt than Dround can abide by; however, since Strauss's trust uses money to gain favors, Harrington's company has no choice but to do likewise or be put out of business. Although the owner speaks against civic corruption, the firm of Dround bribes for special favors. Dround confronts Carmichael about it; Carmichael, furious with Dround's lack of business sense, quits, saying "I don't go broke with you, not for all your college talk and prin-ci-ples" (111). Dround finds that Harrington agrees with Carmichael about rebates, bribes, and secret schemes; "perhaps he began to realize what it meant to stand alone against the commercial system of the age" (112). Harrington takes Carmichael's place on his own terms, and, as Dround ceases to take an active interest in the firm, Harrington then begins to plot his own schemes.

Harrington realizes that more profits can be made by combining or taking over the railways and smaller competitors, and that his firm must grow to combat Strauss's growing trust. Harrington plots a takeover bid of several concerns and attempts to bribe the manager of one company to sell to him. Harrington is double-crossed, and a judge puts a restraining order on his bid; he bribes the judge to change his mind, and his bid goes through. However, the newspapers make a huge scandal of the judge's bribe taking, which tars Harrington's reputation. Harrington does not care, as long as he can expand his economic power: "no one asks, if you *succeed*" (141). His next several years are spent keeping one step ahead of payments on the bonds he issued to pay for his acquisitions and keeping Strauss from driving him out of business.

When the Spanish-American war comes, Harrington takes time away from his attempts to keep his stock scheme afloat to perform a patriotic service. Although unwilling to fight himself, Harrington demonstrates patriotism by outfitting a regiment. Meanwhile, the markets have crashed through wartime manipulation, and Harrington's scheme, built on unbacked stock certificates, is in danger of crashing and taking the savings of many people with it.

At the climax of his largest scheme, he is saved not by his own genius, but by the financial reserves of Mrs. Dround, who has lived a rapacious, acquisitive life vicariously through Harrington. Her money and her stock reserves enable Harrington to run a corner just as Strauss and others are attempting to sell his stock short; his improved bargaining position allows him to sell out to Strauss at his own price.

So far as the public is concerned, Harrington's has become an almost unqualified success story. He has worshipped the great god Success and has been amply rewarded; however, Herrick forces the reader to acknowledge the cost, as well. While discussing his career with the ambitious Mrs. Dround, he realizes the pointlessness of his exertions: "The work I was doing seemed senseless. Somehow a man's happiness had slipped past me on the road, and now I missed it" (233). These doubts do not last for long, however; together with Carmichael, he begins laying the groundwork for a new round of getting, aided by the packing monopoly which he has helped to create; economic activity is an end in itself. Harrington uses his newly acquired riches to secure an appointment to the United States Senate. Although he has been tarred by scandal, his money and the favorable press it buys overcome the widespread objections to his candidacy.

In *The Memoirs of an American Citizen*, Herrick paints a bleak picture of materialism triumphant; those forces of the older order which do not approve of Harrington's doctrine of material success at any cost have washed their hands of him and people like him, but have left the economy of the United States in their hands. In a pointed jab to the reformers and antitrust advocates, Harrington observes that he does not believe "that a power existed which could check our operations . . . nor do I know a man conversant with the modern situation of capital who believes that with our present system of government any effective check upon the operations of capital can be devised" (239). As a demonstration of this proof, he climbs the steps of the Capitol with the money he has earned through the meatpacking trust.

Herrick portrays, with some disapproval, the ways that the language of corporate capitalism dominates first the market and then the government; he recognizes the weakness of the rhetorics that oppose that expansion. Harrington, Sumner, and others preach a "gospel of getting" that underpins Carnegie's vision of capitalist beneficence, *The Gospel of Wealth*. The tenets of this gospel are simple: those who have wealth have it because their superiority demands that they have it; by giving other people jobs and selling them goods and services, the capitalist does more good for society as a whole than a thousand brigades of the Salvation Army. The harshness and elitism of this vision is tempered by the promise that individuals who have the potential will become rich, regardless of their start in life. This combination of progressive benevolence and individual reward bolstered support for the capitalist system by showering material rewards on those who supported the "system."

The anarchists were unable to divert the drive toward corporate organization and centralized bureaucratic structures. By 1905, the anarchist movement in France was folding itself into the syndicalist movement, advocating organized action over individualism. Anarchists moved toward more reformist, hierarchical labor organizations, or renounced political action in favor of radical, aesthetic, individualism. Barbara Tuchman observed that "anarchist passion on the whole passed into the more realistic combat of the syndicalist unions. In the United States it was absorbed into the International Workers of the World, founded in 1905, although in every country there remained irreconcilables who stayed lonely and true to the original creed."[65] The corporate model of human organization had overtaken the last bastion of radical individualism.

5

Anarchism Disarmed

THE DIVIDE BETWEEN ANARCHIST DISCOURSE AND THE DIALOGUE OF THE
larger culture narrowed in the early years of the twentieth century.
Millenarian fears of revolution eased, and the early 1900s were
more notable for the expansion of police authority and corporate
power than they were for anarchist outrages. The revolutionary anarchists who had been inspired by Bakunin were maturing, and the
anarchist "movement" (which had renounced "propaganda by the
deed" ten years earlier) had split into a working-class syndicalist
movement and radical individualists. The few anarchists who remained active in public causes (Emma Goldman being one notable
example) were still persecuted, but the threat posed by anarchist
ideas had lessened, clearing the way for a more constructive dialogue between anarchism and the larger culture. Strains of anarchist discourse were adopted into the general dialogue, losing their
radical status in the translation. The comic and satiric potential of
anarchism and its usefulness as a metaphor for modern society
were exploited during the first years of the twentieth century by
those sympathetic and those hostile to the historic anarchist movement. Although the formal movement would continue in Spain and
parts of Russia, anarchism as a growing, self-defined position
within American or British culture faded and was replaced by an
anarchism which was enmeshed in the social dialogue, a latent potential within the language of culture which would be occasionally
revived throughout the century.[1]

"Propaganda by the deed" had always been a controversial strategy, pursued only by an impulsive minority of the anarchist community. As each bombing or assassination brought only increased
repression, even the most extreme anarchists had forsaken propaganda by the deed in favor of either individual activism or syndicalism. Those assassinations that were committed by anarchists were
done by loners, or by people with only tenuous ties to other anarchists. Csoglosz, the assassin of McKinley who claimed to be an an-

archist after having attended one of Emma Goldman's lectures, was suspected of being a police spy by other anarchists and had a history of mental disturbance; although hagiographies of McKinley dutifully traced the fell history of the anarchist movement as it led up to the assassination of the President, there was little material in Csoglosz's story on which to build a massive conspiracy.

Despite the relative peace that surrounded the anarchist movement in the early years of the twentieth century, governments (responding to the outrages of the earlier decade) continued passing laws which repressed anarchist freedoms of movement and speech, especially in the United States after the McKinley assassination. Despite no evidence of an immediate threat, legislation was passed in reaction to a clichéd form of anarchism—the anarchist stereotype of the mad bomber had entered the cultural consciousness, and could still be useful in political grandstanding.

As fewer acts of terrorism were perpetrated, press coverage of anarchism decreased. Anarchism as a movement was gradually divorced from the fears of revolution and degeneracy which had been associated with it in the 1890s, and the triumph of centralized institutions made the anarchist language of decentralization seem more utopian and less threatening. Many former anarchists embraced anarcho-syndicalism, which merged anarchist tactics with the institution of the trades union; in the process, the language of individualist or aesthetic anarchism was divorced from working-class economic anarchism. Anarcho-syndicalism was seen as an aggressive form of trade unionism, and its glorification of violence appealed to writers on both the left and the right (notably George Sorel). The movement gained strength by forsaking the individual and decentralization, becoming, in effect, something other than anarchism.

Individualist anarchism lost much of its political meaning and entered the general discourse. Rather than transform society, ideas of decentralization, disorder, and lack of authority transformed the cultural perception of society. In order for anarchist language to make the transition into the broader discourse, the words first had to be divorced from the unsavory history of anti-anarchist propaganda, and then placed into the newer, more general context through individual use. In America, the Haymarket Affair was revisited through works of fiction, with Frank Norris' *The Bomb* recasting the story to support a more contemporary socialism, and Charlotte Teller's *The Cage* retelling the story to pull the genre of sentimental fiction into the realm of the overtly political.

The disassociation of anarchism from the fears of degeneracy, revolution, and random violence which had marked it in the propaganda of the popular press occurred slowly, as people began discussing and writing their reminiscences of the 1880s and 1890s. Away from the fears of the moment, writers gave a more judicious appraisal of anarchists and the threat posed by anarchism. Some writers, such as Ford Madox Ford and "Isabel Meredith" (the pen name of Helen and Olivia Rossetti), went so far as to purge anarchism of any threatening aspect whatsoever by characterizing it as an adolescent lark, or a pose which one quickly outgrew.

NARRATIVE REINTERPRETATIONS OF HAYMARKET: CHAROLOTTE TELLER'S *THE CAGE*

Although many adventure writers were using the conspiracy narrative as a setting for their own heroic stories, some writers chose to focus on the darker side of the Haymarket Affair. The abuse of police power, the haughtiness of the new corporate giants, and the mistreatment of the poor and the working classes which were minimized in the adventure narrative become the focus of narratives within other genres which use the events surrounding 4 May 1886 as a setting. Many of these novels come out of the older middle-class tradition, using the values of charity and civic virtue to condemn the extremist violence of which both the radicals and the police were guilty.

Everett Carter's essay "The Haymarket Affair in Literature" discusses William Dean Howell's role in the Haymarket Affair and its role in *A Hazard of New Fortunes* (1890), in which Basil March must defend a German radical against their mutual boss at the risk of his job. Carter claims that Frank Harris' *The Bomb* (1909) is "the only full-length novel which deals exclusively with the Haymarket bombing." Carter's description of the novel itself, a "potpourri of Socialism, Christianity, anarchy, and hero-worship," is accurate enough.[2] However, Carter does not mention another full-length novel that deals directly with the Haymarket Affair. Charlotte Teller's *The Cage*[3] also retells the events of Chicago in 1886, casting them in the language of sentimental fiction. By framing the bombing within a story of love that defies social conventions, Teller turns her story into an implicit defense of anarchism.

Published in 1907, *The Cage* draws on the tradition of sentimental fiction, telling a story of people on all sides of the labor conflicts that shook Chicago in the spring of 1886. In the novel, the domestic sphere comes to represent real human dialogue and understanding and is opposed to the hypocritical and authoritarian nature of inter-action in the civic and commercial spheres. Consequently, domestic values support the goals of economic and human justice toward which anarchism and socialism strive, and oppose the quick judg-ments and immorality of public laws and conventions. In addition to the use of sentimental conventions in the domestic plot to produce sympathy and support for economic radicals in the United States, Teller creates a social dialogue through the major characters' artic-ulation of coherent positions within contemporary debates on mo-rality and social justice. These debates are dominated by the capitalists, who use their control of the media (from newspapers to church pulpits) to deny workers' advocates a fair hearing. Nonethe-less, the workers have their own understandings, and these con-flicts (worker and capitalist, economic jargon and sentimental narrative) structure the conflicting ideas of Teller's novel. By pres-enting competing narratives that undermine capitalist authority, *The Cage* reinterprets the Haymarket narrative as a story in which conventionality wins the battle against the radicals, but only by em-bracing the radical ideals of justice and social dialogue that those conventions had previously resisted. The combination of domestic plot with dialogic structure within the novel transforms the public defeat of the radical cause into a promise of a future triumph: the conventional order had morally bankrupted itself, while those who seek justice are now sustained by the human values of love and jus-tice to continue their struggle.

Although the struggles of the workers in the lumberyard that dominates the neighborhood are constantly in the background of *The Cage*, the novel's main plot involves the relationship between Frederica Hartwell, a clergyman's daughter who has been sheltered from the world's struggles by her own idealism, and Eugene Harden, a socialist activist from an upper-class Hungarian family who, true to his name, has a rigid sense of honor and justice. Hard-en's efforts to unionize the local lumberyard workers in the neigh-borhood of Dr. Hartwell's mission expose Freda to the many ways in which the conventional order falls short of its own rhetorical ide-als, while Freda's innocence and idealism provide Harden with the inspiration necessary to carry on his work in the face of constant attacks from supporters of corporate capitalism and social conser-vatism.

From the beginning of their relationship, Freda and Harden dis-cuss social issues. Eugene Harden first visits Dr. Hartwell, Freda's widower father, in order to enlist his help in forming a union to se-cure justice for the local workers. Dr. Hartwell is a preacher who has given up a secure post in a rich parish in order to minister to the poor. He is assisted by Anne Forester, who has followed Dr. Hartwell from her own financially secure position, and his idealistic daughter Frederica, whose innocence prevents her from understanding much of the conflict which permeates the working-class neighborhood.

Like earlier sentimental novels with political themes, the domestic plot in *The Cage* is informed by a continuing dialogue between members of different groups within the larger society. This dialogue concerns the ways in which people in society treat others and focuses on the related words "law" and "convention." Characters give voice to languages which specific ideologies, from the discourse of Christian charity espoused by Hartwell to the behavioristic mechanization of policeman Flanagan. The novel's dialogue reinforces the main plot's message by emphasizing the political ramifications of many seemingly innocent, yet authority-laden phrases within the culture of late nineteenth-century Chicago.

Dr. Hartwell is a Christian idealist who represents the best of the old civic and religious tradition regarding charity. Hartwell professes a traditional model of charity as moral instruction for the poor provided by the rich. Although his sponsor, Sloane, has ulterior motives for having his workers counseled to accept their lot, Dr. Hartwell is sincere in his belief that material poverty stems from moral failings, and that moral instruction will produce a material improvement in the lives of the poor. At any rate, material goals are unimportant to Dr. Hartwell and Anne. They have left a comfortable life on Chicago's east side for homes nearer to the poor whom they wish to help.

Only one member of his old church could be persuaded to support a mission into the poorer neighborhoods of Chicago: Mr. Sloane, the owner of the local lumber mill, which employs nearly everyone in the neighborhood. In keeping with the affluent Christianity of his sponsor, Dr. Hartwell believes that most poverty is caused by immorality, and, when everyone is good, no one will be poor: "if men are good individually, each one filled with the Christian spirit, everything else [will] settle itself."[4] This view encourages the division of society into distinct spheres—spiritual, public, and private—and forbids experts in the spiritual realm from interfering in the public (and commercial) realm. This division of society into separate realms is one strategy for stifling criticism: the only ones granted authority to speak on economic issues are the ones with a vested interest in maintaining the status quo. Hartwell's acceptance of this division of labor at the beginning of the novel is clear: "First the law

of love, . . . then the laws of men" (26). Although he is generous and
willing to help, his basic message to the poor people he serves is the
same message that anarchists condemn for its naked usefulness to
the propertied class. The poor are to behave and be content with
the wages and treatment that the rich give them; their virtue will be
its own reward.

Anne, who is in love with Dr. Hartwell, has followed him into the
poorer neighborhoods of Chicago. Although she has enough money
to live in upper class society, Anne has been inspired by Dr. Hartwell to improve the conditions of the poor and to aid Dr. Hartwell in
his own work. However, she maintains a fastidious distance from
actual poor individuals, finding the neighborhood squalid, and the
people well-meaning but narrow. Whereas Dr. Hartwell believes in
spiritual goodness apart from material conditions, Anne's abstractions are exclusively in terms of broader municipal reform:

> It always irritated her when Dr. Hartwell discussed heaven, even as a
> "state of being." She was, to be sure, spiritual in a practical way; but
> had she been closely questioned she would have had to admit that in her
> heaven—if she were to look forward to it with comfort—the mansions
> must be numbered, the golden streets named, and the city hall properly
> ventilated. Heaven was a definite municipal ideal. Chicago was its an-
> tithesis, and there was nothing mysterious or abstract in the conditions
> of Chicago. (34)

Anne and Dr. Hartwell have a curious relationship which mimics
the dialogue between the spiritual reform which many churches
worked for and the more materialistic municipal reform advocated
by muckraking journalists and other civic-minded professionals.

True to the conventions of the sentimental narrative, Anne and
Dr. Hartwell frame a public debate within a domestic relationship:
Anne is inspired by Dr. Hartwell's spirituality, yet, at the beginning
of the novel, Dr. Hartwell is unaware of Anne's feelings; similarly,
the muckrakers and reformers were often ignored by missionaries
who thought that conditions were the symptom, not the cause, of
bad morals. Neither Anne nor Dr. Hartwell appreciates poor people
as complete individuals. One addresses only the spirit, the other addresses only the environment, and the two idealists do not enter
into dialogue with each other. Teller uses the strategy of framing a
public discourse within a discussion of a private relationship
throughout the novel. This strategy also contains the destructive
potential of the political, and renews the corrupt conventions of private life as described within a sentimental narrative.

   Teller demonstrates the corrupt nature of Chicago conventionality (and, by extension, American public morality) through the stories of the family of a neighborhood policeman, Officer Flanagan.
Despite being one of the more honest policemen on the force, Flanagan cannot escape the culture of exploitation and violence that the
police are instrumental in upholding, and that moral failing manifests itself in the lives of his children. Frederica catches Michael
Flanagan, the son of a neighborhood policeman, "gambling"—that
is, playing marbles. Adopting a policeman's voice, Frederica says to
Michael:

> "Now, Michael Angelo Flanagan," she asked, "are yez goin' straight
> home?"
>   The boy of six nodded.
>   "And now, listen," she said, with a serious undertone; "you are not
> going to gamble any more, are you?"
>   Michael, with newly aroused shame, looked down at shoes too large
> for him, and made no reply.
>   "You are going to grow up to be a good man, aren't you, like your
> father?"
>   "He's a policeman," piped Michael, who was off at the end of his am-
> biguous response, and into the rear of the house. (16)

Michael's "crime" was in winning marbles from another boy, Tim.
Frederica, unironically, relates her role in the story to Anne:

> "I stopped it; I boxed Tim's ears; he wanted all the marbles back that
> Mikey had won from him."
>   "And you let Mikey keep them?" Anne asked.
>   "Of course not." Frederica was condescending to Anne's density. "I
> took them. I acted the part of the law." (16)

Frederica, who has grown up in the workers' neighborhood, understands the role of the police to be the enforcement of certain moral
tenets (such as "no gambling") through violence and confiscation;
the police enforce good behavior through force, not moral authority.
   Before Frederica meets Eugene Harden, she believes the surface
rhetoric of justice and fairness as the American way. Breaking up a
fight between two of the Flanagans' other children, she drills the
children in the rhetoric of citizenship: "we are a free and noble people; we believe in justice; and the American citizen fights only for
his liberty" (18); Frederica is satisfied that she has done enough,
but does not realize "that Adolph, fleeing from the light of American
principles, had dragged Fritz into the cellar, where he sat on him

until he got what he desired. Frederica was not one to recognize the place of a dark cellar in a democracy" (18). The force that the policeman uses explains Michael's ambiguous response to Frederica: his father is neither good not bad, simply part of the machinery of law enforcement. Beneath the moral rhetoric of the police is the material reality of brute force; the repression which the police inflict on the poor goes only so far as the police can reach and teaches the "moral" that might makes right.

Frederica's true education begins when she meets Eugene Harden, whose allegorical name signifies his role in "hardening" Frederica's soft, sentimental moral principles. She begins to develop an understanding of American culture that does not pretend, as Dr. Hartwell does, that class divisions do not exist within the American democracy. Harden, inspired by Freda, convinces the working men to strike for a shorter workday. Frederica falls in love with Harden, and he teaches her his radical doctrines of social justice.

As the representative radical, Harden is given many different descriptions over the course of the novel that remind readers of the various characterizations of radicals in the popular press. Harden is introduced as "a socialist" who "looks foreign" with hair that "curled wherever he had let it grow long enough to have its own way" (27). In Frederica's first impression, Harden is a polished version of the stereotypical anarchist—foreign, with unkempt hair. The way other characters in the novel describe Harden reflects anti-labor language. A reporter, seeking to dig up unflattering reports on Harden after the union votes to strike for an eight-hour day, talks about "the walking delegate, Harden, that has made all the trouble for Sloane" (109). Other characters emphasize Harden's foreign heritage. The capitalist Sloane summarizes his judgment of Harden: "I told you he was crooked. Any man who comes into a free country and meddles in its business affairs, stirs up discontent among the workingmen—is always crooked" (202). Only once is Harden described as an anarchist—by Sloane, who wishes to destroy Harden's reputation in order to destroy the union. Sloane forbids Dr. Hartwell to allow Harden to speak in the church Sloane supports: "No more anarchists or socialists in *my* church" (154). In keeping with the general attitude of the time, Sloane equates labor agitators with anarchists while being totally uninterested in giving Harden's ideas a hearing. Part of Sloane's strength is his ability to deny a hearing to those who do not share his views; the newspapers, most of which participate in capitalist discourses, would print anything Sloane wanted them to print, but would never accept Harden's

(true) story of collusion on the part of a group of lumberyard owners to break the union; he considers himself to have ownership of
even the church by virtue of his money. Speaking as a radical,
Harden is shut out of the authoritarian discourse of capitalism and
convention.

Harden's activity has personal ramifications in the Hartwell
home because the owner of the lumber yard, Sloane, also supports
Hartwell's mission and pays his salary. Also, Sloane's son, Alec, has
secretly planned on marrying Freda. Although Alec Sloane's assumption that Freda will marry him smacks of ownership, he does
blame himself for not seizing the opportunity to marry her before
Harden entered the scene. His father, however, combines the union
activism with the slight to his son and takes on a personal hatred of
Eugene Harden, whom he labels a "foreign firebrand" in imitation
of the anti-radical rhetoric used by the press. Alec and his father
assume that Harden had aggressively won Freda; neither can con-
ceive that Freda would be attracted to the man for his ideas, because they find those same ideas so abhorrent. Sloane's attitude
toward women is identical to his attitude toward commerce: aggression and quick thinking are sufficient to ensure success. It is only
after the events escalate into tragedy that Sloane remembers the
human values of compassion and fairness.

Although the Sloanes believe that Harden has been aggressive or
underhanded in his courtship, the opposite is the case. Freda and
Eugene share a mutual attraction, but both resist the relationship:
Freda from the timidity of youth, and Harden because he has a complicated past. Harden in particular is well-bred and respectful of
Freda and her religious father. The respect for religion and eti-
quette make Harden an ideal suitor but those characteristics also
divest Harden of the features of radicalism (a tendency toward violence and a lack of respect for Arnoldian high culture) which liberal
members of the middle class would find most objectionable.

Although Harden is introduced as a socialist, the novel avoids
providing details of his political philosophy and does not connect
Harden directly to the anarchist movement. Instead, Harden's anarchism reveals itself in his attitude toward "the law," referring both
to the laws on the statute books and the codes of conduct and prejudice which govern behavior in American society. Through the
framework of the romantic plot, Teller frames anarchism within the
idea of a love that transcends social conventions. The love which
Harden and Frederica feel for each other explicitly parallels the devotion which both feel for the cause of social justice. Harden's anarchism is his contempt for laws which are not just, whether those

laws are statutes designed to help employers against workers or conventions designed to control people's affections or play on their prejudices.

In Harden's own history, his respect for women and his desire for justice are paralleled. Out of a sense of duty, he married a selfish woman who was blackmailing his brother; that marriage did not prevent the woman from dishonoring him, and that dishonor combined with his sense of social injustice led Harden to leave Europe. The parallel between Harden's love for the masses and his treatment of his former wife is explicitly made by an old friend who knew Harden in Europe but does not share Harden's passion for the worker's cause: "I find you have but one mistress—the mob. You defend the mob as you would your wife's honor, and neither one has honor—nor—reason" (141). Harden comes to America, but the land of liberty does not fulfill its promise of social justice. Inspired by Freda, Harden decides that America is capable of social change, and he begins to work on behalf of the labor movement. His old friend notes this as well:

> "Love has so many masks, but this of yours—it is most original. A common aim—the uplifting of humanity"—he raised his hand as a premiere danseuse would toss dainty kisses to the first row—"the freeing of men from the hateful yoke of industrial slavery." Then rising on his toes, and making a bow with arms spread outwards, "Beneath the filmy shade of telegraph poles she passed her shadow fingers over the blunders he made in his manuscript—the manuscript of a book which would show the world how great are the down-trodden . . . I revel in this new dream of love!" (142)

Harden's faith in the workers rises and falls with his faith in Frederica. By winning her from Alec Sloane, Harden has demonstrated the worthiness of his own ideals against the unimaginative assumption of possession that the propertied characters in this novel profess. Harden has offered Frederica a love that is based on passionate activity in the larger world; Sloane offered her a life of material comfort and commodity.

Frederica's own love also parallels her understanding of the events in the larger world. Portayed almost as a child in the beginning of the novel, she is innocently faithful in American rhetoric and institutions, despite her experiences with the struggles of the poor and the routine corruption of the police. Harden awakens in her an adult passion and an awareness of the larger social questions of the day. Although she was always intelligent, her optimism had acted in such a way as make her innocent; often, Frederica does what she considers the right thing (such as side with the strikers, and claim to a reporter that her father does as well) without understanding how her words will be twisted to fit the procrustean narratives of the upper-class press.

The beginning of her education in the ways which everyday events can be twisted by ideology occurs when she goes to Harden in his hotel room in order to ask him to cancel his speaking engagement so as not to embarrass her father after Sloane has ordered Hartwell not to let Harden speak in the church. This conversation opposes the private world of their love with the public reality of a law and convention. When Frederica professes her love, Harden tells her that he is married, not in affection, but under the law. Frederica replies that "my father has always said that we should live according to the higher law—according to 'the righteousness of God without the law'" (148). By invoking her father's words in the context of this romantic scene, Frederica creates a dialogue between convention, love, and social justice. The scene participates in the conventions of the sentimental novel, arousing the readers' sympathies for the lovers against cold social convention; the notion of a "higher law" of the spirit creates sympathy for the anarchists by undermining the laws and conventions which the propertied class use to bolster their authority. Knowing that no one in America knows of his previous marriage, Harden has been tempted to marry Frederica despite the fact that the divorce has not come through on his previous marriage. Frederica encourages them to flout the law: "it is very strange, isn't it, if we love each other and believe in each other that words—the words of the law should come between us?" Harden replies

> even if you had the courage and I was willing that the world should look at you and misjudge you—we should not be free—to work together. My enemies . . . those who think I want to destroy society, who think I want to destroy all law—they would use our life—no matter how beautiful it was—against us. They would have the right, as the world is now. (150)

Frederica understands him only when Sloane and her father walk into the room, and Sloane reproaches Hartwell for allowing his daughter to go unescorted into a man's rooms. Frederica suddenly realizes that Sloane, the capitalist, will eagerly employ the conventional prejudice against sexual license to destroy Harden and protect his own economic interests: "There was no longer any doubt in her mind that he was the "world" which Eugene had said would de-

stroy his work should it suspect him. She was meeting convention
for the first time, and it had come upon her in the guise of destroyer" (156). Although he is a kindly man and a fairer employer
than most, Sloane is cast as the villain of the romantic plot, and this
narrative frame creates sympathy for Harden's anarchism. Just as
Frederica and Harden work together, so the romantic and political
plots of *The Cage* reinforce each other.

Frederica marries Harden, partially in order to protect his reputation, but Sloane's agents discover evidence that Harden was married in Europe. Sloane attempts to destroy Harden's reputation with
the strikers by accusing him of bigamy. Frederica, who finds herself
believing the story because of her husband's silence on the issue,
leaves the house and returns to her father. Harden senses his wife's
lack of trust, and, instead of going to the Haymarket on that fateful
day to make a speech, goes in search of Frederica. Harden is rewarded for valuing the personal relationship over political grandstanding by not being present when the police break up the meeting
and the fateful bomb is thrown.

Harden is juxtaposed against another minor character, Schneider, who is made a martyr for the bombing at Haymarket and is in
some sense a composite of the defendants during the trial. Although
Harden and Hartwell have been arrested and released, Schneider
is being transformed by a fanatic police investigator (modeled
closely on Captain Schaack) into the leader of a violent conspiracy
that aimed to destroy American civilization. With the benefit of
hindsight, Teller builds on the liberal critiques of the trial by Altgeld
and others to find Schneider guilty only of holding radical ideas and
using violent language:

> He stood abreast in thought with all the economic leaders of Europe.
> And that was so far ahead of any economic thought in America that he
> was now to pay a heavy price for a pioneer position. The fact of his lead-
> ership could be used against him; the fact that he had used the word
> "revolution"; that he had said that some day the poor man might come
> to take dynamite as a weapon—this would be used against him, too. In
> the German newspapers were many columns of his in which he had put
> forcibly and fearlessly the principles which he was advocating . . . with
> all the public opinion stirred against those things for which he stood,
> believing that if a man said "dynamite" he was capable of using it, it
> would be hard to expect leniency or even justice for him. (328)

Schneider, like the real Haymarket defendants, is found guilty of
radical ideas and provocative rhetoric, not actual violence. Harden,
who had always been more restrained in his rhetoric, manages to

escape the public wrath by not being associated with the words "revolution" and "dynamite." Just as the liberals who dared to speak against the verdict were careful to disassociate themselves with the violence of the anarchists, so Teller is careful to disassociate her own hero from the violence within the novel.

Unfortunately, the forces of repression are much stronger than those in the novel who pursue the spirit of justice as well as the letter. The bomb invites a severe crackdown and popular hysteria against radicals. Teller divorces the Haymarket bomb itself from any anarchist connection: in the novel, the bomb is thrown by the same worker who set a lumberyard fire, a man who feels a personal grudge against Sloane for firing him when he needed money to help his sick child. Even in the case of the bomb, personal motives take precedence over public causes.

The propertied classes, like the police that represent them, have no respect for the ideals expressed in their laws as they appease their fear. Even Dr. Hartwell is arrested: "there had been no warrant for the arrest, and the ordinary formalities of the law had been absolutely set aside" (303). Personifying the forces of reaction which hide the basest motives behind the loftiest rhetoric is the malefic police investigator, patterned after Captain Schaack:

> Chicago was stricken with panic. A bomb had been thrown. There was an anarchist conspiracy, a plot to destroy the city. With wild, unreasoned conclusions the press called for the suppression of all free speech and public meetings. Police, detectives, and newspaper reporters began to rush from place to place, hunting for evidence which might prove their story of a monster conspiracy. A police officer, enamored of his role of savior of the people, was the most excited of all; and because of what he was by nature it cannot be brought against him that under the necessity of maintaining his honors and position, he invented the only plot which ever had any connection with the Haymarket riots. (308)

For the police captain creating conspiracies in order to win the press's adulation, the power that the narrative offers is too much to resist, and he ignores justice in order to create the concrete details which will support his own role as public defender. Like the rest of the city, he is caught up in a morality play which is tragically disjunctive with the real human situation; the shared narrative of the revolution that the propertied classes had feared for so long was going to be fulfilled, in fantasy if not in actuality.

Although Harden is not responsible for the violence at Haymarket, he is tied to that violence in personal ways (connections that have more force in this conventional romance plot). One of the defendants, Lange, is secretly Harden's brother. Lange shows his lack of discretion and judgment when he seduces the daughter of Officer Flanagan. Her father forces Maggie to flee from his legalistic judgment. Sloane pays Lange to be a secret agent within the union and to encourage violence that would destroy the union's reputation and justify extreme measures against the labor movement. In a superficial way, Lange parallels the actual defendant Lingg, who was also a dashing ladies' man; like Lingg, Lange kills himself in prison by exploding a dynamite cap in his mouth. In the end, the most reprehensible (and responsible) man is the one in the pay of the corporation; the violent, undisciplined Lange is tied to both the radicals and the capitalists.

The secret machinations of the capitalists succeed, and the waves of repression and hysteria that follow the violence near Haymarket shatter the labor movement. The lack of understanding and trust between the upper class and the working class mirrors the lack of understanding between Freda and Eugene. Like the city as a whole, their marriage suffers as they forget the ideals of justice and fairness and do not look beyond the superficial stories to the human realities. After the force of the law has crushed the labor movement, and Sloane's propaganda and her own innocence have led Frederica to distrust Harden, Harden retreats from the world into solitude: "to him were revealed the limitations of a fledgling democracy; and he wished that he had not come to America. . . . [H]is days were a recurrence of activities without spirit, and his nights of empty loneliness in his own home" (309). The triumph of convention over the spirit, and the break in his relationship with Freda, have vanquished his own spirit, and he is unable to throw himself into the public work of inspiring the men of the union. The defeat of his efforts in the hysteria of the Haymarket riot has left him as spiritless as the city around him.

As in many other sentimental novels, the domestic sphere must come to the rescue of the public sphere; *The Cage* twists this formula by asserting the woman's active role in the public sphere rather than a retirement to the private world. Frederica, who began the novel as an innocent, has completed a painful education in the ways of the world in the course of one year. That year has taught her the difference between the innocence and simplicity of most people, and the true nature of courage:

> I think a great many things like honesty and morality just come because men and women have not imaginations. And you have got to go through a long stretch of imagination, and you have got to know just how big a

fight it is not to let the things you see in your mind affect the things that you are going to do before you can get back those virtues again. Then you know how to hold your tongue; then you know what it is to be honest. (327)

Frederica has completed her education and brought Harden back to himself not by reasserting the simplicity or wholesomeness of the domestic sphere, but by asserting their identities as individuals in the larger world. As the business of aiding the Haymarket defendants continues, they realize that "the world had entered upon them; and it had brought them both back to themselves as parts of it" (332). The narratives of popular ideology are simple stories, incapable of describing the subtle complexities of actual lives; the true source of virtue is grappling with those complexities and maintaining your sense of justice. Although the forces of capitalism and convention have destroyed many lives, those who oppose injustice in society are prepared to carry on in the struggle. By having the socialist wed the heroine, and the two remain happy together despite the injustice of "respectable" persons, Teller creates a narrative of vindication which transforms the romantic cliché of a transgressive love into an act of political and social anarchism.

This transgressive love is paralleled by a "marriage" of older and newer rhetorics of justice. Eugene Harden's socialism is more radical and materialist than the ineffectual preaching of Hartwell, yet more aggressive and revolutionary than Anne's civic reform. He is stereotyped in the capitalist press as a walking delegate and foreign meddler, but he possesses a keen intellect and an honest appreciation for the situation of the common worker. Although Hartwell initially refuses to accept the notion of class division in the American democracy, Harden correctly argues that the interests of the employer and the employed are often at odds, and that Hartwell's refusal to recognize that fact has prevented him from reaching the men in his area. Eventually, Harden partially convinces the preacher—and the other workmen—by adopting America's rhetoric of democracy and justice. In turn, Hartwell turns passages from the Bible into texts on the current economic situation: "the camp of the Midianites was in darkness as great as the darkness which prevails over the camps of Capitalism to-day" (116); however, Hartwell still favors arbitration as the meek and proper way to settle differences. As one wife of a worker comments immediately, "if your father'd ever been a union man he's see it ain't no good to arbitrate, at least not until they've got the bosses in a corner" (117). Harden, the radical, comes across in his own speech as a perfect patriot, one who has come from Europe to America because of America's noble ideals, who now realizes that workers must strive to achieve the goals America sets forth in the Constitution. Although Harden is characterized as a radical, his appeal is made more palatable by being grounded in the older liberal civic tradition.

Just as Frederica and Eugene discover a better life outside of conventional economics and romance, Sloane is punished for his manipulation (and ultimate loyalty to) convention and capitalism. The stories that inform his language, imbedded in the authoritarian rhetoric of late nineteenth-century capitalism, prevent him from seeing the actual people around him until the shock of the bomb (and the action by the other members of the lumber cartel to drive him out of business) force him to recognize the human consequences of his actions and attitudes.

Sloane is broad minded enough to fund Dr. Hartwell's mission of charity, but his understanding of charity is much more grounded in selfishness than Hartwell's. Like many capitalists, he sees conventional morality as a useful way to preserve a social order that benefits him greatly, and he is willing to use the power that he has to silence those who would speak on economic issues outside the discourse of capitalism. When Sloane learns

> that Dr. Hartwell was making much of a foreign socialist, whose work was to destroy the industrial system whereby he was enabled to make immense profits without much personal effort, he became conscious of his power as master of the situation, and expressed himself without hesitation to his highest employee, Dr. Hartwell. (154)

Teller echoes the criticism of religion that was made by Bakunin, Marx, and others: religions are in the service of the rich. Teller, working within a liberal tradition which values civic institutions, turns that criticism around by placing the culpability for this situation solely on the capitalists, who undemocratically presume to control every aspect of the lives of their employees.

Sloane embraces the social divisions that capitalism fosters by repeating the argument that only those who are versed in capitalism are capable of commenting on economic issues. In particular, clergymen should not comment on the market and foreigners should not criticize any aspect of American culture. This imperative blunts discourse and impairs Sloane's understanding of events. His refusal to enter into dialogue with others (he is repeatedly described as being uninterested in what others have to say) paints him as the villain through the novel's structure.

The judgment of Sloane as villain is confirmed within the marriage plot of the novel. Sloane confirms that the discourse of capitalism has blunted his human feeling when he tries to use Eugene and Freda's relationship to help destroy the union. The echoes of his villainy on a personal level undercut his claims of authority by equating the rhetorical act of not listening to unacceptable economic ideas with the personal act of hindering love. Although Sloane uses a discourse that carries much power in the real world, he loses his authority when his words are forced into interaction with other languages and other understandings.

In addition to his attempts to destroy Harden's reputation, Sloane, pressured by the trust to which he belongs, secretly hires workers who lack self-discipline in order to undermine the union effort, and then gets his agent, Lange, to hire a worker to set fire to a shed of inexpensive wood. The goal of destroying the union even contradicts the normal tenets of good business practice and in the end backfires on Sloane. The worker whom Lange employs to set the fire had lost a child to sickness when Sloane had laid him off years earlier; he uses the job as an opportunity to seek revenge on Sloane by burning the prime shed, causing much damage. Through all of these actions, Teller creates a picture of capitalists as people who reject America's ideals of justice and democracy and create desperate men through their injustices. The employers do not want peace and arbitration; instead, they want a war they know they will win and use all means to provoke one. The extreme means that are secretly used to force the union to violate conventional standards of behavior reveal the moral vacuum of capitalism and the political nature of unrelated social conventions. The force of convention, inherently a conservative social force, is on Sloane's side, and he eagerly manipulates events to gain an advantage, whether in personal relationships or business dealings. Although Sloane would hold others to a strict separation of public and private discourses, his actions betray an understanding that the personal can be political.

Charlotte Teller's novel *The Cage* juxtaposes the living complexities of a diverse society with the deadening authority of conventional understanding. Within the novel's marriage plot, order becomes a destroyer, and anarchy is a means for revitalizing society through a direct appreciation of human realities. Like many liberals of the time, Teller de-emphasizes the provocative narratives of violent revolution that formed such an objectionable part of anarchist culture, and instead creates a story of a culture which is trapped in its own paranoid narratives and destroys the ideals which it claims to uphold. The only conspiracy present in *The Cage* is that of the lumberyard trust, which uses immoral measures to ensure its victory over the unions; the violence of the bomb is an act of personal anguish.

The Cage, published in 1907, had the advantage of being written at a time when fear of anarchism was ebbing, and writers were revisiting the preoccupations of the previous decade with a more sober eye. Teller's novel, which rejects the fears of revolution and conspiracy which dominated the cultural dialogue of the previous generation, is one of many novels which translated anarchism from a political rhetoric into a metaphoric language which could be used to describe everyday life. By emphasizing the "anarchistic" qualities of love against the mendacity of the forces of convention, Teller transforms anarchism from an ideology of the "other" to a normal state of affairs.

Laughing at the Threat: Anarchist Memoirs

As the fears of revolution subsided with better economic times and the consolidation of corporate hegemony and commercial culture, it became possible to discuss anarchism and anarchists from a less polemical perspective. Many writers in the early years of the twentieth century turned their attention to the actual anarchist movement in an attempt to correct the mistaken narratives that had silenced anarchists throughout the nineteenth century. Ford Madox Ford and Helen and Olivia Rossetti were but a few of the writers on both sides of the Atlantic who wrote stories of life among anarchists, portraying them not so much as nihilistic demons as charming eccentrics, or well-meaning but misguided dreamers. In all of these memoirs, the extreme measures used by the forces of order against anarchists are remembered as well. The anarchist memoirs become a memorial to dreamers, written in the context of a mature—if perhaps *too* ordered or settled—age. The threat of anarchism has vanished, along with anarchism's promise of liberty from convention; after the forces of convention have triumphed, anarchism is framed as an adolescent lark, a childish earnestness that one quickly outgrows.

In England, Ford Madox Ford and his cousins, Helen and Olivia Rosetti, were both acquainted with many prominent members of the radical community. Ford Madox Ford knew Morris, Shaw, Kropotkin, and others through his connections in intellectual circles; although he was not political himself, he was surrounded by those who were, and he observed them with a combination of affection and satiric distance. The Rossettis, who were allowed to follow their ambitions as children, actually edited and published an anarchist journal (the *Torch*) in which many anarchists from across Europe were published. All three published reminiscences of their earlier careers (Ford through numerous sketches and autobiographies, and the Rossettis through the collaborative novel *A Girl Among the Anarchists*, published under the pseudonym Isabel Meredith) which made anarchism seem less threatening by incorporating anarchists into the social fabric of the period and characterizing them as mostly harmless eccentrics and cranks, rather than the bloodthirsty nihilist of the stereotype.

Ford Madox Ford was a prolific writer of "impressions"—short sketches in which he attempted to convey the atmosphere of a given place and time, although not necessarily the historical facts. One of his first collections, titled *Memories and Impressions*,[5] takes a self-conscious distance from the events which it relates; Ford claims to write the book as a way to remember his own childhood among the giants of the late Victorian period. By addressing the book to children, he writes for people with no living memory of the events he describes, allowing him to adopt a very distant tone to the subjects themselves, placing "the Victorian great figures" in a distant past that does not impinge upon the present: "Nowadays we have no great figures, and I thank Heaven for it, because you and I can breathe freely. With the passing the other day of Tolstoy, with the death just a few weeks before of Mr. Holman Hunt, they all went away to Olympus, where very fittingly they may dwell."[6] The social conflicts that the Victorians waged as they crafted modern society have now been settled; now that the possibility of cataclysmic revolution has passed, it is safe to talk about, and even laugh at, anarchists, and to appreciate their motivations.

Ford frames the frightening narrative of revolution and international terrorism with the everyday world of clerks and offices with one story about the Italian anarchist Mazzini. This story, mildly humorous, captures many of the elements of the narrative which rehabilitated anarchism in the early years of the twentieth century. Mazzini, exiled in London for a brief time, lived in a solicitor's attic. After both Mazzini and the solicitor had died, the solicitor's firm grew larger, and converted the attic to office space.

> One day one of the partners was dictating a difficult letter to a clerk in such an attic. He stood before the fire and absent-mindedly fingered a dusty, spherical object of iron that stood upon the mantelpiece. Getting hold of the phrase he wanted, he threw, still absentmindedly, the object

into the fire. He finished dictating the letter and left the room. Immediately afterward there was a terrific explosion. The small round object was nothing more nor less than a small bomb . . . [which] found its predestined billet in the maiming of several poor clerks. I do not know that there is any particular moral to this story. (162–63).

The bomb, like the struggle for the revolution, has been forgotten, and is now a poorly understood relic on the mantel. The bomb, like the terrorist, only becomes dangerous when the leaders of society (in this case the lawyer of the firm) get careless, and, when it does blow up, it does not hurt the leaders themselves, but only their underlings. In much the same way, the terrorists of the previous generation caused much noise, but rarely hit their intended targets; more at fault were the people actually in charge, who, distracted by their own rhetoric, did not understand what they were doing.

With the destructiveness of the anarchists turned into an historical curiosity and a joke, Ford can playfully draw caricatures of anarchists that emphasize their impracticality and relative docility, making the extreme police repression of the late nineteenth century seem all the more unjust. Ford is especially fond of Peter Kropotkin, whose courage and scientific idealism form (for Ford) the ideal balance between heroism and endearing eccentricity. He remembers one debate with Kropotkin:

> I cannot imagine about what we can have wrangled. It was rabbits, I think. Kropotkin immensely admired the rabbit. It was for him the symbol of perdurability—and mass production. It stood out against selection. Defenseless and adapted to nothing in particular, it had outlived the pterodactyl, the Hyrcanian tiger and the lion of Numidia. The coneys, in short, were a feeble people, yet had their homes in the everlasting rocks. I don't know what I had to say against that. I obviously found something or the arguments could not have taken place. What I did say must obviously have had some sense, or he would not have returned to argue with me. (*Return to Yesterday*, 75)

Ford finds this affection for the homely rabbit to be comically absurd. The narratives that were used to combat anarchism have been forgotten, and without those narratives, the struggles of anarchists to communicate their ideals seem somewhat absurd, and the struggles against anarchists doubly so. The world of corporate organization and commercialism have won and retreated into the background; the anarchists seem quaint dreamers, delightful relics of a lost cause.

That the anarchists were harmless, Ford does not doubt. He remembers the funeral procession for the young man killed in the explosion near the Greenwich Observatory (which Ford matter-of-factly blames on agent provocateurs attempting to inspire a crackdown on anarchists in Britain), and the thousands who marched with the body: "there was not one more capable than myself of beginning to think of throwing a bomb. I suppose it was the spirit of romance, of youth, perhaps of sheer tomfoolery"[7] that Ford claims is very hard to find in the sober Edwardian age. Anarchism was part playacting, part adolescent rebellion, and, if the occasional foreigner did in fact blow something up, it was very distant, and the perpetrator always executed. The social order was never in doubt.

Ford remembers also the vitriol with which other radicals held the anarchists, despite (or because of) the similarity of their ideologies and the general harmlessness of the English anarchists. The socialists "were always holding meetings, at which the subject of the debate would be: 'The Foolishness of Anarchism.' This would naturally annoy the harmless and gentle anarchists, who only wanted to be left alone, to loaf on Goodge Street, and to victimize anyone who came into the offices of *The Torch* and had half-a-crown to spend on beer."[8] Ford resurrects the stereotype of the anarchist as loafer, not to condemn anarchism, but to condemn those who demonize anarchists.

The *Torch,* the anarchist paper published by Helen and Olivia Rossetti, was in fact a gathering-place for London anarchists during its brief period of publication, from 1891 until the Rossetti sisters and their brother moved on to other pursuits in 1896. They first published the paper in their parents' home, leading to (hyperbolically described by Ford) the house being "so beset with English detectives, French police spies and Russian *agents provocateurs* that to go along the sidewalk of the respectable terrace was to feel that one ran the gauntlet of innumerable gimlets."[9] The Rossetti sisters' semiautobiographical account of their years with the *Torch, A Girl Among the Anarchists*,[10] described anarchists as eccentric, charming, inspiring, and lazy; unlike Ford, they have their protagonist, Isabel Meredith, recognize the suffering, isolation, and mental instability produced by the anarchists' idealism and the hostility of a cruel society.

In *A Girl Among the Anarchists*, anarchism is seen as a kind of adolescent enthusiasm. As a young girl, Isabel Meredith is inspired by stories of the French Revolution and other narratives of revolt against oppression. An older relative, after hearing Isabel spout revolutionary rhetoric, remarks to her father that "you will have to keep a look-out or she will be making bombs soon and blowing us all up." Isabel's fondest childhood wish is to "die on the scaffold or a barricade, shouting Liberty, Equality, Fraternity."[11] Instead, Isabel devours works of modern economics, passionately sympathizes with the oppressed poor from her country house, and learns Socialism from her brother's radical friend. Inspired by Kropotkin's essay, "Appeal to the Young," Isabel writes an essay, which is published in the local anarchist newspaper. Having firmly established her radical credentials, she gains entrance to a local anarchist meeting.

Isabel's idealism and ignorance of the world are painfully obvious from her anticipation of the socialist meeting: "So great was my ignorance of the world, so wild my enthusiasm, that I imagined every socialist as a hero, willing to throw away his life at a moment's notice on behalf of the 'Cause.' I had had no experience of the petty internal strifes, of the jealousies and human frailties which a closer knowledge of all political parties reveals" (14). Anarchism as an ideal and the venality of the world are constantly at odds in this novel; the characters whom Isabel encounters in her time among the anarchists all unsuccessfully balance their idealism with their situation. The nature of their success or failure at this task is determined by their basic temperament, allowing the Rossettis to distinguish anarchist "types." Much of the novel is a parade of these anarchists, each representing some type within the movement. The mental dissolution of those who work most sincerely for the revolution convinces Isabel that it is hopeless to attempt to change society, and she eventually rejects anarchism as a revolutionary doctrine in favor of an individualist stoicism more suited to the Edwardian age.

A Girl Among the Anarchists presents several types of anarchists that tend to confirm most anarchist stereotypes, except for the violence: "the anarchists and their queer associates might be regarded as a fairly temperate set" (142). The only truly violent anarchists are foreign: one has fled from France after a café bombing, and the other is an Italian whose reason gives way to paranoid delusions and who commits suicide by attacking a Spanish minister. The crowd or the mob, which plays such an important role in anarchist narratives from the previous decade, is absent from the novel. All the anarchists are individuals, although some are faulted for behaviors that, contrary to Isabel's idealism, confirm stereotypes of the poor: a drinking habit, a filthy dress, an apathetic attitude, and a cowardly sense of self-preservation at all costs. Other anarchists are faulted for living too much in their idealism, to the point that they cannot be happy in the actual world because it resists their

dream of revolution. Isabel's depictions of anarchists minimize the
threat by confirming the negative stereotypes of anarchists as lazy
or deranged. All of the anarchists are eccentrics; the office of the
Tocsin attracts eccentrics of other kinds as well, especially religious cranks. With their colorful personalities, they present a stark
contrast to the police, who constantly shadow the anarchists with a
businesslike malevolence.

The most common anarchist is "the loafer type," who adopts
communistic principles in order to justify sponging off others. The
most striking example of this type is the ostensible compositor of
the printing press, a man named Short, who has "discarded dress-
ing and undressing as a frivolous waste of time" (79), lives in the
offices of the paper, and rarely, if ever, does work. Short became a
socialist out of "envy and sloth" (134). Other loafers use their "anarchism" to justify not even working through the poorhouse; one
person, claiming to be an anarchist, engages in petty thievery and
labels it "expropriation" (82); another man "looked forward to the
Social Revolution as the only escape from" a nagging wife (143).
The rank and file of the English anarchist party "used long words
they barely understood, considered that equality justified presump-
tion, and [had] contempt or envy of everything they felt to be superior to themselves. Communism, as they conceived it, amounted
pretty nearly to living at other people's expense" (272). They have
reconciled anarchism to reality by completely forsaking idealism;
they form the most common variety of "anarchist," and are, for the
most part, cowardly deadwood.

The narrator alludes to Lombroso's theories when describing the
psychology of the more committed anarchists: "there has been of
late years a remarkable, and, on the whole, a very futile tendency
among certain men of science to dissect and classify abnormal people and abnormal ideas, to discover that geniuses are mad, and that
all manner of well-intentioned fanatics are born criminals" (187).
This is simply not the case; fanatics differ from others only in their
radically different perspective toward life, which a normal person is
incapable of understanding or judging. "Among the Anarchists—
who may be said to represent the intellectual rather than the material side of the Socialist movement—there were many fanatics"
(187–88). The fanatics were especially drawn to acts of extreme violence, although often for very different reasons. The book mentions
several examples: Emile Henry, who bombed a Parisian café, was
"a theoretical dynamitard" (188) who concluded that his actions
were appropriate. On the other hand, there are terrorists such as
Ravachol, who are motivated out of a sense of personal revenge,

and who care little for anarchist theories as such. In the same class are Christian anarchists, who are so fanatically devoted to nonviolence that the policemen and even other radicals routinely beat them up while they offer no resistance. The police, imbued with their own sense of the justice of violence, are described as being especially frustrated by Christian anarchists.

Some anarchists start out so fanatically that they see the entire world through their fanaticism. Kosinski, an anarchist single-mindedly devoted to the revolutionary cause, despises women because they do not make committed revolutionaries. For a while, he accepts Isabel on his own terms, claiming "you are not a woman: you are a Comrade" (101). When Isabel has a change of heart and begins to doubt that the struggle for the Social Revolution is worth the misery it causes, it is Kosinski she confronts: "To what idol of our own creation are we sacrificing our happiness? We Anarchists are always talking of the rights of the individual, why are you deliberately sacrificing your personal happiness, and mine?" (267–68). He responds only that "an anarchist's life is not his own" (268), and Isabel realizes that he has never had a deep friendship with her, only a comradeship within the framework of the "Cause." The fanatic struggle for revolution, Isabel realizes, leads one to give up the very happiness for which one claims to be working.

Some anarchists start out as competent, even heroic, men, but their idealism erodes their grip on reality. The man whom Isabel feels the strongest connection to during her time with the anarchists, Dr. Armitage, represents the idealist who becomes an anarchist out of his fanatic pursuit of perfection. Dr. Armitage is a talented medical doctor, and he is totally committed to the cause, to the point that he cannot understand hypocrisy: "Dr. Armitage was a fanatic and an idealist, and two convictions were paramount in his mind at this time: the necessity and justice of the 'propaganda by force' doctrine preached by the more advanced Anarchists, and the absolute good faith and devotion to principle of the men with whom he was associated" (51). A police informant who betrays the movement during the Greenwich bombing is totally incomprehensible to him, and he chooses to ignore reality rather than question his own idealism. This preference for ideals over reality leads him to vegetarianism and "clothing reform,"[12] and he eventually abandons Isabel because she will not help him pursue his ideals. When he abandons all human connections, he becomes yet another useless crank.

Giannoli is another talented man who loses his mind in the anarchist cause. Unlike the purely theoretical Armitage, Giannoli is a committed revolutionary from both emotion and theory: "his desires and actions were responsible for his views. They coloured and distorted his opinions and destroyed all sense of proportion. An incident in his private life would stand up giant-like in the way of all the doctrines of the world, dwarfing opinions and creeds" (195). Despite (or because of) his fanaticism, Giannoli is an honorable and exceedingly talented individual. In the course of his revolutionary career, he has been forced to leave city after city and is constantly worried that he will be betrayed by a comrade and arrested. This fear develops into a full-fledged paranoia, in which he trusts no one. He flees London, and, ignoring Isabel's attempts to help him, resolves to kill himself by attempting an anarchist assassination.

When he resolves to commit an outrage, Giannoli acts alone, in accordance with the anarchist belief that terrorism must be an individual act: "like many other anarchists he entertained an almost maniacal prejudice against plots and conspiracies of any kind, maintaining that such organizations were merely police traps and death-gins" (212). This observation is a direct refutation of the wild conspiracy theories spun by conservative elements in the previous century. Nevertheless, after he fails in his assassination attempt and is arrested, the journalists create a conspiracy and the police arrest other anarchists anyway: "The police do not credit the idea that he has no accomplices, and during the evening extensive arrests have been made in Madrid and Barcelona" (290). Mainstream society, too, has its own fanaticism: paranoia, backed up by the police and the newspapers.

All of these latter anarchist breakdowns occur as the novel nears its end, creating the impression of a total breakdown by the best of the movement, leaving only the dregs. The hard work and misery that have overtaken Isabel during her time among the anarchists have led her to reject the possibility of revolution and instead to pursue her own individual happiness. She comes into agreement with her sister, who finds that "it is your stern moralists and humanitarians who cause the most unhappiness in the world" (281). She instead embraces the writings of Marcus Aurelius, "who knew how to create in his own soul an oasis of rest, not by practising a selfish indifference to, and isolation from, public matters—not by placing his hopes in some future paradise, the compensation of terrestrial suffering, but by rising superior to external events" (287). With Aurelius's public-minded yet individualist stoicism, Isabel finds the balance that the revolutionary anarchists tragically lacked, enabling her to leave the movement for a more mature understanding of the world. When a vindictive police officer uses the assassination in Spain as a pretext for suppressing the *Tocsin* (the fictional name for the *Torch* in this novel) Isabel seizes her chance to wash her hands of the revolutionary movement, and leaves "a sadder if a wiser woman" (302).

A Girl Among the Anarchists ends with a rejection of revolutionary extremism on both the left and the right. The anarchists are shown to be deranged, but not nearly as dangerous as the conspiracy narrative depicts them to be. With their justification undercut, the extreme paranoia of the newspapers and the vindictive oppression of the police are also linked as part of delusional narratives which help to keep people miserable. Although Isabel Meredith rejects anarchism, she comes to a position closer to the nonrevolutionary individualist anarchists such as Benjamin Tucker in the United States. In a society filled with vindictive, exploitative, and stupid people, the best position is a kind of stoic individualism—a quiet, as opposed to revolutionary, anarchism.

The narratives of Ford and the Rossettis were part of a reevaluation of the historical anarchist movement that occurred after anarchism as a distinct social vision had been defeated by corporate commercialism. Ford found this new world order to be somewhat tidy and inconsequential when compared to the vast designs of the Victorians; society had become predictable for him. Other writers, such as Conrad and Chesterton, instead adapted the language of anarchism to reveal the inherent disorder in society. By translating the language of a minority group into the larger dialogue, these writers planted the seeds for the twentieth century's enduring interest in anarchism.

6

Anarchy and Culture

Joseph Conrad and G. K. Chesterton, writers who would never have supported anarchism as a political movement, transformed the language of anarchism into a useful way of describing the modern condition. The anarchist ideal of each individual creating his or her own understanding was seized as a way of depicting the alienation, explosion of print sources, and radical social segregation of the modern world. The chaos which endures in spite of (or even because of) our attempts to regulate the world could best be described through the discourse of anarchism. These writers brought anarchist ideas and anarchist assumptions about society into the mainstream of Western thought. Conrad gives his fullest treatment to anarchism as a theme in *The Secret Agent* (1907). G. K. Chesterton depicts the more absurd aspects of an anarchistic carnival in *The Man Who Was Thursday* (1908). Chesterton's satire, contained within a larger order, brings laughter; Conrad's pessimism finds its anarchistic expression in the ultimate futility of human-imposed order, in the inability of the individual to control her or his own fate amid the social machinery.

By bringing anarchistic ideas into the broader dialogue, writers could control the associations through a broader narrative frame, or circumscribe the threat of anarchism with laughter; anarchism created fear only when no dialogue was seen as possible. The anarchist as bomber lived on in the comic strips in *The Yellow Kid* and later in "Spy vs. Spy" in *Mad Magazine*; Charlie Chaplin's tramp transformed the anarchistic fears of the poor into an expression of an Everyman, only tenuously in control of his surroundings. The transformation of anarchist into a figure of jest began in the early part of the century with the effort to defuse the fears associated with anarchism.

THE SECRET AGENT: SOCIAL DISORDER AND THE LANGUAGE OF ANARCHISM

Joseph Conrad's *The Secret Agent*[1] comes at a time when there is a huge difference between the essentially moribund anarchist movement in actuality and the virulent threat represented by the anarchist movement as a symbol. Although he knew little of the historical anarchist movement, Conrad shifts the associations that the symbol of anarchism holds. In *The Secret Agent*, anarchy is not so much a radical political position as it is an essential feature of human society; the anarchist moves from the borders of mainstream understanding to the very middle of things.

Although Conrad claimed that his awareness of the historical details of individual anarchists was slim, the theme of anarchists and revolutionaries was one that held an intense fascination for Conrad. Several short stories and novels deal either directly or indirectly with the idea of revolution or the repression that combats it. Conrad wrote *The Secret Agent* with a full awareness of the discourse surrounding anarchism as a subject. Matthew Arnold's equation of anarchy with the social values of the working class, opposed to the great tradition of Europe's elites, had transformed anarchism into a scapegoat for society's own doubts about the effectiveness of its institutions. Conrad recognized the power of the anarchists as lying in the larger narrative of cultural decline, accounting for the numerous members of the upper class (described in the short story "The Informer")[2] who faddishly espoused anarchism as a way of dealing with their own boredom and self-loathing. In anarchism, Conrad finds a symbol that, in its associations with the increasing political power of the lower classes, allows him to discuss the problems of modern urban life and issues of human comprehension and control that form the central theme of *The Secret Agent*.

Nevertheless, Conrad is not writing a reactionary novel like Richard Savage's *The Anarchist: A Story of To-Day*, which advocates increasingly repressive measures in the maintenance of social order which the hated Russian, Vladimir, encourages England to adopt. Conrad's sarcasm finds both the oppressor and the revolutionary equally inviting targets. In his preface to *Under Western Eyes*, Conrad sees anarchy in government as well as in revolt: "The ferocity and imbecility of an autocratic rule rejecting all legality and in fact basing itself upon moral anarchism provokes the no less imbecile and atrocious answer of a purely Utopian revolutionism."[3] Although Arnold may have characterized anarchism as the antithesis of culture, Conrad sees the demise of Arnoldian "culture" in the face of rampant self-interest; anarchism as a political force is irrelevant. Fleishman noted that "Conrad's view of democratic governments focuses on their reflection of capitalist interests and their inability to resist the will of the middle classes, which dominate the body politic. His faith in democracy is based on its breaking with capitalism."[4] Conrad's dislike of societies based in individualistic greed can be seen in many different works. In "An Anarchist," the capitalists are just as reprehensible—and more dangerous—than the "citizen anarchist" in the story.[5] In *Nostromo* the Europeans are depicted as caring much more for silver than they do for other human beings.[6] Although Conrad is uneasy with the growing influence of greed and the market in all aspects of human culture, he is no more an "anarchist in disguise" than he is an apologist for the upper classes.

Many misunderstandings of *The Secret Agent* have resulted from a desire to see anarchism in purely political terms. Anarchism is not to be understood as a political position in *The Secret Agent*. Rather, Conrad uses anarchism as a theme for the associations it brings. Anarchism was seen as a threat to everything in the established order, from the most exalted government to the institution of marriage itself. Following the tradition of Arnold and Henry James, Conrad recognized anarchism's association with the general sense of social decline as voiced by Lombroso and his pupil, Max Nordau, whose *Degeneration* caused a sensation in 1895, the year after the Greenwich Park explosion which provides the historical basis for the novel.[7] In *The Secret Agent*, Conrad describes a world that is distracted from capitalist dehumanization by the fiction of a political revolution.

Although Conrad uses his reader's associations of anarchism with fear of the masses and the breakdown of social institutions, he undercuts the political confrontation between the revolutionaries and the police by having both "anarchists" and "public servants" despise or fear the public and be motivated out of a similar vanity and self-interest. For Conrad, human selfishness has already produced a kind of anarchy, and nothing that the revolutionists or the police can do will affect the inertia of the masses. One of the chief absurdities of the novel is the relative powerlessness of any individual to bring about any kind of change; even the bomb itself, which profoundly affects the lives of a few individuals, causes barely a ripple in the overall discourse of society.

The novel's criticism of the power of the masses is reinforced by a kind of "scarcity theory of value" by which anything that is common becomes worthless, from newspapers to political assassinations. The declining value of the commonplace is Vladimir's main reason for hatching the plot to blow up the observatory. "Normal" terrorist acts have become too common to be useful: "all this is used up; it is no longer instructive as an object lesson in revolutionary anarchism. Every newspaper has ready-made explanations to explain such manifestations away" (66). Just as murder "is almost an institution" (67), terrorism has become common enough to lose its effectiveness through the deadening power of common language.

In his preface to the novel, Conrad said "I was an extreme revolutionist" (42), a statement most critics have used to point out the parallels between terrorism and challenging art which occur in the novel. The irony of the novel is an attempt to break out of the deadening formulas of established discourse patterns, just as the terrorist bomb is an attempt to shake up perceptions of reality. On one level, *The Secret Agent* is a novel about the social uses of language, the deadening of speech genres, and the pervasive effects of received narratives on individuals. Moreover, the novel shows the inherent anarchy of the modern city, in which millions of people, all governed by their own narrative understandings, are placed in often violent juxtaposition. It is this fear of the multitude inherent in the cultural associations of anarchism that allows Conrad to create a common purpose between the bomb and the book, although Conrad does not have high hopes that any individual or institution can influence the unthinking direction of society.

The city itself, teeming with people and objects, becomes the central symbol of the devaluing effect of the common. Verloc, leaning his head against his window, has only "a fragile film of glass stretched between him and the enormity of cold, black, wet, muddy, inhospitable accumulation of bricks, slates, and stones, things in themselves unlovely and unfriendly to man" (84). The city represents an accumulation, ugly and hostile. The dehumanizing effect of the buildings is extended to the inhabitants as well. Several times in the novel, people on the street—faceless, yet always present—are referred to as insects: "they swarmed numerous like locusts, industrious like ants, thoughtless like a natural force, pushing on blind and orderly and absorbed, impervious to sentiment, to logic, to terror, too, perhaps" (103). The effects of mass culture, not revolutionary doctrines, threaten to make individuals insignificant and worthless. The extreme distance that the narrator takes from his subjects encourages us as readers to see the characters not as individuals, but as parts of the crowd, stripped of their individuality. Despite their efforts to establish themselves as individuals, the characters in *The Secret Agent*, like the members of corporate, industrialized, society, never escape the dehumanizing effect of the crowd.

The Secret Agent is filled with scenes which take place in public locations—people walking or taking cabs from place to place, people running into each other on the streets, and meetings in bars, clubs, and other places. Even the one domestic space in the novel—the Verloc's home—is a quasi-public store, and even their kitchen is a meeting-place for Verloc's acquaintances and contacts. In addition to the public nature of the settings of the novel, the sounds of the street play a role in many important scenes. The constant presence of the "public" in the novel reinforces the latent associations of anarchism with the unsavory aspects of city crowding, social control and mass culture.

Ironically, even an "anarchist" such as the Professor loathes the public, and "public servants" such as Inspector Heat and the Assistant Commissioner are baffled and bemused by the random turns of public opinion which interfere with their own games. The common situation of both the defenders and enemies of social institutions undermines a purely political interpretation of the novel and forces the reader to see both sides fighting a losing battle against the dehumanizing effects of modernity. As several critics have noted, "it is a moot point whether any of the so-called anarchists of *The Secret Agent* are true anarchists."[8] Inspector Heat's initial reaction to the explosion can serve as a key to the novel's main theme: "he had not been thinking of any individual anarchist at all. The complexion of that case had somehow forced upon him the general idea of the absurdity of things human" (110). Walking the public sidewalks, every pitiful character in the novel is engaged in a mostly futile attempt to wrestle narrative order out of the anarchy of the crowd.

Crowd noise plays an important role in several scenes. Characters resist the threat of meaninglessness and chaos by fulfilling roles within chosen narratives. The success of an individual's attempt to order his situation is indicated by the relative presence of the crowd within an individual's consciousness: when the crowd noise subsides, the character has succeeded, and when the crowd noise dominates, a character's sense of order is overwhelmed. One good example of this effect is the confrontation between the Professor and Chief Inspector Heat. The Professor (who had previously been disheartened by the thought of the vast crowd, oblivious to even his most fearsome weapon, terror) regains his equilibrium when he meets the Chief Inspector, which brings him back to his own role within his narrative of defiance: "The blended noises of the enormous town sank down to an inarticulate low murmur . . . the unwholesome-looking little moral agent of destruction exulted silently in the possession of personal prestige, keeping in check this man armed with the defensive mandate of a menaced society" (104). His confrontation with the police gives the Professor a role within his own narrative order, reestablishing his own self-importance by filtering out the knowledge of the vast crowd that surrounds him. The only way the characters can individuate themselves within the narrative is by reducing themselves to a defined role within some larger social game; to preserve their individuality they must lose it.

Even the police and other public servants maintain an ambivalent relationship to the public at large. The Assistant Commissioner in particular feels the weight of the crowd: "he felt himself dependent on too many subordinates and too many masters. The near presence of that strange emotional phenomenon called public opinion weighed upon his spirits, and alarmed him by its irrational nature" (116). The Chief Inspector wants to arrest Michaelis, not because he has anything to do with the bombing, but because the police have the legal right to do so, it will satisfy his own vanity, and it will give them a scapegoat for public consumption: "it seemed to him an excellent thing to have that man at hand to be thrown down to the public should it think fit to roar with any special indignation in this case" (126). The Commissioner, "chained to a desk in the thick of four millions of men" (125), heeds the voice of upper-class dilettantism and his own need for domestic harmony (Michaelis's patron is his socially prestigious wife's friend) in resisting the urge to arrest Michaelis on a pretext. This infuriates Heat, who realizes that, if Michaelis is not a scapegoat, the investigation will lead to his own secret sources. Heat is more interested in preserving the "sense of superiority the members of the police get from the unofficial but intimate side of their intercourse with the criminal classes, by which the vanity of power is soothed" (132) than he is interested in presenting the truth to a "public" he contemptuously serves.

All of the characters in *The Secret Agent* attempt to maintain control by separating themselves from interactions that do not fit within their narrative sense of identity. However, no character successfully maintains his or her own narrative in the face of the relentless pressure of the populace. Verloc's domestic life is intruded upon by the public and commercial spheres of discourse, both in terms of his job as secret agent and his cover as porn-shop owner, and other characters must face the constant threat of having their private narrative understandings overwhelmed by the sheer numbers of people surrounding them. Just as the newspapers diminish rather than convey meaning, so the crowd encourages segregation rather than communication. Even this strategy for maintaining individuality loses its meaning through iteration. The world of *The Secret Agent* is symbolized by Stevie's drawings, which are "innumerable circles, concentric, eccentric; a coruscating whirl of circles that by their tangled multitude of repeated curves, uniformity of form, and confusion of intersecting lines suggested a rendering of cosmic chaos, the symbolism of mad art attempting the inconceivable" (76). Each character attempts to be self-contained in her or his own simplified understanding of the world (especially the nihilistic Professor), and intersects with other characters only randomly; the overall effect of numerous simple shapes randomly related to each other, however, is not order but anarchy.

The self-contained, ineffectual order of the supposed revolutionaries of the novel points to the underlying anarchy of reality. Although critics have argued that each of the anarchists represents a stereotypical anarchist "type," Conrad satirizes both Michaelis and Yundt not so much for their particular creeds as for their jargonfilled visions that have little to do with reality. Sherry describes Michaelis as combining the postimprisonment physique of Michael Bakunin with the indomitable optimism of Peter Kropotkin, and employing the language of Karl Marx and Edward Bellamy (the latter two most certainly not anarchists, but utopian radicals).[9] Michaelis's first lines are filled with jargonized idealism, despite their ironic opening:

All idealization makes life poorer. To beautify it is to take away its character of complexity—it is to destroy it. Leave that to the moralists, my boy. History is made by men, but they do not make it in their heads. The ideas that are born in their consciousness play an insignificant part in the march of events. History is dominated and determined by the tool and the production—by the force of economic conditions. (73)

The irony is that Michaelis does not recognize his own (nor Marx's) jargon as yet another idealization—another oversimplification that "beautifies" the chaos of actual existence by making it appear comprehensible, predictable, and controllable. Although individual ideas are pronounced unimportant by Michaelis, he is eager to accept the advance for a book, and his memoirs include a utopia organized like a hospital—a beautified world. The enclosed nature of Michaelis's idealization can be seen in the fact that "he talked to himself, indifferent to the sympathy or hostility of his hearers, indifferent to their presence" (75). His long imprisonment has perfected his self-enclosure, and his optimism allows him to have faith in his vision despite all evidence to the contrary. He has become a darling of upper-class radicals, who can, in their Princess Casamassima-like ennui, embrace a revolutionary who is completely harmless; his corpulence is a commentary on his beatific vision.

Like Michaelis, Yundt is lampooned for the incongruity between his idealized narrative and physical reality. Yundt, who (Johann Most-like) has always talked of dynamite and serious conspiracy without actually engaging in any plots himself, has "always dreamed . . . of a band of men absolute in their resolve to discard all scruples in the choice of means, strong enough to give themselves frankly the name of destroyers, and free from the taint of that resigned pessimism which rots the world"; unfortunately, "I could never get as many as three such men together" (74). Physically, "his worn out passion, resembling in its impotent fierceness the excitement of a senile sensualist" (74) undercuts the vision of implacable conspiracy which is practically lifted out of Nechaev's *Catechism of a Revolutionary*. For all his talk of conspiracy and dynamite, Yundt has never actually performed an act of terrorism; the only danger is that some simpleminded fool (like Stevie, or like McKinley's assassin, Leon Czogłosz, appeared to be) will take him seriously. In his life, however, Yundt was unable to find three people who would do so.

Ossipon, the scientist and corrupt womanizer, is a revolutionary only when he finds it to his advantage. In many ways, he is the perfect "modern": a firm believer in science (to the point of blindly swallowing Lombroso's theories), he objectifies and uses people in the pursuit of his own self-interest. Whereas Yundt and Michaelis try to maintain narratives that cast them in crucial roles (explicator of history or conspiratorial center), Ossipon uses the language of science itself to order the social universe around him and mask his own base desires. When confronted with real disorder (when Winnie comes to him for help after murdering Verloc), he has no choice but to consciously deny the complex chain of events surrounding the explosion: "for fear of adventuring his intelligence into ways where its natural lights might fail to guide it safely he dismissed resolutely all suppositions, surmises and theories out of his mind" (246); when he actually sees the dead body, he is "terrified scientifically" (254) but still carries through with his plan to rob Winnie of her money. In a world of people governed by materialistic self-interest, Ossipon represents nothing so much as the corrupt status quo.

In contrast to the decrepit impotence of Yundt and Michaelis or the corruption of Ossipon, the Professor, "the perfect anarchist," is the only 'anarchist' in the novel who has the potential for violence. He is the only revolutionary with access to explosives, which he would give to anyone who wanted them. The Professor, more nihilist than anarchist, wants the destruction of all "legalisms"—those internal disciplines which lead people to obey the social norms that allow England to maintain such good order. The Professor would prefer a society of naked force, such as he imagines the United States to be: "they have more character there, and their character is essentially anarchistic. Fertile ground for us, the States—very good ground. The great Republic has the root of the destructive matter in her. The collective temperament is lawless" (96). He desires anarchy as defined by its opponents: a Hobbesian world where might makes right. His sense of his own superiority echoes the egotism of Max Stirner and Nietzsche.

The Professor criticizes the other "revolutionaries" for their own dependence on dogmas: "you are as unable to think independently as any respectable greengrocer or journalist" (93). The Professor correctly sees the great narrative that governs the interactions of the police and the supposed anarchists: "The terrorist and the policeman both come from the same basket. Revolution, legality—counter moves in the same game, forms of idleness at bottom identical" (94). Unlike all other characters in the novel, the Professor lives his life in accordance with his rhetoric and refuses to compromise out of his sense of superiority.

However, even the Professor's narrative is undercut by the apathetic masses. Philosophically convinced of his own superiority, he can get no one else to recognize it; his search to force people to accept his understanding of himself leads him to the search for the perfect detonator. In many ways, the Professor's work is an analog for art. He seeks an "intelligent detonator" which will help him to make "a clean sweep" (97) and force people to question their faith in society. He works on this detonator alone and with a great single-mindedness of purpose, and would "shovel my stuff in heaps at the corners of the streets if I had enough for that" (97), just as an artist (such as Conrad) desires the greatest possible audience for his work and hopes that the work will change minds.

Unfortunately, the Professor's biggest enemy is simple indifference. As Vladimir has pointed out, every bomb becomes commonplace with repetition, losing its ability to change minds. Although Ossipon can imagine people running in horror if they knew that the Professor were a terrorist, the fact is that he can ride the bus without incident; the only people who recognize him are the police, with whom he plays a game every bit as empty as the game he describes the other "revolutionaries" as playing. When confronted with the vast indifference of the population at large, the Professor is disheartened: "he felt the mass of mankind mighty in its numbers . . . what if nothing could move them? Such moments came to all men whose ambition aims at a direct grasp upon humanity—to artists, politicians, thinkers, reformers, or saints" (103). As an artist, the Professor is poor and alone; also like most artists, he will never achieve his goals. The masses are too many to move, even with explosives.

If the anarchists are unable, despite their efforts, to effect any changes on the population, then the police are quite often unwilling to deal with the public at large. From Inspector Heat's "game" with the criminals of London, to the Assistant Commissioner's political deference and separation, to the willing myopia of the Home Secretary, the police in *The Secret Agent* are just as unable to actually change the course of events as the anarchists they engage in cat-and-mouse games. If the anarchists cocoon themselves in their own narratives in order to avoid facing the indifference of the masses, then the public servants of the novel have built institutions which (rather than fulfill their ostensible mission) offer stability and protection from the actual disorder produced by millions of individuals.

Throughout the novel, the police are characterized as tools of the propertied classes, echoing a standard anarchist critique of legal institutions. The first mention of this understanding of the police comes from Yundt as he criticizes Ossipon's faith in Lombroso's ideas: "Teeth and ears mark the criminal? Do they? And what about the law that marks them still better—the pretty branding instrument invented by the overfed to protect themselves against the hungry?" Here, however, Yundt's passion is undercut by his description as a demagogue who never actually acted on these principles of justice. However, Winnie later explains the role of the police to Stevie as "so that them as have nothing shouldn't take anything away from them who have" (170). She says this "without irony" (169); it is simply another way that, as Stevie has earlier observed, it is a "bad world for poor people" (168). The anarchists may offer no useful solution to the problem of justice in human society, but the police are in no way superior in their response to the moral ills of the human condition.

Inspector Heat avoids the moral implications of police work by structuring his life and his understanding though a set of informal "rules of the game." Heat has transformed these rules, loosely based on the code of police conduct and the law, into an elaborate system of rationalizations which allow him to lord over the criminals with whom he associates and to secure his position within the police bureaucracy without actually engaging in dangerous investigative behavior. He is unwilling to confront the Professor, whom he fears may be really dangerous, but he is quite willing to withhold information from his superior and arrest the wrong man for the crime just to have a scapegoat for the public.

As the only individual in the police bureaucracy who is in regular direct contact with the public, Heat is the individual expression of an institutional problem. Heat identifies more with the thieves he is supposed to fight than he does the higher "public good" he is supposed to serve:

> The mind and the instincts of a burglar are of the same kind as the mind and the instincts of a police officer. Both recognize the same conventions, and have a working knowledge of each others' methods and of the routine of their respective trades. They understand each other, which is advantageous to both, and this establishes a sort of amenity in their relations. (110)

Heat's job has been transformed by repetition into a deadened formula, a set of generic rituals and exchanges that are ossified and unable to interact with outside discourses. The novel portrays this rigid set of conventions in explicitly linguistic terms. The punishment which Heat inflicts on those burglars unlucky enough to be caught—"defined in its own special phraseology as 'Seven years' hard'" (110)—is understood by Heat within the language of the thieves. When he confronts the Professor, Heat uses "perfectly proper words, within the tradition and suitable to his character of a police officer. But the reception they got departed from tradition and propriety" (111); the limited nature of his language and understanding are revealed. Heat and the Professor cannot communicate, each refusing to employ the other's language; Heat can only promise that he will eventually capture the Professor on his own terms, within his own understanding, but he does not know how.

Heat's willingness to ignore the Professor stems from the Professor's stance outside of Heat's "game," or discourse. The closed-off nature of Heat's logic, shaken by his inability to predict the Greenwich Park explosion or communicate with the Professor, forces him to find a solution within his own sphere—the arrest of the "ticket-of-leave apostle," Michaelis. Heat wants to arrest Michaelis not because it would help discover the truth, but because it would be a permissible action against anarchists within the discourse of the legal profession. Heat understands the anarchists as simply another gang, somehow all connected; like all the other characters in the text, he attempts to impose his own language and understanding outside its competence.

Inspector Heat avoids the contradiction between his use of illicit informants (such as Verloc) and his role as an agent of law enforcement by avoiding "the game" entirely when he talks with Verloc. He sheds his identity as a policeman: "it was in the character of a private citizen that walking out privately he made use of his customary convenyances. Their general direction was towards Mr. Verloc's home" (190). He cannot express an intention to use an informant and be part of the police force at the same time.

The filter of the discourse of the "game" colors every interaction that Inspector Heat has with the police department as an institution. This mixture of loyalty and contempt that allows Heat to perform his job also prevents the institution from being effective.

> By a benevolent provision of Nature no man is a hero to his valet, or else the heroes would have to brush their own clothes. Likewise no department appears perfectly wise to the intimacy of its workers. A department does not know so much as some of its servants. Being a dispassionate organism, it can never be perfectly informed. (109)

Heat's superiors, who are a part of the institution and not a part of the "game" on the street, are manipulated to obey the wishes of their subordinates. Heat has seen individual Assistant Commissioners come and go, and he gives them only limited respect because they do not know the "game" as well as he does.

Although the previous chiefs were quite happy to be manipulated by Heat, the current Assistant Commissioner is uncomfortable with his role as alienated middleman. Uncomfortable in the "confined nature and apparent lack of reality" (141) of a bureaucratic role, he remembers fondly the time when, as a colony administrator, "he had been very successful in tracking and breaking up certain nefarious secret societies among the natives" (116). He still casts himself as an investigator, even if he is only investigating the reliability of his subordinates; however, the feeling that "strings" of conspiracy exist leads him to bypass the normal channels and resume his role as investigator of political plots.

Although Norman Sherry calls the Assistant Commissioner the novel's hero, his role shows the limitations of his own chosen narrative frame. The Assistant Commissioner fancies himself a political investigator, who will discover a secret plot against the government and extract a confession from the perpetrators. Despite the ludicrous nature of the event, the Commissioner is able to follow it to its forced "conclusion" because his own narrative is just as skewed; "I have been always of opinion" (148), he tells the Home Secretary, betraying his predetermined stance. It is his obsession with ferreting out secret societies which enables him to follow the insane actions of the agent provocateur all the way to Vladimir; it is this same narrative of investigation which keeps him "in ignorance of poor Stevie's devotion" (203), and to the violent potential of the "domestic drama" he finds comic (204). His narrative ends with Verloc's confession, and, in doing so, he misses the only true anarchist in the book, Winnie. Like Heat, he thinks like his antagonists, an arrangement that allows him to follow his own narrative to a satisfactory conclusion. Trained in politics, he values the political over the personal. This tendency is carried to an extreme by the Home Secretary, who can only think of his domestic policy when he hears the word "domestic."

The Home Secretary, with his constant fear of details, is an easy caricature of the politician who operates completely cut off from reality. Although he is vaguely aware that he has no control over his subordinates—"I'm glad there's somebody over at your shop who thinks that the secretary of State may be trusted now and then" (144)—he nonetheless is content to operate above the details of actual living. Ironically, his very abstraction leads him into the same socialism which his subordinates are fighting; his bill to nationalize the fisheries, which consumes all his energy, is more socialistic than any effort on the part of the supposed "revolutionaries."

If neither the police nor the revolutionaries have any effect on the direction of the masses, then the institutions that are supposedly able to influence thought are even less suited to the task. Even the newspapers, which can whip up a popular frenzy, have only a limited appeal. Compared to millions of people, no one thing can be significant: "the trade in afternoon papers was brisk, yet in comparison with the swift, constant march of foot traffic, the effect was of indifference, of a disregarded distribution" (101). Moreover, the newspaper itself is guilty of oversimplifying reality in a most distasteful way. When he first reads the newspaper account of the bombing, Ossipon reacts "the rest's mere newspaper gup. No doubt a wicked attempt to blow up the Observatory, they say. H'm. That's hardly credible" (95). The papers, in their own fanatic pursuit of the "outrage," fit the events into their own sensational narrative. The newspaper sums up the story in an equally unsatisfactory manner, even as Ossipon himself tries to forget his own knowledge of the events: *"an impenetrable mystery seems destined to hang for ever over this act of madness and despair"* (266). The novel, like the papers, disconnects the phrases from their context and repeats them over and over, emphasizing the emptiness of the words themselves. The newspaper, like all other public, shared, endeavors, is unsuitable to the task of giving order to society.

If no public institution can impose a meaning on the anarchistic interactions of numerous individuals, then it is customary to assume (as is often the case with the sentimental tradition of domestic fiction) that the true ordering power lies in domestic relationships. Here, too, Conrad undercuts the conventional narrative by placing domestic discourse in an alien linguistic context and showing the unsuitability of conventional romantic narratives to adequately describe reality. Verloc's retreat from cynical realism to a belief in his own fictions is a counterpoint to the only character who escapes her own "legalisms"—Winnie.

When the novel begins, Verloc recognizes that his position as a secret agent depends upon a propagated fiction, not an actual threat to society. Although differences in wealth and social status create the problems of poverty and theft, Verloc understands that the social belief in violent revolution is a ludicrous fiction: "at the notion of a menaced social order he would perhaps have winked to himself if there had not been an effort to make in that sign of skepticism" (52). As someone who knows the luminaries of the social revolution, yet remains outside their narrative, he recognizes both their actual impotence and the advantage he can accrue by playing to the fears those revolutionaries represent. The Baron, his previous employer, was motivated by the general sense of the coming end of civilization and readily believed Verloc's exaggerated stories of attempts on the lives of various dignitaries; Vladimir, the Baron's successor, is grounded in the spirit of the mass culture. The old stories do not move him; he requires an actual explosion, a novelty which does not fit into established genres. Vladimir wishes to have Verloc fulfill more precisely the role of agent provocateur within the anarchist movement in order to get his money's worth, but Vladimir is completely ignorant of the realities of that movement:

> He confounded causes with effects more than was excusable; the most distinguished propagandists with impulsive bomb throwers; assumed organization where in the nature of things it could not exist; spoke of the social revolutionary party one moment as of a perfectly disciplined army, where the word of chiefs was supreme, and at another as if it had been the loosest association of desperate brigands that ever camped in a mountain gorge. (65)

The ambassador's understanding of anarchism comes straight from the contradictory stories in the newspapers and magazines of the period, which confused all of these issues as completely as does Vladimir and likewise overestimated its potential influence. Like the Home Secretary, Vladimir dwells completely within narratives and does not trouble himself with actualities. Nonetheless, his threat to Verloc's income is very real; the desire for money leads Verloc to his atrocity, just as the cab driver's cruelty is inspired by his desire for the fare. Verloc's lassitude and lack of professionalism are quickly overcome by Vladimir's threat to his domestic life.

What truly motivates Verloc is not his work, but his idea of domestic bliss. A married anarchist, Verloc "cultivated his domestic virtues" in the pornography shop which is his "cover." Cynical about his work and the public sphere, Verloc relies on his domestic relationship to order his life and to filter out the threats which the vast, indifferent masses represent to his own individuality. When Winnie confirms their relationship, Verloc forgets the pressures of the commercial world: "not a whisper reached them from the outside world. The sound of footsteps on the pavement died out in the discreet dimness of the shop" (185). Just as the Professor's confrontations with police shield him from the threat of indifference, so does Winnie's attention shield Verloc.

Unfortunately, Verloc misunderstands the very basis of his relationship with Winnie. "In his affairs of the heart Mr. Verloc had been always carelessly generous, yet always with no other idea that of being loved for himself. Upon this matter, his ethical notions being in agreement with his vanity, he was completely incorrigible" (226). Mr. Verloc believes in the fiction of domestic bliss; unfortunately, Winnie's understanding of their relationship is firmly grounded in the language of the marketplace, a contract for services rendered. Her understanding of marriage as an essentially economic relationship echoes the opinions of many anarchists and freethinkers of the time. Her entire life is understood through her relationship to her brother, and her marriage to Verloc is simply one of the arrangements she has made for her brother's sake. Before Verloc leads Stevie to his death, she feels that she gets a good bargain. Her own silence, "the foundation of their accord in domestic life" (216), allowed Verloc to fulfill his own narrative, unthreatened by Winnie's simple calculation; his role as ideal husband leads him to show caring for Stevie despite his own lack of concern.

Winnie is the only character in the novel who actually escapes the dominant narrative of her life, and her escape is due only to the senseless tragedy of the explosion. Without Stevie, her relationship to Verloc no longer makes sense; her recognition of this lack of order frees her mind: "At that precise moment Mrs. Verloc began to

look upon herself as released from all earthly ties. She had her freedom. Her contract with existence, as represented by that man
standing there, was at an end. She was a free woman" (226). Her
freedom from the order of her life is signaled by her silence, because
true freedom is incompatible with language. Until she murders Verloc and reenters the social world, she utters only one word:

> "Yes," answered obediently Mrs. Verloc the free woman. She com-
> manded her wits now, her vocal organs; she felt herself to be in an al-
> most preternaturally perfect control of every fibre of her body. It was all
> her own, because the bargain was at an end. She was clear sighted. She
> had become cunning. She chose to answer him so readily for a purpose.
> She did not wish that man to change his position on the sofa which was
> very suitable to the circumstances. (233)

By maintaining the illusion of marital bliss, Mrs. Verloc can more
easily kill her husband because, no longer bound by her understood
contract, he is useless to her; her fiction is at an end.

Verloc, however, does not let go of his own language so easily.
Despite the fact that a tacit misunderstanding had been the basis of
their relationship, Verloc finds himself needing communion with
her, perhaps because the rarity of her speech has made itself precious. Winnie's silence throws his domestic fictions into chaos. Verloc ironically resorts to the same fictions which had worked with his
first employer, the Baron; he tries to reestablish his worth to Winnie
by convincing her of his importance in the maintenance of social
order: "there isn't a murdering plot for the last eleven years that I
hadn't my finger in at the risk of my life. There's scores of these
revolutionists I've sent off with their bombs in their blamed pockets,
to get caught on the frontier. The old Baron knew what I was worth
to his country" (217). The same stories he had scoffed at earlier
become his only source of refuge, but even that is insufficient because "the excellent husband of Winnie Verloc saw no writing on
the wall" (218). His own words mean one thing within the closed
circle of his thought; to Winnie, he seems to be bragging about killing her brother. Verloc has never understood Winnie's language,
and so is completely unprepared for her revenge.

After she has killed Verloc, exacting the penalty for the broken
contract, Winnie quickly descends back into the commonplace narratives that govern her world. As is the case with other characters
in Conrad novels (such as Jim in *Lord Jim*, Nostromo in *Nostromo*,
and Razumov in *Under Western Eyes*), Winnie quickly realizes that
it is impossible to live totally apart from human connection. Recog-

nizing the import of the dead body in her house, she shudders at her own vision of hell, the newspaper accounts of hanged murderers:

> Mrs. Verloc, though not a well-informed woman, had a sufficient knowledge of the institutions of her country to know that gallows are no longer erected romantically on the banks of dismal rivers or in windswept heartlands, but in the yards of jails . . . the murderer was brought out to be executed, with an horrible quietness, and, as reports in the newspapers always said, "in the presence of authorities" . . . the newspapers never gave any details except one, but that one with some affection was always there at the end of the meagre report. Mrs. Verloc remembered its nature. It came with a cruel burning pain in her head, as if the words "the drop given was fourteen feet" had been scratched on her brain with a hot needle. (238)

Despite her momentary sense of freedom, Winnie falls back into another social narrative. The newspaper accounts of hanging, designed to instill fear, have worked, and Winnie adopts the role of the murderer, attempting to escape the authorities. Winnie, desperate to play the role of the escaped murderer, turns to Ossipon, whose narrative of seduction and plunder deprives Winnie of both her active role and her only practical means of escape.

The novel ends as Ossipon and the Professor part on the public thoroughfare, and the actions of Winnie and Verloc have been captured by a journalistic formula. The Assistant Commissioner, who has faith that "the wealth and precision of detail will carry conviction to the great mass of the public" (208), is mistaken. The newspaper creates a facade of order and control by replacing individual detail with circular statements and dead formulas. The narrator, brutally distant and mocking of the characters in the novel, invites the reader to engage in this same mocking dismissal, but the only way to do so is to repeat the misunderstandings of the characters themselves. In reality, the countless interactions of independent individuals resemble Stevie's drawings: simple figures repeated so often that the effect is chaotic. Conrad expands the concept of anarchy from its nineteenth-century associations with the anxieties of the coming power of the lower classes into a modernistic conception of society itself as fundamentally anarchistic.

The provisionality of any linguistic understanding combined with the sheer number of different possible languages creates an anarchistic Babel, but despite the inability of effective coordination, the construction of modern, commercial society goes on. In *The Secret Agent*, anarchism is transformed from a political agenda into a metaphor for the human condition, and its failure as a movement in the late nineteenth century parallels the failure of the human mind and human institutions to comprehend the complexity and direction of society as a whole. Rather, individuals will continue to bend to the inevitable demands of the market; Ossipon ends "marching in the gutter as if in training for the task of an inevitable future" (269). Fittingly, the Professor ends the novel, commenting on the role of the artist, a crafter of narrative understandings, in this world of mass culture. The Professor "had no future . . . he passed on unsuspected and deadly, like a pest in a street full of men" (269). Mocking Michaelis's optimism, *The Secret Agent* reminds the reader of the anarchy lurking within the juggernaut of history. Originally a symbol of what threatened society from outside its language, anarchism lurks in the center of all our stories.

HUMAN ANARCHY AND COSMIC ORDER: CHESTERTON'S PARODIC OPTIMISM

G. K. Chesterton's *The Man Who Was Thursday*[10] signifies a dramatic shift in the depiction of anarchism and anarchists. Rather than associating anarchism with threats of revolution or degeneracy, Chesterton sees the comic potential in anarchy. In the novel, the surface disorder of the world becomes an argument favoring an anarchistic understanding of the world and allows Chesterton to gently satirize the pretensions of the powerful. At the same time, however, Chesterton contains the nihilistic potential of anarchist discourse by framing it within the language of Christianity, much as the events of the novel are framed as a nightmare.

The novel *The Man Who Was Thursday* is subtitled "A Nightmare," and most of the book is a fanciful daydream on the part of Gabriel Syme, a poet fanatically devoted to order and respectability, after a confrontation with an "anarchist" poet, Lucian Gregory. Chesterton takes pains to remind his reader to interpret the events of the book symbolically; Gregory tells Syme, while the latter is enjoying Lobster Mayonnaise and champagne at a pub near Chiswick, "You are not asleep, I assure you. . . . You are, on the contrary, close to the most rousing moment of your existence" (17). The novel itself becomes a set of Chinese boxes, one inside the other, alternately exposing the anarchy which follows human attempts to order the universe, and the order which underlies the universe's apparent anarchy.

Chesterton does not have actual anarchists in mind, although he does lampoon several historical anarchists in the course of the novel. The anarchism that Chesterton describes has more in common with the theatrical posture of revolt described by Ford Madox Ford and Helen and Olivia Rosetti. By 1908, the first wave of anarchist agitation had passed nearly everywhere in Europe; anarchism was becoming institutionalized as syndicalism among the working classes, and the fears of revolution which had haunted the West for the previous thirty years were subsiding. Anarchism had become institutionalized as a villain of the forces of order, and Chesterton's novel satirizes the clichéd status of anarchist revolt as well as the histrionic attacks on anarchism by the powerful.

Despite the failure of political or revolutionary anarchism, individualist anarchism, which had always been more popular among artists and the upper classes, continued to exert an influence on culture. The target of Chesterton's satire is not political anarchism, but the vanity he finds lurking behind the individualist (and atheistic) assertion that people are capable of ordering the universe for themselves. He finds a similar hubris in those who vehemently oppose anarchists, who place such a faith in their own ability to order the world that they are blind to the actual chaos that they create. Although Chesterton had not yet converted to Catholicism when he wrote *The Man Who Was Thursday*, he satirizes both anarchy and human order by showing their insignificance within a larger, religious context. By explicitly framing anarchism as a human-constructed narrative, Chesterton transforms anarchism from a code for fear of the masses into a metaphor for the fallen human condition.

The Man Who Was Thursday begins calmly enough, with a polite conversation in Saffron Park, an "artistic colony" of sorts. The area, "the outburst of a speculative builder," is marked for its historical dubiousness and its chaotic ground plan. The novel gently satirizes the pretensions of the so-called "artists" in the neighborhood, because "it never in any definable way produced any art. But although its pretensions to be an intellectual centre were a bit vague, its pretensions to be a pleasant place were quite indisputable" (5). In a neighborhood identified with pretense rather than art, it is unsurprising to find many who have pretensions to mastery of one sort or the other but possess nothing of the kind. One man in particular, although unnamed, presents a satire of Peter Kropotkin, who had been living the genteel life of the exile in London since 1886: " that scientific gentleman with the bald, egg-like head and the bare, bird-like neck had no real right to the airs of science that he assumed. He had not discovered anything new in biology; but what biological creature could he have discovered more singular than himself?" (5–6). The whole community, in fact, is "to be considered not so much as a workshop for artists, but as a frail but finished work of art. A man who stepped into its social atmosphere felt as if he had stepped into a written comedy" (6). The entire anarchist community in this London suburb is to be understood not as a place where things are produced, but as an artificial, theatrical creation. It is a place where people pose and talk but offer no real threat to the social order.

One particular evening, notable for a sunset which "looked like the end of the world" (7), two poets confront one another on the subjects of anarchism and order. The anarchist poet, Gregory Syme, repeats the concepts of the symbolist poets of France and Oscar Wilde: "An artist is identical with an anarchist . . . the artist disregards all governments, abolishes all conventions. The poet delights in disorder only" (8). He is opposed by a newcomer, Gabriel Syme, who delights in order: "It is things going right . . . that is poetical! Our digestions, for instance, going sacredly and silently right, is the foundation of all poetry. Yes, the most poetical thing, more poetical than the flowers, more poetical than the stars—the most poetical thing in the world is not being sick" (10). In this battle of paradoxes, Syme gains the upper hand by being more disorderly in his defense of order than Gregory had been in his celebration of anarchy; he accuses Gregory of not fully understanding his own intellectual position, which infuriates Gregory. In effect, Syme finds all anarchists of this type well meaning but misguided, incapable of actually throwing bombs or any other form of mischief. This extremism in the name of order becomes a theme throughout the narrative.

After talking rapturously with Gregory's sister, Syme loses track of time and slides into his nightmare. From this point until the end of the novel, the fictions surrounding anarchism are revealed to be farcical exaggerations that satirize the limited ability of human beings to order the universe. The first step, away from the harmless anarchist poseurs of Saffron Park and reality and toward the manufactured threat of the global anarchist conspiracy, is to translate anarchism from an insignificant political movement into a metaphor for all that lies outside human control: "there is your precious order, that lean, iron lamp, ugly and barren; and there is anarchy, rich, living, reproducing itself—there is anarchy, splendid in green and gold" (13). The shift from reality to nightmare also signals a shift from a narrowly aesthetic language to a broader consideration of humanity's role in the universe.

In a secret basement of a Chiswick pub with astonishingly good food and drink, Gregory, out to prove the sincerity of his anarchism, takes Syme to the secret meeting of the local revolutionary circle. The ludicrousness of this conception is pointed out at every opportunity: the contrast between the homely pub and the exquisite food lampoons the assumption that homely pub-goers could produce a revolution. The oxymoron of a disciplined anarchist conspiracy is exploded first, as Gregory gives a password before entering the underground anarchist armory: "'I must ask you to forgive me all these formalities,' said Gregory; 'we have to be very strict here.' 'Oh, don't apologize,' said Syme. 'I know your passion for law and order'" (19). The basic contradiction of a disciplined conspiracy of anarchists is made into a joke, just as the idea of huge storehouses of weapons and bombs underneath seedy pubs is seen as the stuff of nightmares, not reality.

While sitting "expansively" in a room shaped "like the inside of a bomb" (20), Gregory carries anarchism to its symbolic extremes, dismissing the goal of abolishing government as a trivial pursuit in favor of "abolishing God":

> "We wish to deny all those arbitrary distinctions of vice and virtue, honor and treachery, upon which mere rebels base themselves. The silly sentimentalists of the French Revolution talked of the Rights of Man! We hate Rights as we hate Wrongs. We have abolished Right and Wrong."
>
> "And Right and Left," said Syme with a simple eagerness, "I hope you will abolish them too. They are much more troublesome to me." (20–21)

Gregory's rhetoric is so extreme as to be absurd, as Syme points out with his joke. To carry the joke further, Gregory tells of his attempts to disguise his anarchism from the world by assuming the role of a bishop, a capitalist, and a major in the army. In every case, he plays the anarchist caricature of the role, which is so removed from reality as to be easily found out: "I defended capital with so much intelligence that a fool could see that I was quite poor" (22). More to the point, it is absurd to think that such a vast conspiracy as is posited by the detractors of anarchism could exist without causing any concern; Gabriel's disguise, underscoring the fact that the entire anarchist threat exists within people's fantasies and nowhere else, is to play the role of an anarchist. Everyone really knows anarchists to be harmless.

Gabriel plays the role of the anarchist because the great secret leader of the worldwide anarchist conspiracy told him to; the very description of this shadowy figure, code-named "Sunday," emphasizes the delusional quality of the conspiracy narrative, in which the very lack of evidence is taken as proof of a cover-up: "Caesar and Napoleon put all their genius into being heard of, and they *were* heard of. He puts all his genius into not being heard of, and he is not heard of" (22). The leader's code name, Sunday, reflects the symbolic organization of the seven anarchist leaders into the seven days of the week; the London delegate is "Thursday," and Gregory has come to the meeting expecting to be elected to the position: "oh, the wild joy of being Thursday!" (24) he exults absurdly. The position comes with its own costume, a cloak and sword-stick quite similar to the costume worn by Chesterton himself.

Just as Gregory confesses his own hopes and secrets to Syme, Syme confesses to Gregory that he is, in fact, a police agent, part of a super-secret group of fanatics whose job is to ferret out anarchists. Syme had become a detective because "he was one of those who are driven early in life into too conservative an attitude by the bewildering folly of most revolutionists . . . his respectability was spontaneous and sudden, a rebellion against rebellion" (38). In his own way, he is as absurd as the anarchists themselves, assuming that the ordinary is in need of extraordinary protection. The sudden turn from Gregory's anarchist conspiracy to Syme's police conspiracy underscore the fact that both delusions are sides of the same coin, a self-enclosed confrontation. Neither can expose the other without exposing himself; it is an intellectual duel, but an indirect one.

The very indirection and baselessness of the discourse surrounding anarchism is itself lampooned. Gregory, speaking before the group, points out that

> those who talk about anarchism and its dangers go everywhere and anywhere to get their information except to us, except to the fountain head. They learn about anarchists from sixpenny novels; they learn about anarchists from tradesmen's newspapers; they learn about anarchists from *Ally Sloper's Half-Holiday* and the *Sporting Times*. They never learn about anarchists from anarchists. We have no chance of denying the mountainous slanders which are heaped upon our heads from one end of Europe to another. (31)

Information about anarchists is generally based on sources that are more interested in sensation and exaggeration than accuracy and that almost never actually quote an anarchist. Anarchists were usually quite absent from the public discourse surrounding anarchists, which usually concerned the threat they represented or their role as a symptom of modern degeneracy. The novel implies that their reputation, however pleasing it may be to an anarchist's vanity, is entirely the result of other people's conversations, and not because of any real viciousness on their part. The previous Thursday, organized "the great dynamite coup of Brighton which, under happier circumstances, ought to have killed everybody on the pier" (but obviously hurt no one) despite the fact that he was a vegetarian because "cruelty, or anything approaching cruelty, revolted him always" (29). This paradox, like the others in the novel, underscores the essential ludicrousness of the anarchist stereotype, who murders for the sake of humanity.

Nevertheless, even anarchists wish to believe that they have the power to destroy. Gregory, aware that Syme is a police spy, gives a mild speech emphasizing the meekness of the conspirators, which offends their vanity. Syme, the police agent, acts as an agent provocateur by giving a wildly violent speech in response, passionate enough to get himself elected to the position of Thursday: "I am not a man at all. I am a cause" (34). As a police agent exaggerating the threat of anarchy, Syme is not dealing with reality, but with causes—in this case, the cause of increased power and social order. Syme concludes "to the fat parliamentarian who says these men are the enemies of order and public decency, to all these I will reply, 'You are false kings, but you are true prophets. I am come to destroy you, and to fulfill your prophecies'" (35). The forces of order are dependent upon the fictions of anarchy to justify their existence; as Syme shows, if there were no anarchist threat, the police would create one.

In fact, the extraordinary police effort to uncover the anarchist conspiracy was born in the head of a detective, of whom Syme only sees his broad back, who "has long been of the opinion that a purely intellectual conspiracy would soon threaten the very existence of civilisation. He is certain that the scientific and artistic worlds are silently bound in a crusade against the Family and the State" (42). Syme, who is "one of those men who are open in a degree to all the nameless psychological influences in a degree a little dangerous to mental health" (54), believes the story and volunteers to help root out this menace. The threats to contemporary understanding which scientific advances and avant-garde art represent become translated, in the mind of this detective, into another kind of criminal conspiracy: the intellectual crime. The absurdity of this notion is found in the application: "the ordinary detective goes to pot-houses to arrest thieves; we go to coffee-houses to detect pessimists. The ordinary detective discovers from a ledger or a diary that a crime has been committed. We discover from a book of sonnets that a

crime will be committed" (42). In their very rage for order and stability, these crusaders have transformed normal human activities
into evidence of a monstrous conspiracy; the very power which re-
sides with the modern state makes their need for justification all
the more extreme.

After winning election to the position of Thursday, Syme pro-
ceeds to the secret anarchist congress. Carrying the hiding-in-plain-
sight strategy to extremes, the conclave of anarchist leaders takes
place on a balcony overlooking Leicester Square. At the congress,
he meets people who parody every conceivable anarchist stereotype: the first man Syme meets, Monday, has a crooked smile, and
"a dead voice that contradicted the fanaticism of his face" (51).
Tuesday, a Pole known as Gogol, is described as "the common or
garden Dynamiter . . . a bewildering bush of brown hair and beard
that almost obscured the eyes like those of a Skye terrier" (55).
Wednesday is an aristocrat, a man who "carried a rich atmosphere
with him, a rich atmosphere that suffocated. It reminded one irra-
tionally of drowsy odours and of dying lamps in the darker poems
of Byron and Poe" (57). Friday, the "Professor de Worms," was "in
the last dissolution of senile decay" (59). Saturday is completely
normal except for "a pair of dark, almost opaque spectacles . . .
those black discs were ugly to Syme; they reminded him of half-re-
membered ugly tales, of some story about pennies being put on the
eyes of the dead" (59). Sunday himself is a mountain of man, reminiscent of Bakunin or Michaelangelo's God on the Sistine Chapel
ceiling, with broad shoulders and billowing white hair. Syme's emotional reactions to the "anarchist's" physical characteristics resembles those of a child frightened by a stranger; every characteristic
assumes a sinister aspect because of fear, not something inherent
in the person. The stereotypical anarchist types are dead roles that
evoke clichéd responses.

Just as Gregory's attempt to act like a conservative exposes him
as an anarchist, so Gogol's attempt to act like an anarchist exposes
this most stereotypical of anarchist madmen to be a police agent.
Sunday, discussing plans to bomb the Tsar while the latter is in
Paris, observes that Gogol "insists on acting like a stage conspira-
tor" (55). Although Syme wants to expose the conspirators and help
the police agent, he does not, because he is certain that Sunday has
an almost mystical power to kill him. When Gogol is exposed, Syme
faints from relief that Sunday did not expose him as a police agent;
Gogol is allowed to leave as the meeting disbands. After the meeting
Syme begins his quest to avert the plot on the Tsar.

What follows is the gradual exposure of each member of the council as a police agent. First, the aging Professor de Worms is revealed to be a young man in disguise after Syme runs throughout London trying to elude the surprisingly nimble Professor. Together, they discover that Bull, the anarchist with the glasses, doesn't intend to take a bomb to France because he, too, is a police agent. Syme and the others go to France in order to prevent the Marquis from carrying out the bombing alone; he reveals himself as an agent as well. Despite the fact that the agents outnumbered the anarchists, all of them still fear Sunday and his mysterious power; each has an acute awareness of his essential solitude, despite the companionship of the other agents, in the face of Sunday's power. They believe a crowd of people to be an anarchist mob on the hunt for them, precipitating a flight across the French countryside in which they believe everyone they meet is a possible anarchist; their own credulity is matched only by the rich people they meet, who are just as willing as these police fanatics to see an anarchist lurking beneath every bushel.

In fact, the rich are seen to be more anarchical than the dreaded mob, because they are more selfish and can be more secure without aid from the government. The poor, who were always associated with anarchism and were, in fact, ardent supporters of anarchism in France and Spain, are here characterized as inherently conservative when compared to the rich:

> The poor have been rebels, but they have never been anarchists; they have more interest that anyone else in their being some decent government. The poor man really has a stake in the country. The rich man hasn't; he can go away to New Guinea in a yacht. The poor have always objected to being governed badly; the rich have always objected to being governed at all. (132)

The secure are the ones who chafe at order or any kind; the poor, those who have to live with hunger and manual labor, are grateful if a government will provide them security they cannot get themselves and revolt against a government which does not provide that service. Therefore, the police agents reason, the mob must actually be guided by the dreaded Sunday, following his will like so many machines.

With everyone turning out to be the opposite of what they appear to be, Syme is understandably confused: "he had found the thing which the modern people call Impressionism, which is another name for that final skepticism which can find no floor in the universe" (131). The confusion comes because Syme's narratives no longer adequately explain the cosmos in which he finds himself. After they realize that their anarchist pursuers were nothing more than echoes and a group of people understandably alarmed by the policemen's mad flight through the country, Syme and the others return to England, determined to find Sunday. In London, they meet Gogol, the first one exposed, who remarks that the quest "is six men going to ask one man what they mean" (158). Their whole institution, built on the fiction of an implacable anarchist foe, is crumbling around them; their attempts to root out disorder have only produced a greater disorder within themselves.

They have completed the quest, and now feel that they have earned answers. The six police agents report to Sunday at the next breakfast meeting of the anarchists and confront him. Anarchy has exploded from the confines of a social movement to become a metaphor for existence, and the profound confusion this has produced in the agents of order makes them desperate for a new set of answers in which they can package reality. The questions they ask are profound, concerning their very existence, the types of questions one might imagine asking God after death:

> "We have come to know what all this means. Who are you? What are you? Why did you get us all here? Do you know who and what we are? Are you a half-witted man playing the conspirator, or are you a clever man playing the fool? Answer me, I tell you."
>
> "Candidates," murmured Sunday, "are only required to answer eight out of the seventeen questions on the paper. As far as I can make out, you want me to tell you what I am, and what you are, and what this table is, and what this Council is, and what this world is for all I know. Well, I will go so far as to rend the veil of one mystery. If you want to know what you are, you are a set of highly well-intentioned young jackasses." (160)

By "rending the veil," Sunday is casting himself in the role of God to these misguided seekers of truth. Sunday describes himself as the ultimate mystery, which neither science nor art can penetrate: "Since the beginning of the world all men have hunted me like a wolf—kings and sages, and poets and lawgivers, all the churches, and all the philosophies. But I have never been caught yet" (161). In fact, he is the man who made all the agents policemen, just as he made them all anarchists. Although the search for him has given these fanatics of order a purpose, he himself defies all their attempts at order.

What follows is a mad chase through London, involving cabs, fire engines, an elephant, and a hot-air balloon. While being chased through the streets, Sunday hurls scraps of paper with bits of writing on it, addressed to the various agents, all of which contain fragments of writing that echo the languages of advertising and popular fiction. The chaos that Sunday represents leaves its traces in the chaos of language in the modern world. Sunday himself, escaping in a hot-air balloon, is compared indirectly to an orator: the balloon is referred to as a gasbag, and then Sunday is "jolly like a balloon himself" (170). Even the words and concepts they have used to define their lives and their absurd mission turn to meaningless strings of words, and each agent is left to define Sunday based on his own prejudices, like the proverbial blind men describing parts of the elephant. Syme sums it up by saying that "when I think of Sunday I think of the whole world" (171). Syme reflects that they have only seen Sunday's back (just as Moses could only see the back of God), like they only see the back of the world. Sunday represents ineffable reality, the true forms of things beyond human language and human understanding.

When the chase ends at Sunday's castle outside London, the police agents find themselves cast as their respective days of the week in a masquerade staged by Sunday. There, as they complain of the hardships they suffered on their quest, Lucian Gregory comes, in the role of Satan, to accuse them of security and comfort, of being too confident in their roles as guardians of the law. Syme, sitting on his throne of power, replies that they have suffered on their quest "so that each thing that obeys law may have the glory and isolation of the anarchist. So that each man fighting for order may be as brave and good a man as the dynamiter. So that the real lie of Satan may be flung back in the face of this blasphemer" (190). To this assertion that the powerful has been a victim as well, Sunday, swelling to an awful size, ends the nightmare by asking Syme "Have you ever suffered? Can ye drink of the cup that I drink of?" (191). Syme suddenly finds himself strolling down a country lane, discussing "adorable triviality" (192) with Lucian Gregory. Whatever conflicts Syme experienced during his nightmare have been resolved peacefully.

Syme's nightmare of suffering in the cause of order does not entitle him to assume Godlike powers, the "thrones" of the earth. The idea that one can earn power over other individuals by working hard at one's own goals—that conservative brand of individualism that was part of the discourse of capitalism—is found lacking within the Christian context of Christ's sacrifice. Syme's hardships have all been a product of his own fancy: the dire threat of anarchism was simply a pretext for the quest that justifies his power.

The expansion of police powers by the state, with the full cooperation of the wealthier classes, is likewise based on the fantasy of a
threat to civilization; anarchists may be misguided, but they are
rarely as dangerous as the police who pursue them.

The Man Who Was Thursday recognizes the comic potential of
anarchistic discourse, sweetening the satiric bitterness which dominates *The Secret Agent*. In both of these novels (by people not entirely sympathetic with the anarchist movement) anarchism is
transformed into a metaphor for society as a whole. In the case of
The Man Who Was Thursday, anarchism is taken far from its atheistic roots: God is categorized as the ultimate anarchist, pricking
the balloons of people who are deluded by their own security. As
anarchism faded as a political movement and abandoned "propaganda by the deed," anarchistic discourse would find its way into
the cultural dialogue, making it possible for Chesterton to write a
popular comic treatment of anarchism.

Epilogue

THE SITES OF SOCIAL CONFLICT CAN BE LOCATED WITHIN THE KEY WORDS and conflicting narratives of a given historical period. In the late nineteenth century, the words, phrases, and narratives that were associated with anarchism became the site of a battle over the direction of society. The concept of anarchy, which had previously signified simple disorder, took on a larger significance as the more centralized, authoritarian industrial state subverted the democratic promises of the Enlightenment. The rhetoric of liberty and rights that the middle classes had used to wrest power from the aristocracy was now used by advocates of the lower classes to attempt to wrest control from property owners, which led the middle classes into an alliance with the upper classes they had resisted a century before. In this new political situation, "anarchy" (as used by Matthew Arnold and others) came to represent the challenge to the authority of the property owners by the working classes.

The "problem" of the working classes was one of the chief topics in the dialogue of the day. As iniquities in the early industrial system produced squalid urban living conditions and extreme differences in wealth, police and military power were used more and more often to defend the extensive property rights of the upper classes. As rural workers were forced off their lands and into the overcrowded cities, people were increasingly alienated from one another by a socioeconomic segregation that made neighbors seem sinister and mysterious. The "masses" (the word itself is dehumanizing) were depicted as increasingly hostile, prone to violence, and opposed to every refinement with which the propertied classes identified themselves. Advocates of corporate institutions promised a better future through material prosperity (the "mass culture" of capitalism) and centralized control; they used their domination of public discourse (through publishing houses and journalism) to define anarchism and push the movement and its ideas to the margins of public discourse. Faced with political, economic, and cultural authority actively working to preserve their control through centralization, some radicals argued that control itself—any kind of authority over others—was the problem.

Although the idea of anarchy as a political doctrine was a logical outcome of Godwin's Enlightenment positivism, it was Proudhon who translated Godwin's arguments on the evils of authority based on property into a narrative of working-class liberation. Bakunin, reacting against the despotisms of Eastern Europe, saw in anarchism the ideological framework most suited to his idea of creative revolt. Faced with the historical fact that every government had acted as a partisan of the rich against the poor, anarchist revolutionaries argued that government itself should be abolished. Some extremists argued that everyone should be completely autonomous, but most saw an alternative society in which people assumed direct control of their lives—a direct attack on the increasing distance between the individual and the economic and political forces which controlled his or her life under the domination of the corporation and the nation-state.

As some anarchists dreamed of overthrowing the current order and starting again like Rousseau's noble savage, individuals in the propertied classes (aware of the symbolism of the end of the century) began to dread a coming cataclysm, either the social revolution (brought about from outside middle-class discourse by the working classes) or a collapse into total degeneration (caused from within discourse by decadent literature and dangerous ideas). Advocates of corporate organization shut anarchists out of the cultural discourse by distorting their terms—anarchist opposition to income-producing property was transformed into a threat to private property; Rousseau's noble savage was translated into Hobbes' rule of might. The civic and political institutions were constrained by the narrative of social Darwinism: nothing should interfere with the ravages of corporate capitalism. With alternative discourses silenced, the grinding poverty that permeated city life in America and Great Britain was understood as an inescapable fact of existence.

For activist radicals, the revolution was a central narrative, binding together a movement that rejected institutional controls. Anarchists celebrated the failed and thwarted attempts at revolution which had occurred over the last century—the French Revolution, the American Revolution, the revolts of 1848—and looked to every large strike and riot as the harbinger of the Social Revolution they felt was imminent. This "movement culture" was strongest in Europe (especially parts of Russia, Italy, Spain, and France) and in immigrant neighborhoods of London, New York, and Chicago. The narrative of revolution also garnered anarchists a place, albeit a circumscribed one, within the larger cultural dialogue which shut them out on so many other issues. Never numerous or powerful, anarchists could shake the institutions which they opposed through the threat of revolution—terrorism.

At the same time, other anarchists rejected "propaganda by the deed," preferring instead to live as individuals and not force a change on others. Individualist anarchism was popular in the United States because of its affinities with the language of the Constitution. Many European artists were drawn to this libertarian discourse, including the symbolist poets and Oscar Wilde, who celebrated the liberation of the artist from both official and conventional censorship in "The Soul of Man Under Socialism."

Nevertheless, the threat of a mass movement and mass culture to the artistic traditions which the propertied classes assumed as their own led many artists (and revolutionaries) to see the revolution as the end of high culture, not its fulfillment. Henry James dreads the revolution which he fears will chop up art into little bits so that everyone can share equally; Griffith's Hartmann, who sees art and architecture as the symbol of the oppressor, would destroy both with his flying machine.

Although some artists advocated a retreat into the aesthetic life in order to avoid the constant threat which urban life had become, most people found it harder to ignore the reports of unrest which came with increasing frequency through telegraph news services. In the face of horrible conditions and a lack of individual control, people created a scapegoat for the dystopia of emerging capitalism in the idea of an anarchist conspiracy. This narrative made the same radicals and workers which they feared the cause of all social problems. The conspiracy was a dark twin to the corporate order: international, hierarchical, autocratic, and controlling. This narrative allowed people to blame acts of terrorism on something other than conditions—and gave police forces an easy way to repress political undesirables.

The idea of conspiracy permeated anarchist narratives of the 1880s and 1890s and was even written into law in Illinois. The Haymarket Affair, in which eight people were found guilty of murder solely because they were outspoken anarchists, was the first "red scare" in history. The police, private detectives, and the newspapers used the conspiracy narrative as a justification for increased repression of immigrants and leftists and as a way to silence radical discourses. The individual anarchist may appear harmless, they argued, but in reality there is a secret organization of unfathomable malevolence behind each one; only stringent laws and increased police protection would protect property and order.

In the early years of the twentieth century, the advocates of increasing centralization and authority opposed "revolution" (the narrative challenge to their power) by repressing the political anarchist movement in the United States and Great Britain. The threat represented by anarchism was kept alive in narratives and by a transfer of the language of conspiracy to other marginal groups. The parties remaining in the cultural dialogue (capitalists, socialists, and communists) were all forced to agree on the desirability of centralized institutions and the concept of social order enforced by state authority—an overarching monologism which is only slowly being broken down.

Anarchism did not die out; its language was lifted out of the discourse of a small political movement and placed within the larger aesthetic discourse. Artists, some influenced by the symbolists and decadents, others drawn to the novel possibilities and new perspectives of anarchist narratives, made anarchism into a language for understanding society as a whole. Even writers such as Joseph Conrad and G. K. Chesterton, who had little sympathy for actual revolutionaries, were drawn to the tropes of anarchism as a way of describing the disorder within the social order and the alienation of the individual. Even as the actual anarchists were being omitted from history, T. S. Eliot writes in *The Waste Land* of "these fragments I have shored against my ruins"—of the individual forced to construct personal order out of cultural anarchy.

In the twentieth century, the influence of anarchist narratives can be found in works ranging from the paintings of Picasso to the films of Charlie Chaplin. Twentieth-century society occasionally has been troubled by the negative aspects of the anarchistic narratives that inform our perceptions—the tendency toward nihilism, the creative destruction of institutions, the fragility of consensus—because, for the most part, we have shut the cultural forces that oppose authority out of our discourse and therefore out of our consciousness. Only by entering into dialogue with anarchism, in our history and in our language, can we fully understand our own culture, and ourselves.

Notes

Introduction

1. Cesare Lombroso, "Illustrative Studies in Criminal Anthropology," *Monist* 1 (1891): 336–43; and "A Paradoxical Anarchist," *Popular Science Monthly* (January 1900): 312–15.

2. Henry Adams, *The Education of Henry Adams* (Boston, New York: Houghton Mifflin Company, 1918).

Chapter 1: The Haymarket Affair

1. There are several good book-length histories of the Haymarket Affair. The first is Henry David's *The History of the Haymarket Affair* (New York: Russell & Russell, 1936), and more recently Paul Avrich's *The Haymarket Tragedy* (Princeton, N.J.: Princeton University Press, 1984) and Bruce Nelson's study of the culture of the Chicago anarchist movement, *Beyond the Martyrs* (New Brunswick, N.J.: Rutgers University Press, 1988). A more detailed treatment of the events themselves can be found in these books.

2. Carl Sandburg, *Always the Young Strangers* (New York: Harcourt, Brace & Co., 1952) 132–33.

3. This association of acts of violence with foreigners continues to the present day. In 1995, the initial descriptions of those suspected for the bombing of the Federal Building in Oklahoma City emphasized their "Middle Eastern" appearance. In the absence of facts, the narrative of the "Arab terrorist" controlled initial perceptions. After a suspect associated with the right-wing Militia movement was arrested, many newspapers wrote extensively on the right-wing militia "conspiracy" which was behind the bombing and other conflicts between Federal agents and citizens, such as the attack on the Branch Davidian compound in 1993.

4. David, *Haymarket Affair*, 296.

5. Ibid., 297.

6. Ibid., 337.

7. Avrich, *Haymarket*, 292–93.

8. Quoted in Ibid., 340.

9. Ibid., 338.

10. Ibid., 352.

11. David, *Haymarket Affair*, 439.

12. Ibid., 429.

13. Ibid., 463.

14. Ibid., 413.

15. Joseph E. Gary, "The Chicago Anarchists of 1886: The Crime, the Trial, and the Punishment," *Century Magazine* (April 1893): 803–37.

16. M. M. Trumbull, "Judge Gary and the Anarchists," *Arena* 8 (1893): 554.

17. Avrich, *Haymarket*, 424–25.

18. Bruce Nelson, *Beyond the Martyrs: A Social History of Chicago's Anarchists, 1870-1900* (New Brunswick, N.J.: Rutgers University Press, 1988).

19. Ibid., 142, 144.

20. David, *Haymarket Affair*, 118.

21. Ibid., 120.

22. Avrich, *Haymarket*, 170.

23. Ibid., 28, 212.

24. Nelson, *Beyond the Martyrs*, 154.

25. Avrich, *Haymarket*, 177.

26. Quoted in Ibid., 288.

27. Michael J. Schaack, *Anarchy and Anarchists* (Chicago: F. J. Schulte & Co., 1889). The references in this section that are not explicitly attributed to another source are from this text.

28. Avrich, *Haymarket*, 416.

29. An English translation of this document is available at *Countermedia: Information Beyond the Mainstream*, New Dawn International News Service, http://www.geocities.com/countermedia/5.html (30 April 2002).

30. Most disinterested reports (including that of the mayor) undercut Schaack's story, and instead support the story that the police opened fire on a mostly unarmed crowd in the panic after the bomb. "A telegraph pole at the scene was filled with bullet holes, all coming from the direction of the police. The pole was removed the next day and never recovered. Captain Schaack's explanation that it had been 'very prosaically, and in the common course of business, removed by the telegraph company,' is unconvincing" (Avrich, *Haymarket*, 209, quoting Schaack, 490).

31. Avrich, *Haymarket*, 224.

32. The activities of the Pinkerton detective agency in relation to Haymarket are described in lurid detail by a former operative, the "cowboy detective" Charles Siringo, in a small pamphlet called *Two Evil Isms: Pinkertonism and Anarchism* 1915; reprint, Austin, Tex.: Steck-Vaughn Company, 1967). The book as a whole is an extended attack on Pinkerton's agency, accusing it of corrupting elections, bribing juries, and killing people on behalf of its clients. Siringo, who was detailed to prevent the defense from bribing the jury in the Haymarket Trial, says that "My orders from Superintendent David Robinson were to pay no attention to the lawyers for the prosecution as on that side the jury was already 'fixed' " (5), a suspicion later confirmed by a Chicago businessman who did the bribing. The Pinkertons also made up false reports of anarchist activities and speeches in order to give their employers what they wanted to hear and to pad their own expense accounts. The book was suppressed by the Pinkerton agency, and a version published later had names changed and the agency not mentioned by name.

33. In fact, much evidence reports that Schaack would threaten, bully, and bribe people into supporting his story of the conspiracy, and even then most of these witnesses were inconsistent with each other.

CHAPTER 2: THE ANARCHIST BACKGROUND

1. Max Stirner, *The Ego and His Own*, edited by John Carroll and based on the English translation by Steven T. Byington from 1907 (New York: Harper & Row, 1971).

2. George Woodcock, *Anarchism: A History of Libertarian Ideas and Movements* (New York: Penguin Books, 1962), 8; 8–9.

3. Atindranath Bose, *A History of Anarchism*, Calcutta: The World Press, 1967.

4. William Godwin, *An Enquiry Concerning Political Justice and Its Influence on General Virtue and Happiness* (short title: *Political Justice*) (1793; reprint, Toronto: University of Toronto Press, 1946.)

5. Ibid., 174.

6. Pierre Proudhon, *What Is Property?* (1840; reprint, Cambridge: Cambridge University Press, 1994).

7. Adam Smith, *Wealth of Nations*, Bk. V, Ch. I, pt. II (1776; reprint, New York: Modern Library, 1994).

8. Proudhon, *Property*, 171.

9. Ibid., 124.

10. Bose, *History of Anarchism*, 124.

11. It is interesting to note the expansion of cooperative banks that offer "micro-loans" to the poor (such as Bangladesh's Grameen Bank) in many countries. These banks, which use the collateral of "loan circles" and offer small loans at or below the current market rates, are indirect descendants of Proudhon's ideas.

12. Pierre Proudhon, *De la capacité politique des classes ouvrières* (Paris: E. Dentu, 1865).

13. George Woodcock, *Anarchism*, 132.

14. Ibid., 11.

15. Stirner, Ego, 50–51.

16. Ibid., 68–69.

17. Ibid., 90–91.

18. Quoted in Woodcock, *Anarchism*, 139.

19. Ibid., 140.

20. James Joll, *The Anarchists*, 96.

21. Quoted in Ibid., 153.

22. Nathaniel Hong, "Constructing the Anarchist Beast in American Periodical Literature, 1880–1903," *Critical Studies in Mass Communication* 9 (1992): 117.

23. Not everyone believed Kropotkin to be nonviolent. Zenker is particularly vehement in his condemnation of Kropotkin as one who inspires violence, but does not commit violent acts personally: "But Prince Kropotkin, who appears to be such a stern materialist, is a very enthusiast, who gives way to utter self-deception as to human nature. . . . The Anarchists, and especially those who acknowledge Kropotkin as their highest 'authority,' do not wish force used against them, yet use it themselves; they do not wish to be killed, yet they kill others. Can there be a stronger refutation of Anarchist morality?" (Zenker, *Anarchism*, 179–80).

24. Hong, "Anarchist Beast," 117.

25. Benjamin Tucker, *Instead of a Book, by a Man Too Busy to Write One* (New York: Benjamin R. Tucker, 1893), 14.

26. Henry D. Thoreau, *Walden and Civil Disobedience* (New York: Penguin Books, 1983).

27. Quoted in Woodcock, *Anarchism*, 431.

28. Ibid., 433.

29. Ibid., 436.

30. Ibid., 438.

31. See Arthur Redding for his discussion of the problem with the concept of the individual and how that ambiguity makes anarchism impossible to clearly formulate in *Raids on Human Consciousness* (Columbia: University of South Carolina Press, 1998) 77–78.

32. Hong, "Anarchist Beast," 119.

Chapter 3: Revolution, Anarchism, and the Mob

1. See Patrick Brantlinger's *Bread and Circuses* (Ithaca: Cornell University Press, 1983) or the essay collection *Fin de Siècle, Fin du Globe* edited by John Stokes (London: Macmillan, 1992) for a more complete discussion of narratives of social decay during the late nineteenth century.

2. Frederic Jameson discusses this phenomenon more generally under the label of the "Utopian Impulse" in his *The Political Unconscious* (Ithaca: Cornell University Press, 1982).

3. Oliver, *International Anarchist Movement* (London: C. Helm, 1983), 14.

4. Ibid., 13.

5. One English act of political "terrorism" was carried out by the poet Evelyn Barlow, who fired shots into the Parliament Building itself, then, handing the gun to a nearby policeman, proclaimed himself an anarchist who did not want to hurt anyone but who wanted simply to protest the government.

6. Richard D. Sonn, *Anarchism* (New York: Twayne, 1992), 238.

7. Brantlinger, *Bread and Circuses*, 1983.

8. Ford Madox Ford, *Return to Yesterday* (New York: Horace Liverwright, 1932), 107.

9. Edward Gibbon, *The History of the Decline and Fall of the Roman Empire* (1782; reprint, New York: Harper and Bros., 1880).

10. Ignatius Donnelly, *Caesar's Column*, Chicago: F. J. Shulie & Co. 1890. Available http://www.veritel.com.br/gutenberg ctcyt D4/8ccol10L.htm

11. Matthew Arnold, *Culture and Anarchy*, (1869; reprint, New York: Macmillan, 1908).

12. J. A. Jameson, "Is Our Civilization Perishable?," *North American Review* 88 (March 1884): 209–10.

13. Ibid., 212.

14. Fitz John Porter, "How to Quell Mobs," *North American Review* 89 (October 1885): 351.

15. Ibid., 356.

16. "Law and License," *Fortnightly Review* 39, new series (1 March 1886), 297–305.

17. Cesare Lombroso, "A Study of Mobs," *Chautauquan* 15 (1892): 316.

18. Cesare Lombroso, "Criminal Anthropology," 337.

19. Max Nordau, *Degeneration*, (1892, translated 1895; reprint, Omaha: University of Nebraska Press, 1993).

20. Max Nordau, "Society's Protection Against the Degenerates," *Forum* 19 (July 1895): vii.

21. Henry James, *The Princess Casamassima* (New York: Penguin Books, 1977). All references to the text in this section use the pagination of this edition.

22. F. O. Matthiessen, *The James Family* (New York: Alfred A. Knopt, 1971), 592.

23. Quoted in W. H. Tilley, *The Background of* The Princess Casamassima (Gainesville: University of Florida Press, 1961), 18.

24. Ibid., 19.

25. Lyall Powers notes Hyacinth's problems with identity: "'Who am I really?' is the constant, nagging, question that faces him at every turn." See *Henry James and the Naturalist Movement* (East Lansing: Michigan State University Press, 1971), 117. Millie in particular is constantly questioning his identity, and near the end of the novel Hyacinth admits that he does not know himself.

26. Mildred E. Hartsock, "*The Princess Casamassima*: The Politics of Power," *Studies in the Novel* 1 (1969): 305.

27. E. Douglas Fawcett, *Hartmann the Anarchist* (London: Edward Arnold, 1893). George Griffith, *The Angel of the Revolution* (London: Tower Publishing Co., 1893). Richard Savage, *The Anarchist: A Story of To-Day* (Chicago: F. Tennyson Neely, 1894).

28. All parenthetical page references in this section are to the 1975 Arno reprint of the original edition.

29. All parenthetical page references in this section are to the original 1893 edition.

30. All parenthetical page references in this section are to the original 1894 edition.

31. The novel's tone and Savage's earnest characterizations suggest a close identification between the author's opinions and those of his more reactionary characters.

32. This opinion (in a book by an American writer) stands in stark contrast to the British opinion of American social control as voiced by *The Fortnightly Review* ("Law and License," *Fortnightly Review* 39 [new series], 297–305), which praised the American government for having the army fire on workers during the Strikes of 1877.

CHAPTER 4: INDUSTRIALISM AND UTOPIA

1. He was well-known enough to be selected to write the *Encyclopedia Britannica* entry on anarchism.

2. Peter Kropotkin, *Mutual Aid: A Factor of Evolution* (1896; reprint, Montreal: Black Rose Books, 1989).

3. William Morris, *News from Nowhere*. Reprint, London: Routledge & Kegan Paul, 1970.

4. C. R. Henderson, "Business Men and Social Theorists," *American Journal of Sociology* (January 1896): 387.

5. Albion Small, "Sanity in Social Legislation," *American Journal of Sociology* 4, no. 3 (November 1898): 336.

6. The power of this theoretical model continues to the present day in the measurement of the Gross Domestic Product, which, for example, measures the increased need for paid day care and anti-crime systems as an expansion of the economy rather than a loss of family support or private security. See Cobb, Halstead, and Rowe's article "If the GDP Is Up, Why Is America Down?" in the October 1995 *Atlantic Monthly*.

7. The very complexity of the system was used as a way to silence criticism by those outside of capitalist discourse. In an 1897 *Atlantic* article entitled "Are the Rich Growing Richer and the Poor Poorer?" Carroll D. Wright attacks the worrisome refrain of the title by breaking down the industrial "system" into its component parts. The rhetorical claim that the economic realities of the time constitute a deliberately designed system is justified by an appeal to natural laws—the current system, its defenders claim, arises out of natural forces rather than human decisions, and therefore is superior to any human-imposed economic system.

8. Paul Monroe, "Possibilities of the Present Industrial System," *American Journal of Sociology* (May 1898): 729.

9. Ibid., 733.

10. Ibid., 744, 745.

11. Ibid., 747, 747.

12. Ibid., 749.

13. Ibid., 750, 752.

14. "Communism and Common Sense," *New York Times*, p. 6 col. 1, 12 May 1878.

15. Ibid.

16. "Demagogues and Working Men," *New York Times*, p. 4 col. 1, 25 August 1870.

17. Ibid.

18. Ibid.

19. C. R. Henderson, "Business Men and Social Theorists," *American Journal of Sociology* (January 1896), 385–86.

20. The recent presidential bids by such businessmen as Ross Perot and Steve Forbes, which were taken seriously solely on the basis of their business experience and their deep pockets, testifies to the success of this project which began in the nineteenth century.

21. Elbert Hubbard, *Little Journeys to the Homes of Great Businessmen* (Memorial Edition), (New York: William H. Wise & Co., 1916), 205.

22. Bernard Alderson, *Andrew Carnegie: The Man and His Work* (New York: Doubleday, 1909).

23. Ibid., 7.

24. "A Career of a Capitalist," *Atlantic Monthly* 43, February 1879, 130.

25. Ibid., 131, 133.

26. Hubbard, *Little Journeys*, 174, 175.

27. Alderson, *Andrew Carnegie*, 21.

28. Hubbard describes Philip Armour's war profiteering unapologetically. "The War's end found the new firm much stronger and well stocked with large orders for mess-pork, sold for future delivery at war-time prices, which contracts they filled at a much lower cost and to their financial satisfaction. Their guesser was good and they prospered" (177). Rather than label this move as war profiteering, Hubbard lauds Armour for his individual shrewdness; divorcing the individual from the context absolves Armour of any guilt in Hubbard's narrative.

29. Alderson, *Andrew Carnegie*, 25.

30. Ibid., 26.

31. Hubbard, *Little Journeys*, 179.

32. Ibid., 200.

33. Ibid., 359.

34. "Career," 133.

35. Alderson, *Andrew Carnegie*, 61.

36. Andrew Carnegie, *The Gospel of Wealth*, in *The Andrew Carnegie Reader*, ed. Joseph Frazier Wall (Pittsburgh: University of Pittsburgh Press, 1992).

37. Andrew Carnegie, "The Problem of the Administration of Wealth," in *The Andrew Carnegie Reader*, ed. Joseph Frazier Wall (Pittsburgh: University of Pittsburgh Press, 1992), 131.

38. Ibid.

39. Ibid., 132.

40. Ibid., 133.

41. Ibid., 132.

42. Ibid., 138, 139.

43. Hubbard, *Little Journeys*, 390.

44. Ibid., 285.

45. Ibid., 396.

46. Alderson, *Andrew Carnegie*, 140.

47. Edward Bellamy, *Looking Backward: 2000-1887* (1887; reprint, New York: Houghton Mifflin, 1927).

48. Morris, *News From Nowhere,* xxxvii.

49. Michael Holzman, "Anarchism and Utopia: William Morris' *News From Nowhere,*" *ELH* 51, no. 3 (1984): 593.

50. Morris, *News from Nowhere,* 107. All unreferenced page numbers that follow in this section are to *News From Nowhere.*

51. Kropotkin, *Mutual Aid.*

52. William Graham Sumner, from Albert Galloway Keller and Maurice R. Davie, eds. *The Essays of William Graham Sumner.* (New Haven: Yale University Press, 193), 291.

53. Ibid., 292, 297.

54. Ibid., 285.

55. Ibid., 286.

56. Ibid., 329, 353.

57. Available in *Mutual Aid.* All unreferenced quotations in this passage are from that edition.

58. Frank Norris, *The Octopus: A Story of California* (New York: A. Wessels Company, 1906).

59. Robert Herrick, *The Memoirs of an American Citizen* (1905; reprint, Cambridge: Belknap Press of Harvard University Press, 1963.)

60. Donald Pizer, *Realism and Naturalism in Nineteenth-Century American Literature*, (Carbondale: Southern Illinois University Press, 1984).

61. Norris, *Octopus*, 54. All subsequent unreferenced page numbers in this section are to this text.

62. Robert Herrick. All subsequent unreferenced page citations in this section are to this edition.

63. Henry Blake Fuller, *With the Procession* (New York: Harper and Brothers, 1895), 248.

64. In his 1900 novel, *The Web of Life* (New York: Macmillan, 1900), Herrick laughs at the specter of anarchism which haunts affluent Chicago, and its use against strikers: "the anarchist was the most terrifying bugaboo in Chicago, referred to as a kind of Asiatic plague that might break out at any time" (154–55).

65. Barbara W. Tuchman, *The Proud Tower: A Portrait of the World Before the War 1890-1914* (New York: Macmillan, 1966), 109.

CHAPTER 5: ANARCHISM DISARMED

1. Several recent studies make this same claim, including Arthur Redding's *Raids on Human Consciousness* (Columbia: University of South Carolina Press, 1998) and Christopher GoGwilt's *The Fiction of Geopolitics* (Stanford: Stanford University Press, 2000).

2. Everett Carter, "The Haymarket Affair in Literature," *American Quarterly* 2, no. 3 (1950): 276, 277. Carter's study of these two novels in relation to the Haymarket Affair is complete enough not to require further elaboration.

3. Charlotte Teller, *The Cage* (New York: Appleton & Co., 1907).

4. Ibid., 26. All unreferenced page citations in this section are to this edition.

5. Ford Madox Ford, *Memories and Impressions: A Study in Atmospheres* (New York: Ecco Press, 1911).

6. Ibid., xiv.

7. Ibid., 137.

8. Ibid., 135.

9. Ford, *Return to Yesterday*, 112.

10. Isabel Meredith [Helen and Olivia Rossetti], *A Girl Among the Anarchists* (1903; reprint, Omaha: University of Nebraska Press, 1992).

11. Meredith, 8, 10. All subsequent unreferenced citations in this section are to this text.

12. Ford Madox Ford describes a "Comrade P" who was likely the same individual who the Rossettis used as a model. Comrade P's clothing reform consisted of doing without, until a judge forced him to wear a loose shirt, shorts, and sandals as a condition for using the library.

CHAPTER 6: ANARCHY AND CULTURE

1. Joseph Conrad, *The Secret Agent*, originally published 1907. All unlabeled page references in this section are to the Penguin edition (New York: Penguin Books, 1990).

2. Joseph Conrad, "The Informer," in *The Lagoon and Other Stories* (Oxford: Oxford University Press, 1997).

3. Walter F. Wright, *Joseph Conrad on Fiction* (Lincoln, University of Nebraska Press: 1964).

4. Avrom Fleishman, *Conrad's Politics: Community and Anarchy in the Fiction of Joseph Conrad* (Baltimore: Johns Hopkins University Press, 1967).

5. Joseph Conrad, "An Anarchist," in *The Lagoon and Other Stories* (Oxford: Oxford University Press, 1997).

6. Joseph Conrad, *Nostromo* (1904; reprint, Oxford: Oxford University Press, 1984).

7. Martin Ray has traced the influence of *Degeneration* on Conrad's thinking in his article "Conrad, Nordau, and Other Degenerates: The Psychology of *The Secret Agent*" (*Conradiana* 16, no. 2 [1984]: 125–40). Several other scholars have noted the connections as well.

8. Martin Seymour-Smith, in his preface to the Penguin edition (*The Secret Agent*, New York: Penguin, 1990) 21.

9. Norman Sherry, *Conrad's Western World* (Cambridge: Cambridge University Press, 1971.

10. G. K. Chesterton, *The Man Who Was Thursday: A Nightmare* (New York: Dodd, Mead, & Co., 1908). Parenthetical page references in this section will be to this edition of the novel.

Works Cited

Alderson, Bernard. *Andrew Carnegie: The Man and His Work*. New York: Doubleday, Page & Co., 1909.

Arnold, Matthew. *Culture and Anarchy*. 1869. Reprint, New York: Macmillan, 1908.

Avrich, Paul. *Anarchist Portraits*. Princeton, N.J.: Princeton University Press, 1988.

———. *The Haymarket Tragedy*. Princeton, N.J.: Princeton University Press, 1984.

Bose, Atindranath. *A History of Anarchism*. Calcutta: The World Press, 1967.

Brantlinger, Patrick. *Bread & Circuses: Theories of Mass Culture as Social Decay*. Ithaca: Cornell University Press, 1983.

Bellamy, Edward. *Looking Backward: 2000-1887* New York: Houghton Mifflin, 1889.

"The Career of a Capitalist." *Atlantic Monthly* 43 (1879): 129–35.

Carter, Everett. "The Haymarket Affair in Literature." *American Quarterly* 2, no. 3 (1950): 270–78.

Chesterton, Gilbert Keith. *The Man Who Was Thursday: A Nightmare*. New York: Dodd, Mead, & Co., 1908.

Cobb, Halstead, and Rowe. "If the GDP Is Up, Why Is America Down?" *Atlantic Monthly* 276 (October 1995): 59–73.

"Communism and Common Sense." *New York Times*, 12 May 1878, p. 6 col. 1.

Conrad, Joseph. "An Anarchist." In *The Lagoon and Other Stories*. Oxford: Oxford University Press, 1997.

———. "The Informer." In *The Lagoon and Other Stories*. Oxford: Oxford University Press, 1997.

———. *Nostromo*. 1905, Reprint, Oxford: Oxford University Press, 1984.

———. *The Secret Agent*. 1907. Reprint, New York: Penguin Books, 1990.

David, Henry. *The History of the Haymarket Affair: A Study in the American Social-Revolutionary and Labor Movements*. New York: Russell & Russell, 1936.

"Demagogues and Working Men." *New York Times*, 25 August 1870, p. 4 col. 4.

Fawcett, E. Douglas. *Hartmann the Anarchist, or the Doom of the Great City*. 1893. Reprint, New York: Arno, 1975.

Fleishman, Avrom. *Conrad's Politics: Community and Anarchy in the Fiction of Joseph Conrad*. Baltimore: Johns Hopkins University Press, 1967.

Ford, Ford Madox. *Memories and Impressions: A Study in Atmospheres*. New York: Ecco Press, 1911.

———. *Return to Yesterday*. New York: Horace Liverwright, 1932.

Gary, Joseph E. "The Chicago Anarchists of 1886: The Crime, the Trial, and the Punishment." *Century Magazine* (April 1893): 803–37.

Gibbon, Edward. *The History of the Decline and Fall of the Roman Empire*. 1782. Reprint, New York: Harper and Bros., 1880.

Godwin, William. *An Enquiry Concerning Political Justice and Its Influence on General Virtue and Happiness*. 1793. Reprint, Toronto: University of Toronto Press, 1946.

GoGwilt, Christopher. *The Fiction of Geopolitics: Afterimages of Culture from Wilkie Collins to Alfred Hitchcock*. Stanford: Stanford University Press, 2000.

Griffith, George. *The Angel of the Revolution*. London: Tower Publishing Co., 1893.

Hartsock, Mildred E. "*The Princess Casamassima*: The Politics of Power." *Studies in the Novel* 1 (1969): 297–309.

Henderson, C. R. "Business Men and Social Theorists." *American Journal of Sociology* 1, no. 4 (January 1896): 385–97.

Herrick, Robert. *The Memoirs of an American Citizen*. 1905. Cambridge: Belknap Press of Harvard University Press, 1963.

Holzman, Michael. "Anarchism and Utopia: William Morris' *News from Nowhere*." ELH 51, no. 3 (1984), 589–603.

Hong, Nathaniel. "Constructing the Anarchist Beast in American Periodical Literature, 1880–1903." *Critical Studies in Mass Communication* 9 (1992): 110–30.

Hubbard, Elbert. *Little Journeys to the Homes of Great Businessmen (Memorial Edition)*. New York: William H. Wise & Co., 1916.

James, Henry. *The Princess Casamassima*. New York: Penguin, 1987.

Jameson, Frederic. *The Political Unconscious*. Ithaca: Cornell University Press, 1982.

Jameson, J. A. "Is Our Civilization Perishable?" *North American Review* 88 (March 1884): 205–15.

Joll, James. *The Anarchists*. Boston: Little, Brown & Company, 1964.

Kropotkin, Peter. *Mutual Aid: A Factor of Evolution*. 1896. Reprint, Montreal: Black Rose Books, 1989.

"Law and License." *Fortnightly Review* 39, new series (1 March 1886): 297–305.

Lombroso, C. "A Paradoxical Anarchist." *Popular Science Monthly* (January 1900): 312–15.

———. "A Study of Mobs." *Chautauquan* 15 (1892): 314 ff.

———. "Illustrative Studies in Criminal Anthropology." *Monist* 1 (1891): 336–43.

Matthiessen, F. O. *The James Family*. New York: Alfred A. Knopf, 1947.

Meredith, Isabel [Helen and Olivia Rossetti]. *A Girl Among the Anarchists*. 1903. Reprint, Lincoln: University of Nebraska Press, 1992.

Monroe, Paul. "Possibilities of the Present Industrial System," *American Journal of Sociology,* (May 1898): 729–53.

Morris, William. *News From Nowhere, or an Epoch of Rest*. Edited by James Redmond. London: Routledge & Kegan Paul, 1970.

Nechaev, Sergei. "Catechism of a Revolutionary." *Countermedia: Information Beyond the Mainstream*. New Dawn International News Service. 30 April 2002. http://www.geocities.com/countermedia/5.html.

Nelson, Bruce C. *Beyond the Martyrs: A Social History of Chicago's Anarchists, 1870-1900*. New Brunswick, N.J.: Rutgers University Press, 1988.

Nordau, Max. *Degeneration*. 1892, translated 1895. Reprint, Omaha: University of Nebraska Press, 1993.

———. "Society's Protection Against the Degenerates." *Forum* 19 (July 1895): 532–43.

Norris, Frank. *The Octopus: A Story of California*. New York: A. Wessels Company, 1906.

Oliver, Hermia. *The International Anarchist Movement in Late Victorian London*. London: Croon Helm, Ltd., 1983.

Pizer, Donald. *Realism and Naturalism in Nineteenth-century American Literature*. Revised edition. Carbondale: Southern Illinois University Press, 1984.

Porter, Fitz John. "How to Quell Mobs." *North American Review* 89 (October 1885): 531–60.

Powers, Lyall. *Henry James and the Naturalist Movement*. East Lansing: Michigan State University Press, 1971.

Proudhon, Pierre. *De la capacité politique des classes ouvrières*. Paris: E. Dentu, 1865.

———. *What is Property?* 1840. Reprint, Cambridge: Cambridge University Press, 1994.

Ray, Martin. "Conrad, Nordau, and Other Degenerates: The Psychology of *The Secret Agent*." *Conradiana* 16, no. 2 (1984): 125–40.

Redding, Arthur. *Raids on Human Consciousness: Writing, Anarchism, and Violence (Cultural Frames, Framing Culture)*. Columbia: University of South Carolina Press, 1998.

Sandburg, Carl. *Always the Young Strangers*. New York: Harcourt, Brace, & Co., 1952.

Savage, Richard Henry. *The Anarchist: A Story of To-Day*. Chicago: F. Tennyson Neely, 1894.

Schaack, Michael J. *Anarchy and Anarchists*. Chicago: F. J. Schulte & Co., 1889.

Sherry, Norman. *Conrad's Western World*. Cambridge: Cambridge University Press, 1971.

Siringo, Charles A. *Two Evil Isms: Pinkertonism and Anarchism*. Austin, Tex: Steck-Vaughn Company, 1967.

Smith, Adam. *Wealth of Nations*. Reprint, New York: Modern Library, 1994.

Sonn, Richard D. *Anarchism*. New York: Twayne, 1992.

Stirner, Max. *The Ego and His Own*. Edited by John Caroll. Translated by Steven T. Byington. 1907. Reprint, New York: Harper & Row, 1971.

Stokes, John, ed. *Fin de Siècle, Fin du Globe*. London: Macmillan, 1992.

Sumner, William Graham. *The Essays of William Graham Sumner*. Edited by Albert Galloway Keller and Maurice R. Davie. New Haven: Yale University Press, 1934.

Teller, Charlotte. *The Cage*. New York: Appleton & Co., 1907.

Thoreau, Henry David. *Walden and Civil Disobedience*. New York: Penguin, 1983.

Tilley, W. H. *The Background of* The Princess Casamassima. Gainesville: University of Florida Press, 1961.

Trumbull, M. M. "Judge Gary and the Anarchists." *Arena* 8 (1893): 544–61.

Tuchman, Barbara W. *The Proud Tower: A Portrait of the World Before the War 1890-1914*. New York: MacMillan Company, 1966.

Tucker, Benjamin R. *Instead of a Book, by a Man Too Busy to Write One*. New York: Benjamin R. Tucker, 1893.

Wall, Joseph Frazier, ed. *The Andrew Carnegie Reader*. Pittsburgh: University of Pittsburgh Press, 1992.

Woodcock, George. *Anarchism: A History of Libertarian Ideas and Movements*. New York: Penguin Books, 1962.

Wright, Carroll D. "Are the Rich Growing Richer and the Poor Poorer?" *Atlantic Monthly* 80 (September 1897): 300–309.

Wright, Walter F. *Joseph Conrad on Fiction*. Lincoln: University of Nebraska Press, 1964.

Zenker, E. V. *Anarchism: A Criticism and History of the Anarchist Theory*. New York: G. P. Putnam's Sons, 1897.

Index

231

racism, 98–100, 118

Ravachol, 64, 68, 92, 183–84

revolution, 49, 51–52, 185, 195, 200; faith in, 25, 29–30, 65, 88–89, 216; fear of, 31–32, 42, 69, 73–74, 78–83, 90, 92–102, 106–9, 139, 151–52, 217; French, 15, 25, 47–48, 52, 62, 66, 82–83, 182

Rogers, H[enry] H[uttleston], 124, 127–28

Rosetti, Helen and Olivia, 16, 178; *A Girl Among the Anarchists*, 181–86

Rousseau, Jean-Jacques, 136, 143

Sandburg, Carl, 19

Savage, Richard: *The Anarchist: A Story of To-Day* 15, 74, 93–94, 101–9

Schaack, Michael, 19–20, 23, 172; *Anarchy and Anarchists*, 32–44

Sinclair, Upton, 127

Smith, Adam, 49, 114, 116

social Darwinism, 34–35, 55, 103, 106, 110, 112, 116, 120, 123, 129–31, 135–36, 138–44, 146

socialism, 17, 27, 29, 94, 95, 97, 99, 118–19, 121, 130, 164, 166, 181, 183, 199

Spies, August, 18, 20–22, 37–38

Stirner, Max, 50–52; *The Ego and His Own*, 46, 50–51

strike, 37, 129, 157, 168, 177; of 1877, 18, 26, 28, 71; Homestead, 64; McCormick, 18, 37–38, 155

Sumner, William Graham, 112, 116, 136–38

technology, 14, 110–11, 117, 143. *See also* flying machines

Teller, Charlotte: *The Cage*, 16, 163–77

Thoreau, Henry: *On the Duty of Civil Disobedience*, 59

Tilley, W. H., 75–77

Tucker, Benjamin, 58, 186

utopia, 53, 110, 113, 132–35; anarchism as, 16; capitalist, 114, 116

Warren, Josiah, 59

Weitling, William, 53

working classes, 15, 60, 62, 69, 103–4, 111, 119, 121, 168, 174

Zola, Émile: *Germinal*, 28